'Chris Kane's prescient account of the changing workplace couldn't be more timely. As we start framing the required redesign of our post-Covid-19 society we must rethink the shared value creation opportunities presented by our most enduring asset, our real estate portfolios. *Where is My Office?* is insightful, provocative and helpful.'

Seán Meehan, Martin Hilti Professor of Marketing & Change Management and the Dean of the MBA program, IMD Business School

'With the recent onset of remote working and prevalence of flexible outsourced workspaces, the traditional "office" has never been so obsolete. Chris Kane provides fascinating insights into the future of corporate real estate with this timely and engaging book.'

Mark Dixon, CEO & founder, IWG

'This book is a rare offering – a perspective on the future of real estate from a seasoned "client-side" professional. In a sector where most of the narrative emanates from the consultancy and supply side, Chris applies his wealth of knowledge and experience from several decades operating within large organizations to an optimistic and crisply argued case for a better future.'

Neil Usher, author of The Elemental Workplace *and* Elemental Change

'Chris Kane has written an incredibly timely book for leaders thinking through the value and role of the physical and virtual office in a post-Covid-19 "new normal" world. The Smart Value Formula presents a playbook for executives who have an organizational imperative to optimally engage their employees.'

Will Saunders, Founder & CEO, AllyAlign Health

'Chris Kane's radical rethinking of the workspaces that are so central to our corporate lives today is urgent and visionary. He expertly addresses the major challenges commercial real estate faces and offers not only thoughtful, persuasive ideas for engaging and adapting the workforce, but also a comprehensive roadmap for getting it done.'

Fiona Calnan, CEO, Santovia

'Particularly relevant post-Covid-19, *Where is My Office?* is a compelling call for change in the property industry. Supported by insights from experience and bursting with practical solutions, Chris Kane shows how property can be about providing great workplaces and enabling better business outcomes for the customer.'

Steven Boyd MBE, CEO, Government Property Agency

'*Where is My Office?* does a great job of making the confusing world of commercial real estate understandable and, more importantly, it lays out the key transformations that are happening and should happen. The book provides an approach that can help business executives turn their spaces into strategic investments that help organizations become more agile and dynamic while nurturing stronger connections both within the company and with local communities.'

Corey Thomas, CEO, Rapid7

'The idea of "the office" is at an inflection point today more than ever. While the evolving nature of work, and in turn the role of the office, has been a key topic for industry insiders, it is now something that every business leader is asking themselves. This book touches upon these issues and provides a depth of insight that only someone with Chris's experience and innovative spirit could capture.'

Steven Quick, Chief Executive, Cushman & Wakefield

'This timely book from Chris Kane demonstrates much of his deep and insightful expertise. By looking at the dilemmas created by the new ways of working, he offers practical reconciliations – exploring the balance between digital and analogue solutions while also considering the dynamics of individual creativity and teamwork. And there are even answers to the behavioural question of how to create an organizational culture, making this a sustainable process rather than another fashionable quick fix. A must read!'

Fons Trompenaars, organizational theorist, management consultant and author

'Chris has a fascinating insight so clearly driven by first-hand experience at the highest level. He has captured the fundamentals of how important the workplace is to businesses and individuals and has done so in a real, personal and engaging way, giving a critical guide to the purpose of the office.'

Charlie Green, Co-CEO, The Office Group

'Entrepreneur, intrapreneur or provocateur, Chris Kane has been an agent for change in the workplace. His journey through Walt Disney and the BBC charts a prescient trajectory for our post-Covid-19 future.'

Jack Pringle, Principal, Regional Director, EMEA

WHERE IS MY OFFICE?

Reimagining the Workplace for the 21st Century

CHRIS KANE

In collaboration with Eugenia Anastassiou

BLOOMSBURY BUSINESS
LONDON • OXFORD • NEW YORK • NEW DELHI • SYDNEY

BLOOMSBURY BUSINESS
Bloomsbury Publishing Plc
50 Bedford Square, London, WC1B 3DP, UK

BLOOMSBURY, BLOOMSBURY BUSINESS and the Diana logo are trademarks
of Bloomsbury Publishing Plc

First published in Great Britain 2020

A catalogue record for this book is available from the British Library

Library of Congress Cataloguing-in-Publication data has been applied for

ISBN: 978-1-4729-7868-4; eBook: 978-1-4729-7869-1

2 4 6 8 10 9 7 5 3 1

Typeset by Deanta Global Publishing Services, Chennai, India
Printed and bound in Great Britain by CPI Group (UK) Ltd, Croydon CR0 4YY

To find out more about our authors and books visit www.bloomsbury.com
and sign up for our newsletters

To my darling wife Lol (aka Loreto), who has lovingly supported me throughout my journey of writing this book

CONTENTS

FOREWORD

The other day I unfolded my trusty Brompton and cycled fifty blocks through a deserted Manhattan to my office. Once I finished what I'd come to do, I got back on the bike and – breaking every health and safety regulation in the book – took a ride through the interior of the building. Everything was exactly as I remembered it: the work stations, the photos of loved ones, the potted plants. On one desk, five bottles of hot sauce in a row. On another, a cardigan still lying where it had been thrown, one sleeve hanging limply over the side.

The only thing missing was the people.

As I write in May 2020, the office where I used to work is more or less empty. Instead of the five thousand daily security card swipes we normally see at the *New York Times* building, currently there are fewer than forty. The only people venturing in nowadays are security guards and a handful of other essential workers.

We don't expect to even begin re-populating our skyscraper for months yet. Indeed many of us – managers as well as employees – doubt whether we will ever go back to working as we did before. What goes for us, goes for offices across the developed world.

Covid-19 has given the themes of this excellent book added relevance and urgency. By showing how much we can get done *without* offices, the virus has forced us to ask ourselves fundamental questions about how we work, and how often and in what settings we need to come together to get that work done. Once, employers and employees alike accepted the inevitability of office-working despite the costs and inconvenience involved. Now we all know that we have a choice.

The office will only survive if it demonstrably adds value to our endeavours – if it promotes creativity, enhances team-work, breaks down barriers between disciplines, nurtures a community with bonds that go deeper than the effective execution of each individual's allotted responsibilities. This agenda – the re-imagining of the traditional office work-space – has been Chris Kane's preoccupation for more than two decades. He's had not one but a whole series of opportunities to challenge conventional wisdom and put new ideas to the test at scale. *Where is My Office?* tells the story of those experiments and the many insights that Chris was able to derive from them. We need these insights now more than ever.

My part in the re-thinking of the office began in the 1990s. By then I'd spent nearly twenty years at the BBC, an organization that combined astonishing and often anarchic creativity with an office environment redolent of the mid-century British civil service at its worst: drab desks, green and brown decor, flat fluorescent light. Environment and management culture often went hand in hand. It was an inner sanctum and a drinks cabinet for the bosses; open plan and tepid tea for the rest of us.

On the fabled sixth floor of Television Centre, where the most senior executives had their suites, the bathrooms were kept locked, and the one key entrusted to one of the corporation's fiercest assistants to ensure that the leaders of the world's greatest television service would never have to place their posteriors on a toilet seat that had previously been used by an underling.

Of course it couldn't last. By the turn of the century, neither the BBC's physical or technological infrastructure were fit for purpose. It had been obvious for years that the future was digital. By the millennium, we'd also come to realize that it would be *distributed*. Whether news, drama or feature, content would be increasingly made on location rather than in central studios. Talent itself was becoming increasingly portable. The old arguments in favour of a massive concentration of investment and operations in London no longer made either practical or political sense.

Soon a vision of a very different BBC took shape with a re-imagined Broadcasting House in central London and new fully digital broadcast and production centres across the UK. We then began the boldest set of building projects in the history of the Corporation – projects which were often the critical first piece of even more ambitious public/private schemes for urban regeneration. Chris Kane played a significant part in much of this, as you'll discover in the chapters that follow.

But the office revolution went deeper and broader than this. In broadcasting as in so many other industries, the twentieth-century model of a division of labour between separate siloes of expertise, each with their own offices and hierarchies, was also breaking down. Nearly all the new challenges were multi-disciplinary and were best solved by agile teams coordinated by empowered junior front-line leaders. Silicon Valley had demonstrated years earlier that teams like these work best when their members sit together in informal and inspirational shared spaces. The reasons are practical – it's much easier to keep a team in sync when everyone's in the same room – but also psychological: teams who no longer sense the beady eyes of their host departments on them feel far more able to take risks and try new ideas.

This revolution in team-working wasn't limited to the BBC or the media industry. It's been unfolding across sectors and around the world. One of the few positive impacts of the coronavirus crisis may well be a further acceleration of our transition from the regimented offices of the past (and the archaic management philosophy that built them) to something more flexible, more individuated, more human-shaped.

The best new talent requires it. Our more seasoned colleagues have found they prefer it. The sheer speed at which the future is hurtling towards us demands it.

Mark Thompson
Former President and CEO of The New York Times Company
Former Director-General of the BBC

Introduction

The executive corner office is the embodiment of having made it to the top after many decades of climbing up the corporate ladder. However, looking beyond those four-cornered bastions of success and personal achievement, the world of work is changing. Today's leaders only have to open the pages of the *Wall Street Journal*, *New York Times*, *Economist* or the *Financial Times* to be confronted with articles on open-plan workplaces and how management has to be more accessible, authentic and 'in touch' with their employees – how technology and agile or flexible practices are driving change in every aspect of our working lives. Terminology such as hot-desking, co-working, third space working and the gig economy abound. Attracting new talent is a challenge as young interviewees grill management on a company's ethical and environmental stance and retaining them is even harder without an engaging, stimulating workplace.

Is it any wonder that most CEOs and those in management positions are all at sea, as the waves of new-fangled technology, working practices and progress are battering them from all sides? Looking around the executive corner office, it resembles a gilded cage which is beginning to lose its shine as increased governance and accountability are making business leaders more wary. Furthermore, company chiefs of a certain age are seen as boardroom dinosaurs, especially in terms of tech skills, and in reality, how many of them are really comfortable with all the new technology? Perhaps they all rely on executive IT support teams, but the stings of those pitying or irritated looks from today's digital natives when they are not so quick on the uptake of new tech cannot be ignored.

It all boils down to a fairly human condition of helplessness, where many leaders ask themselves: how am I going to manage all of these new developments and lead my organization through uncertain times? The Covid-19 pandemic of 2020 proved to be the unexpected curveball that affected not only business, but our whole way of life. The fact is the corporate sphere now needs to take a Darwinian approach – adapting and evolving in order to cope with uncertainty. This is the primary reason for writing this book. But I have another motive too, which has been honed by my unique experiences spanning a 30-year career, which took me from the unglamorous world of chartered surveying to guiding major global corporations such as The Walt Disney Company and the BBC through challenging real estate-enabled organizational transformations. This meant that as an industry insider – or intrapreneur – I had the responsibility and accountability for both strategy and delivery. I certainly earned my battle scars in helping make the world's largest media enterprises more efficient and productive, by maximizing the potential of their workspaces and deploying agile ways of working.

Although my background is in property, I am considered an industry provocateur for espousing the view that commercial real estate is a disjointed and siloed system of facilities, real estate and design/construction management which can be bewildering to the uninitiated. In other words, the most important people in the equation – the tenants or clients – are completely befuddled by the property world's anachronistic ways, complex procedures and jargon. Added to that there is a real disconnect between the providers of space, the deal makers and those who help run and operate the finished product. This is especially true in the corporate property sector and yet business leaders are expected to deal and communicate with this convoluted and fragmented industry. Furthermore, they risk enormous sums of their organization's money and their reputations in making decisions affecting some of their corporation's costliest assets.

This is another aim of this book: to demystify the complexities of the corporate property sector to make it just a little easier for everyone to understand. This is a problem I have dealt with at every level all over the world. The amount of times I have heard (and sympathized with) those responsible for their company's property portfolio as they cry out in exasperation 'Why are things so damned difficult and complicated?' Worse still, they are paying millions for the privilege of being frustrated by an industry which holds them in disdain and does not even view them as customers. Currently there is no emotional connection between landlords and tenants, maybe the time has come to fill this vacuum?

I have been very fortunate in my career to have come across a variety of people from many backgrounds and professions who have inspired me to broaden my view beyond the insularity of the real estate industry. They have encouraged me to look at property from a different perspective, to go beyond the challenges of its complexities. However, to achieve that, I always felt the need to 'interpret' my industry to the outside world. To this end, I collaborated with freelance journalist Eugenia Anastassiou to help me explain how the corporate property system functions, as well as its changing role in the workplace, in an accessible, engaging way.

Another important aspect of my work has been trying to open the minds and eyes of business leaders to see the importance of the physical workplace in their company's success. Through first-hand case studies such as the regeneration of the BBC's failing real estate, I demonstrate that a company's property portfolio, one of its most substantial, yet underused assets, can

3

be utilized for change and that it can be converted from a cost centre into a value creator.

This helter-skelter journey of change management was a learning curve for me, not only in terms of rising to the challenge of providing this iconic British institution with a fit-for-purpose estate at minimum possible cost. It also instigated commercial partnerships which laid the foundations for two new creative, innovation quarters in the UK, reviving previously neglected areas and turning them into vibrant, attractive places to live and work in.

The BBC change management programme confirmed one important factor: that in order to deliver twenty-first-century workplaces there has to be a 'joining of the dots' between property, people and technology. These three contributors need to align around the corporate goal and collaborate to ensure effective results. This all inspired me to devise the Smart Value formula, which fuses my 'People, Place and Process' philosophy to the potential of an organization's brand and the land it occupies. It forms a template of how property can be used to create business value and by extension can also benefit society.

Another premise of the book is to question the way the property industry works and to challenge everyone, both in the sector and business leaders/management. I help them see that the traditional meaning of workplace and the office is being reshaped, primarily by the formidable impact of technology. Every time I use my smartphone, I am reminded of the huge amount of capability it provides, and furthermore, that I can use it as a tool for work anywhere and at any given time.

With good connectivity widely available, easy access to the internet and effective cloud computing, any space can become a workplace. Which obviously begs that all-important question – where will our offices go? If working from the comfort of our own homes means we can meet our deadlines/work obligations,

4

while also avoiding the wretched daily commute, or working from the convivial atmosphere of a coffee shop suits our lifestyle and actually makes us more productive, does it actually matter where, how and when we work? Or are there other factors?

Covid-19 has provided the impetus for everyone – the property sector as well as corporate executives – to realize and accept that there is a multiplicity of places – home, digital offices, third spaces – which are redefining and reinventing the way we work in the twenty-first century. Everyone has to come to terms with the new reality that we are now entering a new era of 'omni-channel' property/facilities.

The notion of how people work was being discussed as far back as 1959 by the 'father' of modern business management Peter Drucker in his book, *The Landmarks of Tomorrow*. Drucker has been credited with changing the face of corporate America and went on to 'invent' many of the concepts which have now become reality in the working landscape. Drucker coined the phrase 'knowledge work' to describe how working people would generate value with their minds to a greater extent than using their muscle power. He also suggested that the shift from manual work to those who 'think for a living' will be the single biggest influence on our society.

With all this in mind as we look around our twenty-first-century workplaces we should ask ourselves: why do we carry on using offices in the way we do? How do we work differently now in comparison to 20 years ago? Why do so many of us use offices in the same way as our parents did when it is so patently outdated? What do we need to do, if anything, and how might we go about it? We must not forget that today's Millennials are becoming embedded in the management layers of our organizations and their workplace expectations and demands are different from previous generations. These questions are being asked more and more by many business leaders and in organizations globally and it is time that the supply side of the industry stepped up to the challenge. The impact of Covid-19 reinforces this.

Another important issue is that twenty-first-century companies are increasingly becoming more aware of their social responsibility. Savvy business leaders are in the unique position to drive significant beneficial change in shaping the value systems and behaviours of the ways we work, which also benefits their bottom line. Additionally, this also means encouraging the property sector to be more conscious of creating a more sustainable workplace environment. This requires business leaders and the corporate property sector to adopt a different type of leadership mindset. There needs to be a convergence of approaches to create workplaces, which inspire employee engagement, foster creativity and increase productivity, while also improving a company's capacity to compete and create value.

This is a 'clarion call' for everyone to crawl out of their siloed, insular spheres/sectors and take a smarter approach in how spaces and places are used in the best possible way. One of my great inspirations is Charles Handy. Not only is he a fellow Irishman from County Kildare, but like Peter Drucker, he is rightly regarded as a business management visionary. Charles Handy once said to me, 'We need to address the challenge of how to design the modern workplace for creativity and human engagement.' To this, I add that we should all become part of the 'Coalition of the Convinced' – a collaborative endeavour in building bridges to create effective, engaging workplaces, which contribute to a better, more sustainable, 'built' legacy for future generations. These challenges have to be faced not just by property professionals and corporate heads, this also involves HR, IT, Procurement, as well as management at every level, and even those studying business and change management. The book's aim is to act as a guide into how the true potential of an organization's people and workplace can be harnessed and to demonstrate how business success can be achieved by integrating 'People, Place, Process' in an intelligent and innovative way.

Drawing upon case studies, research, data and interviews from global business leaders, academics and experts in the fields of the economics of work, urban planning, architecture, human resources and government, I hope to be able to steer decision-makers in all sectors to formulate their strategic thinking in terms of turning placemaking into profit-making, as well as creating new, more meaningful solutions for the workforce and the workplace. These are the reasons why I am writing this book — to present a game-changing challenge to the existing ways we produce, operate and consume workplaces. This holistic view of an entire industry and the way it impacts on our working lives has never really been explored in this manner. The book also offers 'real-life' solutions, not just theory, into how business leaders and managers can capitalize on their workspaces by deploying smarter ways of working.

It is now an accepted fact that 'business agility is no longer a luxury; it is critical to survival', but what has been ignored so far is that an 'alignment between workplace and purpose is a key tool in managing agility'. This vital link has to be made in order to create successful and productive workplaces. I hope that in this way I can help guide businesspeople to join the dots and make sense of the complex demands of dealing with the twenty-first-century working environment.

Chris Kane, London, 2020

Sources

1. The Stoddart Review. 'The Workplace Advantage'. Raconteur Custom Publishing, 2016, pp.28–9.

Part One

A FRESH PERSPECTIVE ON WORKPLACES

I

Seeing the Forest for the Trees

Progress is impossible without change, and those who
cannot change their minds, cannot change anything.
George Bernard Shaw

'Why don't we use spaces and places differently?' I mused.
It's not often I get so philosophical stuck in a long traffic jam on a roundabout in Twickenham, London, on a typical
Saturday morning and looking enviously at a completely empty
bus lane. Dare I dart forward into that traffic-free lane and get
ahead of the game? After all, it was perfectly legal – bus lane
restrictions are only in force for part of the day and not on weekends. Yet here we all were, car, van and lorry drivers dutifully in
line and waiting our turn; so organized, so automatic, not realizing we could actually use these lanes outside of restricted hours.
I wondered why so few of us took advantage of this and it struck
me that we are all such creatures of habit that nobody bothered
to use the empty lane. This is what triggered my question: 'Why
don't we use spaces and places differently?'

Hardly a 'Eureka' moment in the grand scheme of things, and
not quite in the same vein as Archimedes jumping out of his bath
and streaking around Ancient Athens. It was enough for me to just
escape into that empty bus lane and power down that traffic-free
road while thinking about all those lost opportunities we could

take advantage of, where we do not remain stuck doing the same things over and over again unthinkingly. When in fact we could do something beneficial and productive just by thinking differently.

That roundabout lightbulb moment encapsulated what I seem to have spent nearly 30 years of my life working on: a smarter approach to how we use our spaces and places. Taking on the role of instigator and constantly asking that question: 'why?' Why do we do things in this way, especially in the anachronistic world of property and the workplace since the evolving nature of how we work in offices today is a game-changer?

Confessions of a Lapsed Chartered Surveyor

I guess the importance for changing perspectives in the work-place and wanting to effect change both for people working in offices and business, as well as for the benefit of the property industry and the wider community, stems from my roots. Rather appropriately, those roots lay in property and land since I come from the third generation of a family involved in auctioneer-ing and land management in Ireland. It was growing up with that legacy and understanding the importance of land that led to my interest in the rather unromantic profession of chartered surveying; it was also the reason I came to London in the early eighties to complete my qualifications.

I suspect that being from a small place on a small island always made me something of an outsider and a bit of a maverick since I was not a member of the 'Old Boys' establishment' property world. It certainly makes me question how the industry operates in the UK and beyond, as it is riddled with acronyms, complexity and jargon, all of which are crying out to be reformed and simpli-fied. Despite my different attitude, I was lucky enough to get a job at one of Britain's largest surveyors, Jones Lang Wootton – now known as leading worldwide estate service provider, JLL.

I spent 13 years there and ended up as a partner, after helping to launch a new occupier client facility, their Corporate Real Estate Services. Working for a major world-leading organization, I came to see the power of brand and corporate culture in action – factors which were key to developing a successful business in every sector.

It was in the mid-nineties that I received one of those very unusual calls from a US-based headhunter in Los Angeles, asking me if I fancied a change. After much cloak-and-dagger activity and 17 interviews later, that mysterious phone call led to a job with The Walt Disney Company. This eventually culminated in me becoming vice-president of International Corporate Real Estate, which meant I was responsible for nearly all of Disney's worldwide corporate real estate. This involved much travel, criss-crossing the globe, with the added good fortune of being exposed to diverse work cultures and ways of doing business. So, it was Mickey Mouse who shaped both my journey and understanding of what the workplace really is, how it serves business and indeed the broader community. Walt Disney's famous quote, 'If you can dream it, you can do it,' was also my mantra and it served me well then, as it does today. Additionally, I also learned the ins and outs of the media world. I discovered broadcasting and TV studios – little did I know how useful learning that side of the business would become one day…

In 2003, I received another of those life-changing phone calls. This time from a very traditional English firm of headhunters, with an interesting proposition: a major organization needed someone to help them transform their property portfolio to the tune of £2 billion.

Six months after that call, I arrived at the imposing Art Deco entrance of the BBC's Broadcasting House in London and was given the challenge of driving the biggest modern-day transformation of one of the UK's most iconic cultural institutions. This resulted in a 40 per cent reduction in their real estate footprint, moving over 12,000 people around the country, delivering more than 20 projects, refreshing 60 per cent of the BBC's property portfolio and achieving an annual saving of £47 million in their property by 2016–17. Additionally, it entailed shifting the BBC's London-centric broadcasting production to other regional hubs, such as the flagship MediaCityUK in Salford, near Manchester, and Pacific Quays in Scotland; all done while keeping BBC programmes and broadcasting carrying on seamlessly.

This incredible multi-layered restructuring really opened my eyes to the link between workplace and business performance; many of the BBC's property schemes were actually turned into business transformation projects, so the move to a new building became a major catalyst for organizational change and helped the BBC in its wider transition from analogue to digital.

My time at the BBC was also key to inspiring my Smart Value concept. This enabled me to navigate this vast project successfully, as well as generate unprecedented levels of creative and economic value for the BBC. However, the greatest benefit in deploying Smart Value was that it also considers the wider community, particularly in the cases of MediaCityUK in Salford and White City in West London. The basic premise of Smart Value was using the BBC brand as a catalyst to attract other leading creative organizations to these once-neglected sites, which provided the springboard to develop new attractive, thriving places to live and work in. The other bonus being it also galvanized the local economies by creating jobs, not just through the companies who moved there but also through building links with universities/schools, creating innovation hubs, leisure activities and community centres.

The Smart Value formula will be analysed at greater length in Chapter 5 and the way it impacted on both Salford and White City will be explored further in Part 2 – The BBC Story.

The other important lesson I learned as Head of the BBC's Corporate Real Estate was understanding diverse groups of people, trying to bring them together and lead them to achieve a higher aim or bring about a successful result. This could only be accomplished by breaking down communication barriers and cutting across the silos which often divide sectors and individuals.

This, in a nutshell, is the practical background of where I have come from in the industry; it has been a case of 'working the coalface', and not just in terms of property and Corporate Real Estate. The role has included project and facilities management, but most importantly, it has featured change management and leading assorted teams of people through large-scale regeneration and development at the highest levels. Over my 30-year career I have worn many hats, as well as Mickey Mouse ears too. I have gone from being a typical adviser/surveyor to being on the client and consumer side of property facilities, so I have seen first-hand how all of these complex and convoluted areas of the property world function from all angles.

Also, over these three decades I have seen the shifts, both in the world of work and business itself, and the monumental impact it has had on where and how people can work. I have also concluded that it cannot be overlooked anymore. Nobody can really afford to sit herd-like in the slow lane, watching how much the world around us is changing, peering mindlessly at those taking the opportunity to whizz into the twenty-first century's fast lane without transforming or innovating to keep pace. However, like most people I also suffered from a closed mind and tunnel vision. Along my career journey I was fortunate enough to come across many individuals who made me think that as an industry we have to step back and ask ourselves certain questions: How come we have different perspectives, even within the same sector? Who has the best view of the situation? They encouraged me to see the bigger picture and to challenge the status quo of the property world. They also inspired my other professional goal to integrate all the disparate elements of the real estate industry and the workplace, to instigate change for the better, and to make workplaces fit-for-purpose for the ways we work in the twenty-first century.

Inspiring Instigators and Interpreters

Everyone has their own interpretation of how they view the world and it would be a very boring, dull place if we all saw it the same way, but certain individuals really did broaden my vision regarding my sector and its role in the workplace. Namely former RIBA President Frank Duffy, founder of the pioneering architectural practice DEGW, who was an advisor for many years, and Professor Michael Joroff, former Senior Lecturer at MIT's Laboratory of Architecture and Planning, who kick-started my interest in turning property into strategic assets.

Having access to both Frank and Mike provided me with the perfect mix of viewpoints, which enabled me to navigate the complex world of spaces and places. With this cocktail of thoughtful counsel and MIT's academic rigour, their combined outlooks were invaluable, as well as enlightening. However, the secret sauce to the relationships we developed over the years was that we connected well as people.

Frank Duffy's importance in the evolution of workplace strategy cannot be underestimated: he introduced this US-inspired sector to Europe as far back as the 1970s. Together with his DEGW colleagues, he revolutionized the office environment by emphasizing the importance of an organization's changing nature and the need for the workplace to reflect this. This also extended to incorporating developments in mobile and remote working. He also introduced trailblazing concepts such as the involvement of users in the design and management of their space and the significance of differing life cycles in buildings, from structural core to interior fittings. Instead of viewing buildings as static objects, DEGW looked at them as evolving entities.

I first met Frank when I was at JLL but it was not till I went to Disney that our relationship really blossomed. Frank and his DEGW colleagues were not only creative and innovative in their approach, they were also very thoughtful and passionate in their work. He and his European team assisted me on most of the international TV channel projects at Disney and with his business partner, Despina Katsikakis, they led the charge when I attempted to introduce a workplace strategy at their vast London headquarters in Hammersmith. They also gave me insights into the importance of securing senior management sponsorship and backing for projects of this nature. Frank's wise guidance was also instrumental in helping me with the BBC's estate transformation and in providing strategic support in building up solid engagement with the BBC boardroom.

Since Disney was such a global organization, it also gave me the opportunity to meet the wider DEGW community across the world. Many years later, I partnered with some of the DEGW diaspora on Six Ideas – a worldwide community of people and creative thinkers resolved to tackle issues around the way we work, learn and live.

Professor Michael Joroff specializes in the field of city planning, building technology and real estate development. He is considered a leading expert in twenty-first-century placemaking and pioneered the formation of large-scale entrepreneurial clusters. Mike has helped cities all over the world plan and launch districts designed to engender innovation and entrepreneurship, through large-scale, mixed-use developments designed to serve people's lives and their work. He has been a great influence in my challenges to align real estate strategies with business processes, ever since I did an MIT walkabout with him in May 2005. He was of course hugely supportive in the creation of the BBC's MediaCityUK in the north of England. At my suggestion, he advised the Manchester-based Peel Group, responsible for the development of a run-down area by the canal in Salford into a vibrant, lively, creative community. This now encompasses the UK's two major broadcasters, BBC and ITV, and other media outlets, plus education, business, living and leisure facilities.

Mike also acted as a wise sounding board for me when I was taking up the gauntlet to get involved in the BBC's redevelopment of its White City site. This 60-acre neighbourhood in West London allies the UK's premier science and research university, Europe's largest shopping mall and the world's oldest broadcaster in forming a new innovation quarter, attracting other leading organizations, small businesses and creative centres.

Perhaps one of the great accolades of my career, aside from participating in such groundbreaking projects, is when Mike described me as an 'intrapreneur'. Defined by American entrepreneur and business school founder Gifford Pinchot, this term describes individuals who are passionate about exploring new and innovative directions to produce added value for their employers' organizations, as 'dreamers who do'.

A Confusing Mosaic of Players and Barriers to Change

Unfortunately, the majority of the real estate industry can hardly be described as dreamers or even 'activators' of ideas or progress since it is still firmly set in its outdated ways and resistant to change. Innovation is regarded as a key priority in most sectors, but there is little evidence of real change across the property world. Yet who could blame them since business has been booming in the last decade, so there is no real urgency to change – though it remains to be seen whether life after the pandemic will change this.

Matters are further confounded by the generally negative perception engendered by the real estate world, especially landlords and developers, and this creates a challenging landscape for both the residential and commercial sector. Furthermore, for the uninitiated, it can be quite daunting to pinpoint just how property markets function and who is pulling the strings. It is difficult for those outside the industry, and even those working within it, to understand the operational intricacies of property.

To make it even more perplexing, the sector which supports corporations to help them make the best use of their real estate portfolios is a subset of the overall commercial property world. It is evident in certain parts of the world that many people are confused by the terms commercial real estate and Corporate Real Estate, the difference being that commercial real estate is the umbrella name for the entire system and Corporate Real Estate (CRE) is the internal support function responsible for a corporation's property portfolio. To minimize confusion, the acronym CRE will be used from now on when referring to Corporate Real Estate.

Additionally, another area of misunderstanding rarely addressed is the plethora of titles and descriptions associated with CRE. One can encounter a surveyor, a premises manager, a facilities manager, an estates manager, a CRE person and a workplace manager, to name but a few – and they could all be doing much the same thing. Little wonder that the outside world fails to grasp what we do and what value, if any, we bring to the table.

As I will discuss in more detail in the next chapter, there are many different groups who use these titles involved in the process of providing and consuming real estate. There is also a clear need for a more united approach and one that recognizes that the overall product, i.e. the workplace, is not only an office building but an operational facility which needs to enable people to do work.

Regardless of which side one sits on the real estate spectrum, most attention is placed on doing profitable real estate deals, designing great buildings and delivering good construction solutions, with very little thought given to the operational aspects of the completed facility. For decades a gulf has existed between the delivery of a building and how it functions once it is taken over by a tenant. The various parties involved in producing these edifices have little interest in how the building will run, what is included in its life-cycle maintenance and whole life costs, as their role comes to an end on the practical completion of its construction. Yet everyone accepts this modus operandi because that is how 'things have been done' and mindsets are notoriously difficult to change. However, some chinks in this position have started to emerge in very recent times. For example, Lisa Picard, President and CEO of EQ Office, a US Real Estate Investment Trust (REIT), formerly known as Equity Office, now wholly owned by the Blackstone Group, has a very different take on the market. She cites data from the big brokerage houses, such as JLL, as evidence of a shift, as some 2.5 per cent of the total office stock in the US currently under construction has only a 1 per cent forecast absorption rate. This also begs the question of who will occupy these buildings. As Mark Galbreath, CEO and founder of US workspace network LiquidSpace, speculates, 'Maybe we have hit peak office?'

Never the Twain Shall Meet

One of the most notable legacies of the commercial property model today is the absence of any meaningful links between the two principal players – the provider and the consumer. Better known by their contractual labels as 'landlord' and 'tenant', they are brought together through an intermediary – a broker – and bound by a voluminous legal contract, known as 'the lease'. This non-existent relationship between the 'consumer', in this case senior executives and the property industry, is another obstacle in the overall system.

It is time for a rapprochement between the now outdated worlds of landlord and tenant and encourage the commercial property sector to think more in terms of consumer and provider. Denis McGowan, Global Head of Real Estate at Standard Chartered Bank, is quite emphatic in stating, 'Landlords and tenants are emotionally disconnected. Everyone has different agendas, but we now need to come together.' However, this will not be easy since business leaders suffer distrust and adopt an apprehensive mindset when real estate issues are tabled, fuelled further by the fact they do not have any relationship with the other side. I suspect fundamentally they are reluctant to make real estate decisions since they are usually high-profile in nature, with risks and high-costs attached too. There is always the underlying fear that something will go wrong, especially when construction or fit-out works[1] are involved. Projects can be delayed and budgets exceeded. Worse still, the building might not work for the business. All of which have the potential to damage reputations.

At both Disney and at the BBC I saw the knock-on effects of bad property news on the C-Suite and how they viewed the industry with disdain and distrust. 'What if it all goes wrong?' was a common fear expressed around the boardroom, especially by non-executive directors and trustees.

Regardless of whether occupiers/end users of real estate are right or wrong in their thinking and views, whether they are justified in seeing our industry in such a negative light, this drives me to consider why people view things differently. No

---

[1] Fit-out is the process of making interior spaces suitable for occupation.

doubt it all boils down to how each of us perceives a certain situation, but it also brings to mind that great George Eliot quote from *Middlemarch*: 'It is a narrow mind which cannot look at a subject from various points of view.'

The other area in which people's perceptions often vary is in their view of the workplace. First, most people equate the workplace with the office, yet there are many millions of people who do not work in an office. Second, how Human Resources (HR) perceives the workplace differs fundamentally from how CRE and Facilities Management (FM) see it, especially since HR's primary focus is on people issues. (From now on, Facilities Management and Human Resources will be referred to with their respective initials FM and HR.) However, given the rapidly changing nature of the game for those of us interested in the built environment and particularly regarding the space where people work in today, we need to seek fresh perspectives and start a dialogue to enable us all to see above the parapet, to view the broader picture and be able to discern the forest for the trees.

The Workplace Renaissance

We really do need to challenge some long-standing thinking – not only in relation to the overall system for providing and leasing offices but, more so, in relation to the thinking and service provided by those in the CRE and FM sector. The nature of work has changed and, for the most part, we are struggling to address the issue. We persist in trying to work in a twentieth-century straitjacket of behaviours, processes and procedures as if nothing has happened – as if we have not experienced the seismic shift of the digital revolution.

This, for many in my sector, may be outside our comfort zone, but as Frank Duffy said, 'We live in an increasingly virtual world and we need to justify the role of "place" in the overall jigsaw.'

I contend that the virtual world is approaching far faster than most of us realize owing to Covid-19 and the time for debate and introspection is now over. This has to be approached by using 'joined-up thinking' and not falling into the trap of looking at an issue as an 'either/or' option. Take, for example, the rise of technology and the extent which it frees us from is being shackled to the traditional concept of 'one person, one desk', this in effect being the equivalent of cutting the umbilical cord in terms of how occupiers think about using offices and how they forecast occupancy. Office workers, for the most part, no longer need to use one particular desk with a fixed telephone and a desktop PC – although some prefer to work in this time-honoured fashion and will always do so.

For many observers, freeing office workers from the limitations of that one desk also means the loss of personal space, individual offices and the shift to 'unassigned' working. I used to argue that introducing ratio working was a panacea for securing optimum real estate portfolio efficiency. That was before I learned the smart approach at the BBC, which was to provide a range of work-settings which suited the work required.

Unarguably, over the last two decades moving away from the 'one person, one desk' concept has generated huge efficiencies and become the lynchpin of portfolio planning, to the delight of many CFOs, yet the implications are only starting to be fully understood in recent years as employee engagement, wellbeing and talent issues are beginning to be considered. Nowadays it is all about efficiency and effectiveness, according to the results of a Gallup poll, which tracked US workers daily, measuring their levels of commitment, enthusiasm and involvement in their work and workplace: only 32 per cent of employees were found to be engaged in their jobs as of 2017. The same poll indicated a similar crisis globally, reporting only a 13 per cent level of workforce engagement and with every type of organization asking, what can be done to increase levels of engagement?

One factor which might solve the problem and is fuelling the workplace revolution worldwide is the emergence of agile working. The idea being there is no 'one size fits all' in the way we work; instead it is all about offering people choice as to how, what, where and when they work, provided of course that the job is done professionally and efficiently. Essentially, it empowers employees to deliver results and best value to their organization in the optimal way for the individual and incorporates both the physical workspace and the digital workplace. This significant development in how people work and how enterprises can organize themselves as agile organizations has given rise to a structural change in the nature of the demand for offices.

The cutting of the umbilical cord from the physical office is a factor which stakeholders have either ignored so far or have chosen to overlook, yet for the wider real estate sector, the consequences have far-reaching implications in terms of how offices are funded, designed, constructed and leased. For the most part the supply side – apart from some notable exceptions – are sitting on the fence. EQ Office President/CEO Lisa Picard gives the best picture of the situation: 'Every smart business on the planet, except real estate, spends time understanding what the customer journey is, learning from it and re-casting their product. Real estate just continues to push out the same product over and over again rather than asking – what does the customer need?'

Therefore, I find it extraordinary how anachronistic the world of commercial real estate still is and how slow it is to respond to changing twenty-first-century business demands and working environments. It is a view held by the original 'workplace disruptor' Mark Dixon, founder of serviced office provider Regus, now re-branded as IWG, who established his alternative office service back in the late 1980s. He reiterates, 'One could not find an industry more traditional and more resistant to change than the real estate industry.' Dixon's pioneering serviced office model has only really impacted commercial property in the past 20 years as a result of the rise of a whole host of imitators and competitors in the flexible workplace arena. LiquidSpace CEO Mark Galbreath observes that attitudes are changing slowly in the industry with the ascendancy of alternative office space services: 'We are experiencing a renaissance, where we are seeing a shift from asset to service mindsets.' Will Covid-19 accelerate this?

The Flexible Space Phenomenon

The alternative to the traditional model of either leasing or buying a building to house offices, collectively known as the flexible space sector, has been in development for over a decade. The origins of serviced office/executive suite provision can be traced back to the US in the 1960s; this area was given a significant boost by the formation of Regus in 1989. However, for the most part, serviced office provision remained a quiet backwater in the overall scheme of things. They prospered to a point but remained very much the 'poor relation' compared to mainstream leasing.

That is until two factors emerged which proved to be real game-changers: first, the demands of the business world and the nature of work have changed fundamentally. Second, the impact of the 'WeWork Phenomenon'[2] has changed the corporate psyche as business leaders are beginning to see a viable alternative to the old-school leasing system, which is both flexible and client friendly. Coupled with the eruption of start-ups and the gig economy, the last 20 years has seen an explosion in the demand for flexible workplaces. This has spawned a variety of alternative

---

[2] Founded in 2010 in New York, WeWork's meteoric rise in the co-working/ flexi-space market was fuelled by its reputation for being a hothouse for start-ups. At their peak in 2017, WeWork operated in 280 locations, across 86 cities in 32 countries worldwide (2017 figures).

space products that developed together with the expansion of Regus and other serviced office providers. According to John Duckworth, MD of Instant Group, which runs several million square feet of 'space-as-a-service' and is also a leading listings platform for flex space, this changed in 2017 when mainstream landlords started to pay attention to the activities of WeWork, who had turned into the accelerators of the flexible office market.

Rapidly overtaking Regus/IWG and other established serviced office providers, for a period WeWork became the darlings of real estate markets globally. While many question their business operations, given the spectacular failure of the 2019 IPO, they did achieve bringing about a fresh perspective to how tenants/clients consume space other than through traditional leasing.

In my view, when history is written WeWork will be regarded as the tornado which accelerated the pace of change in commercial property. Through very effective marketing and promotion, coupled with unprecedented activity, WeWork certainly attracted huge publicity. In effect, WeWork let the 'genie out of the real estate bottle'; so much so that many other operators acknowledge that they have done them a huge favour in opening up the market. Conversely, compared to a decade ago business leaders are now more aware of the availability of alternatives to buying or leasing real estate. Unashamedly, since acting as 'poster kids' and influencers, WeWork's approach has shaken up a fairly conservative market.

WeWork certainly think very differently to mainstream real estate. Ronen Journo, Senior Vice-President of WeWork, describes their approach as creating space which 'has a magic sauce that establishes a special energy which is attractive to people'. WeWork and fellow flexible space providers are the start of a much more profound revolution in how we use and consume the built environment and one where business leaders need to take a more active role in shaping this new paradigm.

Although many commentators and property people make the analogy between Regus and WeWork, it is not quite comparable as Mark Dixon focused only on creating a very innovative space solution. What WeWork did was take the workspace model and make it 'cool' and compelling for people and this created an emotional connection with the brand. This is not just about offering their occupiers on-site coffee baristas, free beer on-tap and lunchtime yoga sessions. WeWork were the first of the alternative workplace providers to see the potential of building an ecosystem within its spaces to enable businesses to develop and grow by fostering forward-thinking start-ups globally.

According to We Company's Global Impact Report 2019, 54 per cent of its members around the world credit the company for accelerating their business growth and 80 per cent report an increase in productivity since setting up in WeWork premises. Dr Arun Sundararajan, Professor of Technology, Operations and Statistics at New York University's Stern School of Business and author of *The Sharing Economy*, states that WeWork's 'global constellation of companies and entrepreneurs allows members to tap into and realize value from these economic spill-overs, within their local communities and across cities'.

WeWork and the other new alternative workplace providers have acknowledged the importance of the 'people-factor' over the 'property-factor' – a concept which has certainly bypassed most mainstream commercial real estate players.

Responding to the 'Rubik's Cube on Steroids'

Another factor in the rise of serviced offices and alternative workplace offerings is that they are flexible and agile in response to twenty-first-century commercial demands. The traditional real estate response was that it takes 12 to 18 months to deliver new spaces. This is no longer viable, especially in the last decade, as the pace of business has accelerated beyond all expectation. New ideas and products need to be developed faster, problems or crises require resolution within hours and consequently, customers and clients expect agility.

Peter Miscovich, MD of Strategy & Innovation at JLL, likens the current US corporate environment to 'a Rubik's Cube on steroids' — as the pieces of the business puzzle keep changing, leaders have to keep on figuring out the puzzle while they are putting it together. This 'always on' business model transformation is the new normal which requires innovative levels of agility and flexibility to adapt constantly to changing conditions. Some in real estate like Denis McGowan have realized this and observe, 'We have to be much more nimble as a property function to turn things around.'

Achieving 'Six Impossible Things Before Breakfast'

It is a daunting task to bring about a broadening and altering of perspectives in order to adapt to the changing demands of the workplace. Sometimes we all feel a bit like we have entered the world of Lewis Carroll's *Through the Looking-Glass*, confused and bewildered by all this change. One of the tenets of Six Ideas is that we should attempt to accomplish 'six impossible things before breakfast' and to this end, I have drawn up a list of six impediments that act as barriers to the effective use of the workplace within the real estate system, as it exists today:

- ✦ There is a fundamental disconnect in the system in that the suppliers of the physical workplace see their product as an asset while the consumer sees it as a business resource or utility;
- ✦ Enterprise workforces are changing radically, yet the nature of the places they inhabit and how that space is supported has yet to fully respond to these changes;

+ The workplace as a label means one thing to HR (people focus) and something different to Real Estate and FM (property focus);
+ The space and how it is managed/operated is the key ingredient which enables productivity – the current system fails to recognize this;
+ The support functions (CRE, FM, HR, IT, Procurement) and consumers of workplaces operate in silos and have divergent points of view on how an organization uses and operate its workplaces;
+ Everyone places undue focus on the physical 'workplace', viewing it purely as a destination where work is carried out. The implications of the 2020 pandemic forced everyone to re-think how and where they can work.

Sources

1. 'It is a narrow mind which cannot look at a subject from various points of view.'
Eliot, G. *Middlemarch: A Study of Provincial Life*. London & Edinburgh: William Blackwood & Sons, 1874, p.46.
2. 'global constellation of companies and entrepreneurs allows members to tap into and realize value from these economic spill-overs, within their local communities and across cities.' Dr Arun Sundararajan
We Company/HR&A Advisors, Global Impact Report 2019, p. 23.
3. 'Why, sometimes I've believed as many as six impossible things before breakfast.'
Carroll, L. *Through the Looking-Glass, and What Alice Found There*. London: Macmillan, 1871. p.58.

Epigraph

Bernard Shaw, G. *Everybody's Political What's What?* London: Constable & Co., Ltd., 1944. Reproduced by kind permission of The Society of Authors, on behalf of the Bernard Shaw Estate, p. 330.

Shifting the Status Quo and Changing Perspectives

Change is the law of life. And those who look only to the
past or present are certain to miss the future.
John F. Kennedy

I was only expecting £100! It is remarkable when one reflects on how you see things over the years. The event in question is writ large in my memory, as it was my very first bonus as a very naive and wet-behind-the-ears chartered surveyor. That day in May 1984 seems such a long time ago and whole rivers of water have passed under the bridge since then. Me, a young country lad in London, brought up in a small village in Ireland, where my father and his father before him had dabbled in the property game, this being only a sideline as my father's main activity was owning a country pub. Here I was, walking out of a senior partner's office, over the moon, as my first ever negotiator's profit share was the princely sum of £871! It was a small fortune to somebody who was surviving on a £100 bank overdraft.

Looking back to 1984 and receiving what for me was a large sum of money, made me realize that the industry is hugely dependent on personal gain. I was reminded of this by a young friend of mine, who recently graduated and was seeking advice on which profession to enter. He had formed the opinion that property could give him a very good living without a great deal of effort. An interesting perspective and one which is not completely off the mark.

Personal gain is certainly a very important driver and also influences behaviours and practices in every industry. The property world has the reputation of being where the mega-bucks are made. Even in the mid-nineteenth century, political economist and liberal philosopher John Stuart Mill observed, 'Landlords grow rich in their sleep without working, risking or economising.' In the late nineteenth century, American industrialist Andrew Carnegie went one further, allegedly stating, 'Ninety percent of all millionaires become so through owning real estate. More money has been made in real estate than in all industrial investments combined.' Today, he would be talking billionaires!

To prove Carnegie's point, the estimated value of the commercial real estate market in the US was $16 trillion in 2018. In the UK, it was estimated at £883 billion in 2016, representing 10 per cent of the country's net wealth and contributing £63 billion to the total UK economy. So why change something that has been working for centuries and continues to generate vast profits? Seeing as the wider world is changing, and established customs, beliefs and practices are fundamentally altering, the Brave New Digital World has heralded the Fourth Industrial Revolution. The impact of the age of technology is changing society, from the way we view the world, business and work to how we make money and perhaps questioning how wealth is achieved. We want more transparency and more accountability in the way our organizations are run, in all aspects of their operations: from the way employees are treated to a company's environmental impact. These are becoming increasingly important factors in the way businesses approach their corporate real estate portfolios as their employees and their customers expect them to uphold these progressive and transparent values.

However, we in the property world seem shrouded in complex jargon and idiosyncratic practices and are stuck in the original nineteenth-century Industrial Revolution, as well as being extremely introspective – and for many in the industry, it is still all about 'the deal'. This short-term, 'let's make big bucks' view, coupled with the clichéd developers' attitude of 'build it and they will come', is a very narrow and regressive standpoint. It does not serve the industry well in a world where we need to use space in a smarter and more sustainable manner. We also need to consider the legacy we leave to future generations by creating something meaningful and worthwhile.

We need to challenge the design community to break out of the financial constraints imposed on them that only produces spatially efficient boxes where sustainability features come as a premium. Or, as former RIBA President Jack Pringle puts it, 'Clients should look to their well-informed designers and say, tell us what to do rather than this is what we want you to do.' There should be a concerted effort on better sustainable design that will stand the test of time and not place an undue burden on the environment, as well as being aesthetically pleasing and functional.

To survive, the property world's mantra must change now to a 'sell better, sell smarter' model, which puts the consumer or the occupier first – just like any other progressive twenty-first-century industry – and not just to serve the developer/landlord's profit margins. So far, for the most part and up until now, the supply side of the industry has not seen the need to engage with its customers, nor to provide any innovative thinking and solutions into their real wants and needs, vis-à-vis both living and working spaces. There are, however, some glimmers of light ahead as I uncovered during my research that there are many people who have seen that the CRE winds are changing and now think differently.

The impact of technology cannot be underestimated in creating the era of flexible working. These days we can work from home, at the weekend, on holiday, anywhere and everywhere, provided we have decent internet or cellular network connection. We talk about work–life balance, but this does not necessarily include going to the office five days a week, for the usual 9–5 and often enduring a tedious commute to and fro. In fact, it begs a bigger question that no one is asking: where will offices go, if fewer of us are working in them?

Significantly, it is not just a transformation in terms of where and when office work can be done; something much more momentous is taking place in the world of office work as digital technology is automating processes that people were employed to do and the entire way in which we work is changing dramatically. That is why we collectively need to think more about the purpose of 'office buildings' and the role they play in our working lives, but also in our towns, our cities and, more importantly, in our precious environmental ecosystem. We can no longer accept the status quo and the entire property sector has to come out of its closeted complex world of old-fashioned practices and jargon and broaden its view in accepting the changes now taking place. They have to see how organizations, both large and small, operate in the twenty-first century and in realizing the long-established principles of operating offices are crumbling before our very eyes.

The Antiquated Emperor's New Clothes

Our industry has fallen into a position very similar to the one described in the Hans Christian Andersen fairy tale, *The Emperor's New Clothes*. As real estate industry struts around like the old Emperor, the time has come for the boy in the story to point out the obvious – that 'times are a-changing'. This is an industry which is governed by many regulations harking back to bygone eras, especially in the UK, and these include:

The 1954 Landlord and Tenant Act governs the rights and obligations of landlords and tenants, occupying business premises in the UK. This came into place the year after Queen Elizabeth II's accession, when Churchill was still Prime Minister and food rationing had just ended.

Quarter Days Some other rules go even further back – to when England was a medieval feudal agricultural country and a time when most of the populace was illiterate and the Church played a major role in people's lives. A simple, universal system needed to be devised so that everybody knew when rents had to be paid or collected. Therefore, the easiest way was to follow the religious calendar and subsequently, rents were charged in advance on Quarter Days. For those not familiar with UK leasing practices, these dates are:

+ 25 March – Lady Day, The Feast of the Annunciation;
+ 24 June – Midsummer Day, The Feast of St John the Baptist;
+ 29 September – Michaelmas, The Feast of St Michael and All Angels;
+ 25 December – Christmas Day, The Feast of the Nativity.

Admittedly, some landlords have seen the light and relinquished traditional Quarter Days, with quarterly rents now paid on a more logical system of 1 January, 1 April, 1 July and 1 October. It seems a strange practice, especially to people from overseas who are renting premises in the UK and expect to pay rent on a monthly basis, like every other business expense. I have seen many raised eyebrows when they also learn that rent is paid in advance.

Ground Leases and 'Peppercorn' Rents Apart from mainstream leasing, another legacy from the past is the English practice of granting long leaseholds; in other countries they are known as ground leases. Their origins lie in a desire to retain ultimate control of land, which once again goes back to the feudal system. For instance, much of the land in central London, including the prime locations of Mayfair and Belgravia (the most expensive areas on both the UK Monopoly board and in reality), is owned by the Duke of Westminster. Over the centuries, successive dukes have granted long leases for periods ranging from between 99 years and 199 years, all the way up to 999 years. Such leases usually have a 'peppercorn rent' attached, referring to the nominal annual ground rent for property, land or buildings that dates from the Middle Ages when exotic spices like pepper were expensive luxury commodities.

Nowadays, this anachronism – which is not just confined to a peppercorn but could also be a rose or a £1 coin – maintains the formal landlord–tenant relationship, where a substantial premium has also been paid at the start of a long lease of 99 to 999 years, known as a 'virtual freehold'. Whimsically, the annual 'peppercorn rent' on buildings in London's Covent Garden is fixed at one red apple and a posy of flowers; further afield in Canada, the University of Ontario leases its land from their Legislative Assembly Buildings in central Toronto, for a peppercorn $1 a year until 2892.

Unwieldy Leasing Systems These have been the bane of my career, especially in the early days. Back then, the supply side of the UK leasing market completely dominated and tenants had little or no choice but to accept 25-year terms when renting offices or shops.

One of my clients at that time, in 1989, was Abe Darwish, Head of Real Estate at the 3Com Corporation. We spent a great deal of time together looking at offices in the UK and it became abundantly clear that he had a completely different perspective on real estate. He once told me that the US Chamber of Commerce advised him to tread very carefully when operating and leasing new facilities in the UK. Their advice was, 'Don't rush into any leasing deals, as you will have 25 years to pay for any mistakes you make.' Even today, in the second decade of the twenty-first century, Patrick Marsh, Glaxo Smith Kline's Director of Real Estate & Asset Management EMEA, bemoans, 'Why isn't our physical environment more accessible, more adaptable to our needs? There is zero agility baked into our leasing system.'

Exit Costs/Dilapidations In addition to the cumbersome 25-year leases, there were upward-only rent reviews every five years, plus a full repairing obligation. This last item came as a surprise to many overseas-based clients as they struggled to understand exit costs, such as dilapidations. In the US, for instance, tenants are not required to reinstate an office space to its original condition when they leave so this requirement in the UK to quote one American CRE head, 'really bamboozles US corporates'.

To the uninitiated, most standard corporate leases in the UK contain clauses compelling the occupier to reinstate their office space back to its original condition when vacating the premises. Not only does this mean redecorating, but the outgoing tenant has to remove any additional fixtures and fittings installed as the space reverts to its initial open-plan format at the end of the lease.

This outlay can be exorbitant: for example, a 30-person office incurs an average dilapidations cost of between £25,000 and £35,000. Obviously, the larger the office and bigger the employee head count, the more these costs skyrocket to the hundreds of thousands. The highest I have seen has been for £2.5 million – is it any wonder most people think this is a purely money-making exercise? One Japanese client found this totally incomprehensible, asking me in complete bewilderment, 'How come I have to pay twice? I pay rent which never goes down during the lease, then at the end I have to pay to put the space back to its original "as-new" condition.'

Measurement Variations Another confusing inconsistency has arisen since the UK building industry adopted metric measurements in 1972. The wider property industry took another 20 years to start to get to grips with the metric system. In the mid-1990s there was a great flurry among the commercial property sector to change to square metres or at least to show both metric and imperial units on 'To Let' signs. Yet the real estate industry has curiously reverted back to square feet, while the construction sector has enthusiastically embraced square metres – resulting in a perplexing situation where commercial buildings are built in square metres but are being valued, leased or sold in square feet!

Usable Space Versus Rentable Space in the US Monthly rent for commercial real estate is calculated differently to residential rent, using a variety of complex methods and several types of measurement. These are industry standards all over the US and they are calculated on guidelines set by the Building Owners and Managers Association International (BOMA). Monthly rent on commercial property is based on 'rentable square feet', which encompasses an additional number of square feet comprising the building's shared common parts – e.g. hallways, lobbies, lifts, stairwells – and not just the tenant's 'usable square feet', which they occupy physically.

Commercial Real Estate Leasing in the Rest of the World It is hardly surprising that lease agreements differ across the world. In Europe, despite the attempts of the EU trying to impose uniform legislation across member states, national property laws can vary across the Continent. Most abide by Civil Law/Napoleonic Code, while others adhere to variations on the theme.

As former British colonies most Commonwealth countries, such as Australia, New Zealand, India, South Africa and others, generally keep to Common Law. However, buyer/tenant beware in Canada! Most of the country follows British-inspired Common Law, except for the once French province of Quebec, which adheres to Civil Law.

Being in the fortunate position of having been both a supplier and consumer of real estate, I see many areas of opportunity for the industry to up its game, not just in the UK and the USA, but worldwide too. However, if we continue to hold on to archaic, complex and sometimes illogical practices, which do not help either the industry or the client, there is little prospect of truly moving into the twenty-first century.

Real Estate is a Riddle Wrapped in a Mystery, Inside an Enigma

Paraphrasing from Winston Churchill's famous quote on Soviet Russia, this is probably how those outside of the industry view the property sector and it is important at this stage to try and explain its often Kremlin-like complexity in order to clarify how and why progress has been hindered. To really comprehend how we have reached this state of affairs, it is worthwhile examining the lay of the land in the commercial real estate world.

Figure 2.1 is a basic scene-setter and it is evident the scales weigh heavily on the supply side as the dominant element in this particular economic system. Indeed, I have often wondered how the laws of supply and demand function for real estate markets. Historically, demand for office space has always exceeded supply, with the occasional disruption during times of recession. Canny investors and property owners usually cut back production

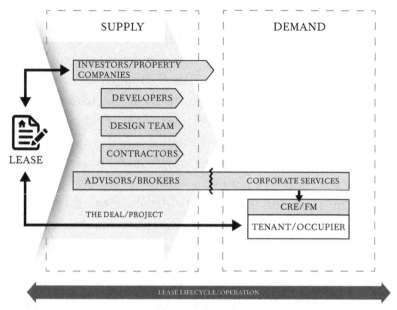

FIGURE 2.1: The Commercial Real Estate Structure

when they see the onset of recession, leaving their core investment portfolio intact.

Taking the UK market as an example, investing in commercial real estate emerged just after the Second World War and it gave birth to the concept of the institutional lease. This proved to be a gilt-edged form of investment in bricks and mortar, because for the most part investors leased buildings for 25 years and just sat back and collected the rent – it was all one-way traffic. Over the years this favoured position has been somewhat diluted, with the stripping away of things such as privity of contract and the reduction of lease terms to 5–15 years; the average lease duration was only 7.7 years in 2018.

As a consequence of this 'licence to print money', a complicated and sophisticated framework emerged to allow for participation in the supply side. To help the core money men, the pension funds and property companies expand their portfolios, the market saw the emergence of the property developer. This gave rise to astute traders, who carried the risk of bringing new stock to the market but went on to reap the rewards by leasing to a tenant on 'institutional terms' and then selling the completed investment package to pension funds or property companies. To facilitate this activity, construction work is executed by building contractors and all of these players use a raft of professional advisors and brokers to effect the multiple and layered transactions required to make the system work – and this is just one side of a very complicated equation.

Another aspect of the property development side is their modus operandi: find a site, get consent to build as much as one can, find a tenant and then move on. Apart from contractual liabilities such as warranties, the majority of those on the supply of space see this as the end of the process. This short-termism highlights one of real estate's greatest fault-lines: as far as the industry is concerned, their 'clients' are the property or investment companies and it is their needs (and profits) which are paramount in the scheme of things. Ironically, the most important group of people in the equation, the tenant who pays rent or the occupiers who shell out fortunes to buy property, are generally discounted as 'the clients' by the industry. Allied to all this is the highly lucrative reward system that has evolved over the years in terms of brokerage commissions and percentage-based investment deal fees. This has been highlighted by many CRE leaders as a major impediment to changing the status quo in the industry.

Delivering a New Office – A Fragmented Process

At this juncture it is worth introducing how the overall system works for delivering and operating commercial real estate. There are some regional variations but the basic steps are pretty consistent the world over, as demonstrated in Figure 2.2.

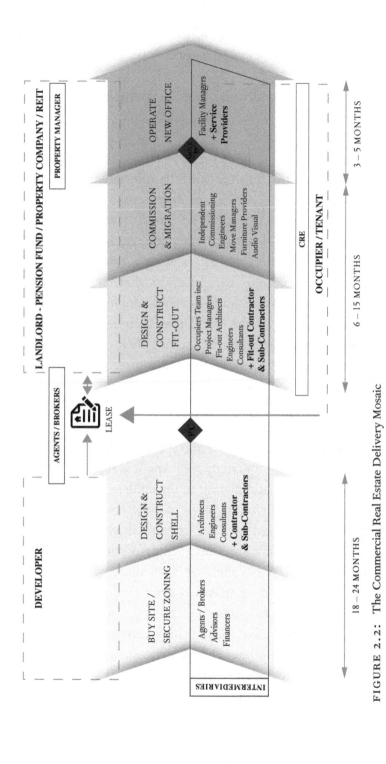

FIGURE 2.2: The Commercial Real Estate Delivery Mosaic

There are two major handoff points in the office delivery story, which are contractual in nature:

+ the practical completion of the shell building;
+ when the office is ready for occupation.

Most new offices are built speculatively with no occupier in mind and are usually finished with the interiors in shell condition. The design and specification are driven by what is deemed to deliver the greatest profit. The input of what an occupier requires in their space is usually provided by intermediaries or brokers who advise on such matters. This is a sweeping generalization and there are lots of exceptions to what has been regarded as the core philosophy for office development for many decades. It was underpinned by the belief that occupiers do not know what they want and are always changing their minds. However, there are certain elements of the procedure, which might be addressed in a better way:

+ 'Build-out' (or in the UK, 'fit-out') refers to the
  process of making the internal spaces of the new office
  building suitable for occupation and it is separate from
  the structural work relating to the edifice. There are a
  wide range of permutations as to how this works across
  global markets and each has its own idiosyncrasies.
  In the US, there are Tenant Improvement allowances applied to the 'shell' or 'raw' space, while in the
  UK such works have spawned a mini industry with
  various options falling into Category A, Category B
  and Category C. For jobs of this nature in parts of
  Asia Pacific one comes across terms such as cold and
  warm shells! In other words, 'cold' spaces with no
  infrastructure, plumbing or heating supplied or 'warm'

with some features, such as heat. In the absence of any real standards, what is included can be very wide-ranging and with so many variations on the theme, the process can end up being 'Fifty Shades of Fit-out'! Therefore, it is essential that contracts between developers and tenants define who is responsible for what is supplied or what work is carried out and ultimately, who pays for it;

+ Most new offices are delivered in shell condition as the presumption is that tenants will need to specify the interior to meet specific needs. Yet the people who know most about the operational needs of the building are facility managers, who rarely get involved in the process until the later stages.

In cases where the tenant or occupier leases space in an existing building, there is no 'Developer's phase'. However, the scope of the fit-out may call for the removal of a pre-existing installation and it has always been odd to see tonnes of material being ripped out of a building which might only be 5–10 years old and transported in skips to landfill sites – surplus or unused building materials make up 40 per cent of landfill waste in the US. British Land's Development Director Richard Madelin, the man behind Europe's largest regeneration project, the redevelopment of London's King's Cross, goes one further to say, 'It is absolutely disgraceful the waste that occurs with commercial office fit-outs.'

Equally, Bryan Koop, Executive Vice-President (Boston Region) of Boston Properties, has some thought-provoking views on the subject: 'The Holy Grail is finding the answer to – how do we create office deals with less tenant improvement fit-outs? This will be more profitable and more sustainable.' Especially considering this REIT is one of the largest owners, managers and developers of office properties in the US. It is interesting to note that Boston Properties is constructing a new home for Google in Cambridge, Massachusetts, using a combination of repurposed and new buildings;

+ Throughout the process there is minimal direct contact between the two principals – the owner and the consumer – but there are numerous intermediaries involved. The delivery system is populated by a plethora of consultants and contractors, who require a high level of co-ordination to deal with the various handovers and transitions. From the consumer's point of view all this takes up much of their valuable management time.

Given all this complexity in the system the consumer or demand side responded with the creation of CRE in-house teams to face off the supply side. In many markets this was a fairly one-sided affair, where a 'take it or leave it' approach used to be the norm, but in recent years this has started to change. Since the mid-1990s, large companies in particular realized that they needed to pay more attention to their real estate holdings and so CRE emerged as a new corporate function.

The Evolution of Corporate Real Estate

CRE is American in origin and has a relatively short history going back to the late 1980s. The aim of its founders was to 'professionalize' the management of a corporation's real estate holdings with an internal perspective. They tended to take a rather purist view without a unified approach into how facilities or an organization's bricks and mortar would be operated within the context of corporate real estate. This has created a 'mixed metaphor' around those specializing in working with the end user or tenant/occupier for the best interests of the company.

It was the arrival en masse of the big American computer companies in the UK during the mid-1980s and the early 1990s which introduced a whole new product into the country's property landscape – the out-of-town business park. Multinational corporations such as IBM, DEC, Data General, Compaq, Silicon Graphics, Sun Microsystems and others drove the demand for campuses and the UK market had to adjust. One of the first was Stockley Park, developed in 1986, which was situated in a former garbage dump near Heathrow airport, chosen for its convenient location so that American executives could hop off transatlantic flights and be behind their desks in no time. This was soon followed by a mushrooming of these out-of-town identikit schemes across the length and breadth of the country.

The arrival of heads of CRE from the US, representing their organizations to set up subsidiaries or teams in the UK and Europe, was another significant development. They also brought with them their professional body, the International Development Research Council (IDRC), the precursor to CoreNet Global, now CRE's biggest professional association. This groundswell of activity in the UK's CRE world created the possibility of a new career as a property or facilities professional within corporations, even though historically, they were two very different groups.

The evolution of CRE during the late 1980s and early 1990s coincided with me working in what was then Jones Lang Wootton, one of the few surveying practices in London with an international network and an inside track in terms of knowing which US corporations were looking for space in the UK. It also turned out to be a tipping point in my career as a chartered surveyor, which became something much more than just selling space, especially since I learned that in the US, it was customary practice for a corporate occupier seeking to lease new space to engage an advocate on their behalf. This was called Tenant Representation and in 1989, I headed to New York to learn more about it and to import this new service to the UK. I came back armed with all sorts of new 'tools of the trade', which were quite innovative for the UK's wider traditional leasing agency world.

This was all part of my personal development and the start of my 30-year journey navigating the business of CRE, which saw me evolve more into a management consultant role and gave me a view of real estate from the consumer's perspective. This led me to develop my capabilities into what back then was the nascent world of Workplace Strategy – yet another subset of an already crowded market.

The most recent development in the evolution of CRE has occurred in the last 10–15 years, when corporations started outsourcing significant elements of this function to surveying companies or commercial real estate services firms such as Jones Lang LaSalle or JLL (formerly my place of work, Jones Lang Wootton), CBRE or Cushman & Wakefield. All of these organizations plus many others now offer a comprehensive range of services bundled onto the core tenant representation offer and known mainly as Corporate Solutions.

The Corporate Real Estate Family and Other Property Animals

There is also an additional layer of complexity within the occupier-focused sector of the commercial property industry, on the one side CRE and on the other its sibling FM. I am often asked, why are there two different professional titles? Most people outside these groups perceive them as having broadly the same responsibilities and functions within an organization whereas those within these functions would hotly debate this view. During my years at Disney, there was a time when these two groups were literally at war and certainly not living up to the ideal of 'The Happiest' or 'The Most Magical Place On Earth'! To clarify things in the simplest way:

+ **Corporate Real Estate**, better known by its acronym CRE, focuses on an organization's property portfolio, including site location, building design, leasing facilities, acquisition, disposition, lease administration, rent reviews, lease renewals; in other words, the life cycle of a corporation's estate from beginning to end. Its role was to engage with its big brother or sister to represent the corporate end user or occupier;
+ **Facilities Management** (FM) is primarily an operational role, which manages the day-to-day running of an organization's facilities, including maintenance, repairs, utilities, furniture acquisition, etc. – in short, in the eyes of some, taking care of the 'bogs and boilers'!

Crucially, CRE professionals are also responsible for an organization's multi-site portfolio; this might include a company's industrial plants, retail and storage space, as well as its offices and HQ, which could be spread all over the world. They are also involved in an organization's long-term strategic planning, ensuring cost efficiency and effectiveness across their property portfolio. This generally gives them a 'neither fish nor fowl' position in a company's hierarchy – not quite C-Suite boardroom, but regarded instead as middle management, even though they provide an essential, yet thankless and often misunderstood service for their company.

To further complicate matters, there are equivalent terms in other parts of the world and the terminology varies from premises department or property division. However, I hold the view that these two functions, CRE and FM, are in fact twins of equal standing, like 'love and marriage' – you can't have one without the other.

Interestingly, during a workshop I held in the US attended by 25 CRE leaders representing major global organizations, my interpretation of the relationship between CRE and FM was hotly disputed. Some of the delegates held the view that CRE has the strategic long-term view, while FM's focus is solely on the operational; others thought that they had a dual responsibility for the two areas. It was also interesting to note that some of the delegates held titles such as VP of Workplace Resources and this resonated with me, as during my time at the BBC, when I changed the name of BBC Property to BBC Workplace. However, this proves once again that there is no right or wrong answer to the CRE/FM debate. Nevertheless, for many years I have maintained that FM and CRE should have a more integrated approach beyond just managing aspects of bricks and mortar and to think more about the workplace as a whole, as part of an ecosystem, which enables them to add value and benefit to the organization they serve. Additionally, both sectors need to consider the enormous changes taking place in how people work in today's office environments. This underpins the need for these two historically disparate groups to converge.

The third leg of the stool which supports the occupier-focused property ecosystem is:

+ **Construction or Capital Project Management**:
  For the most part this activity, which is primarily project and construction management focused, can be subsumed within the two larger groups of the CRE/ FM family, very much as the younger sibling. This group can also be home to design-based professionals such as architects and engineers. Unless an organization

is building new headquarters or has a busy programme of construction-related activity, this is when this group is classified as a stand-alone team.

Looking at how these three distinct groups of professionals interact – CRE, FM and the Construction Management group – an outsider might be forgiven for regarding them all in the same light, but within a typical organizational structure of a large corporation each have different roles and responsibilities. Each of these functions has its own set of characteristics, customs and conventions within their three silos, which one can stereotypically depict as a hierarchy of:

+ Suits – those who claim allegiance to CRE;
+ Boiler Suits and Overalls – the people who operate and service the buildings;
+ Hard Hats and T-shirts – an eclectic group who design the space, construct and build it out.

It is interesting to note that all these sub-groups have their own particular language and modus operandi and it is also worth noting the unique behaviours within these three groups. For instance, CRE works for the most part in square feet, while most design and construction activities use metric. Facilities managers worry about the actual physical occupied space and how it will be serviced, while at CRE, it is mostly transactional and asset management focused. When it comes to construction, CRE practitioners think mostly in terms of net lettable areas; FM worry about occupiable space and to top it all, those in construction focus on gross areas, which is 20 per cent more than net lettable area. Additionally, there are numerous examples of insider jargon and three-letter acronyms pertinent to all these groups; this has always led me to muse on how confusing

49

this must appear to the outside world. Added to this, each particular area has its own culture and value systems, which have been heavily influenced by their respective introduction to the industry, the level of education provided for the professionals within each group and the support of the various professional bodies within the overall property industry.

In commercial real estate, this is shaped by the fact that CRE, and Construction Management, owe their origins to the wider worlds of property; FM, on the other hand, is the only true occupier-focused sector, at least until the outsourcing trend took a grip of many organizations. Additionally, the functions of CRE and Construction Management are transactional and episodic in nature, while FM works on a continuous basis, day in, day out. Moreover, FM has a relationship with all the consumers of the spaces they support, while this is not usually the case for either CRE or design and construction.

Ultimately, as Paul Bagust, Global Property Standards Director at the Royal Institution of Chartered Surveyors (RICS), concedes these labels are meaningless in the eyes of business leaders. This is quite an admission from a director of this august UK-based professional real estate body of 150 years' standing, which has worldwide membership of 125,000. Paul asserts that all management wants is somebody to sort out their property or operational problems and that, 'our propensity to pigeonhole people into asset and facility categories doesn't really work anymore'.

Workplace Strategy: The 'Newish' Kid on the Block

Over the last 20 years another set of players has made inroads into the real estate mosaic – Workplace Strategy experts and teams. Although very small in number compared with the mainstream services, this capability has grown in stature over the last decade on both sides of the supplier/occupier divide. Their focus is to understand the multiple ways of using space today and figuring out how to make the best use of workplace models.

Getting to Grips with Commercial Real Estate:
A Dynastic *Game of Thrones*

So, what does all this mean for anyone who has to make sense of the world of commercial real estate? There are times when I view the convoluted, multi-layered, hierarchical relationships as being comparable to the complex and intriguing power struggles in the storylines of those classic eighties 'glitz and glamour' TV soap operas, *Dallas* and *Dynasty*, or more recently, the epic web of alliances and conflicts among the noble dynasties in *Game of Thrones*. In all cases, the essence of their plots is basically the same. They tend to centre on a family or a dynasty, with strong powerful father figures at the helm, supported by a dysfunctional and scheming set of siblings, children and extended family. The storylines also feature characters who occupy junior roles in the hierarchy and the outliers, who are desperate to gain acceptance and be noticed by the all-powerful head of the family; usually half-siblings conceived out of wedlock or the progeny of prior relationships. This is all underpinned by excessive greed and plenty of Machiavellian conspiracies to gain either greater wealth or wield more control over their respective families, business empires, kingdoms or lands.

Looking at my world, one can see an allegory in the antics of the power-hungry Carringtons from *Dynasty*, *Dallas*'s conniving Ewings and the House of Stark's dynastic battles in *Game of Thrones*. Not that I'm suggesting in any way that the folk who populate the property industry are power-crazed, manipulative dragon-slayers! This interesting parallel best describes a cluttered assortment of players, beliefs, practices, relationships and loyalties, as well as the tremendous influence and immense wealth wielded by those who run the major organizations that own and supply real estate. The metaphor also provides a torturous way of explaining the status of CRE and FM in the overall property ecosystem. The mainstream supply sector probably views itself as the legitimate older sibling, while the internal side – CRE and FM – can be described as the half-brothers and sisters in the court of the property family. In some cases, one might say they are the black sheep – trying desperately to gain acceptance from the 'patriarch', the real estate world.

The half-sibling comparison is useful because CRE and FM are, for the most part, treated as two separate functions, as they are generally organized as stand-alone teams or divisions. In some organizations and some regions around the world, they are treated as one and the same and they are completely unified though. When it comes to the external supply chain, where, until recently, there has been a clear distinction between CRE and FM providers, mainly underpinned by the large discrepancy in profitability – CRE facilities' activity tends to attract good margins, while FM is very much a commodity product, associated with low single-digit margins.

There is a plot twist to this real estate version of *'Dynasty* and *Dallas* meet *Game of Thrones'*, in that those who work in the CRE and FM sectors are directly employed by their respective occupier enterprises, which means people who play these roles straddle two camps: that of their occupier organizations (their employers) and that of their 'paternal' profession (property). This gives rise to an objective on the part of those in CRE and FM teams to act in the best interests of their employers – in other words, the organizations they serve. Yet at the same time, emotionally, culturally and intellectually, they also belong to the property family dynasty with a small 'D'.

One also needs to consider that CRE is a relatively young profession and that FM is not much older. Their relative newness contrasts with the long-established customs, mindsets and practices of the wider property family, which can act as a strong emotional magnet. Given the size of the CRE/FM world, it is most likely individuals would have received their basic training on the supply side, which reinforces the link with the bigger siblings. What bothers me is that the wider property family is, in the eyes of its customers, regarded as dysfunctional, inefficient and is struggling to deal with a rapidly changing world. Given that the little half-brother and half-sister operating as CRE and FM are very much aligned with their bigger siblings in commercial real estate, this is a dilemma.

Many people working in CRE/FM find it very difficult to break out of the mindset constraints imposed by those bigger, older and more powerful siblings. This sometimes brings them into conflict with serving their employer organization, which is their primary responsibility.

The Perfect Storm – Winter is Upon Us!

The *Game of Thrones* storyline provides a useful parallel for all those involved in the commercial property world since it operates smugly secure in the knowledge that its equivalent of the 'Great Ice Wall' is impregnable. For those unfamiliar with the series, this is the same as the way the French armies viewed the Maginot Line before World War II, which we know proved completely useless once France was invaded.

The property sector's Great Ice Wall/Maginot Line is based on the core belief that people and businesses require roofs over their heads and for the most part, there will always be tenants or buyers needing space, encapsulated by the mantra – build it and they will come. This well-worn refrain may have worked very well for many generations and in the past has proved to be a very solid and profitable commercial principle.

However, in the business world, the nature of demand and consumption is changing dramatically and rapidly. In *Game of Thrones*, an oft-used phrase of the dynastic House of Stark is 'Winter is coming' – an interesting analogy for an industry where the status quo has been unassailable for centuries. However, a number of people in the property world are starting to realize that the Great Ice Wall of real estate is now being breached. We can see that 'winter is coming', or may even have arrived already (such as with Covid-19), and that we are in the midst of a perfect storm, whether that is as a result of marauding disruptors who have appeared in recent years or a combination of various micro and macro influences.

The macro factors not only effect commercial real estate but everyone, from senior management to every person working in an organization. Furthermore, they impact society as a whole. Their significance in transforming both the commercial property and business world cannot be underestimated. Undoubtedly, their roles and influence merit greater examination, which will be analysed in the coming chapters, because they are the key drivers in precipitating change in every aspect.

The following have major implications for real estate and twenty-first century workplaces:

+ Ubiquitous and reliable digital capability, which means that work can be carried out anywhere; this is the key factor in breaking the umbilical cord of 'one person, one desk';
+ The economy's increasing digital transformation as a result of the Fourth Industrial Revolution, coupled with the growing demand of finding and retaining skilled digital talent to cover new jobs in areas such

as artificial intelligence, big data, robotic process automation, the internet of things and other new technologies;

+ Changing societal and attitudinal paradigms, especially towards the workplace and the office, highlighted by the now well-known phrase, 'Work is a thing you do, not a place you go';

+ The impact of Covid-19 on the health and wellbeing of its occupants and subsequently on employee productivity. This is coupled with greater public awareness regarding the environment and sustainability in our living/working environments;

+ The challenge of the multi-generational workforce; an unprecedented phenomenon which means accommodating and integrating the diverse needs and attitudes of four generations of people working together at the same time;

+ The emergence of the gig economy and ascendance of freelancers, also referred to as the 'agile workforce' or 'independent workforce'.

There are also significant structural changes building up because of micro or property industry sector related forces. These also have implications for business leaders and a company's decision makers.

The micro factors impacting real estate and how an organization consumes it:

+ The maturing of different types of working and workplace environments, as exemplified by Agile, Activity-Based Work and Flexible Working;

+ The march of the disruptors offering flexible serviced options, such as co-working spaces and 'hybrids' (a mix of co-working and serviced offices in the same building);
+ The digital world's disruption in real estate technology with the onset of Proptech (Property Technology, which uses IT to streamline the process of buying, selling, and managing real-estate);
+ The global property market's shift towards shorter and more flexible leases – the average commercial lease around the world is now between 3 and 10 years;
+ The outsourced facility management sector is also facing a financial crisis;
+ The impact of regulations, such as FASB (Financial Accounting Standards Board) or IFRS 16 (International Financial Reporting Standard) and the consequences of this new accounting standard, which came into effect from January 2019 on property market dynamics.

Macro and Micro Storms Blowing into the Workplace

The combination of this formidable array of factors coming into play at the same time is unparalleled and it is certainly an uncomfortable place for the commercial property sector to find itself for the first time. In many ways it is similar to the dilemmas facing business leaders all around the world today as they grapple with volatility, uncertainty, complexity and ambiguity in the running of their organizations. As the poet John Donne said, 'no man is an island entire of itself' and we as an industry must face up to the challenge of how we can best accommodate and collaborate with enterprises and their people in order to drive organizational success and add greater social value.

Six Steps for Property and Business to Shift the Status Quo

+ Acceptance that the world of work is changing fundamentally – this is especially true of office work, as it is
  no longer anchored in one place;
+ Building understanding – by considering issues not just
  through your own lens of perception, but also through
  the views and perspectives of others;
+ Collaboration is key as this will help unlock solutions
  by finding common cause with those who have diverse
  and complementary experiences;
+ Focusing on the outcomes – rather than the outputs or
  the process/presence; this will yield greater dividends;
+ Holistic thinking is paramount – as we need to look at
  the situation in the round and think of it as an ecosystem;
+ Accepting that necessity is the mother of all invention
  and that it would be better to collectively adapt to the
  post-Covid-19 business world by jointly finding innovative solutions and new models.

Sources

1. 'Landlords grow rich in their sleep without working, risking or
   economising.'
   Mill, J.S. *Principles of Political Economy with Some of Their Applications
   to Social Philosophy*. London: John W. Parker. Book V, Chapter 2,
   1848, pp. 523.
2. 'no man is an island entire of itself.'
   Donne, J. 'Meditation 17', *Devotions Upon Emergent Occasions*. 1624.

Epigraph

From the Papers of John F. Kennedy, President's Office Files, speech
Files. *Address in the Assembly Hall at the Paulskirche, Frankfurt*, 25 June
1963.

Enterprise and Office: The Odd Couple?

Every human benefit and enjoyment, every virtue, and every prudent act, is founded on compromise and barter.
Edmund Burke

One of the overriding challenges of my 30-year career, apart from attempting to broaden the view of the commercial property industry, has been to enable business leaders and the C-Suite to see the 'Missing Link' – to make that all-important connection between how an effective office can add value to their organization and transform their enterprise for the twenty-first century. Historically, such a link has not been fully recognized or appreciated because it has never been needed, but times and demands have changed and it has created this imperative.

In my experience this all boils down to perceptions and rela-tionships, both on the part of business leaders, who for the most part are the consumers of commercial property and the various elements of the property world described in the previous chapter in all their fragmented and dysfunctional glory. Since those who run organizations pay the rent, understandably, they see them-selves as the clients, despite the fact that the real estate industry regards their principal and most important clients as property or investment companies. Naturally, as consumers, they ask the

question, 'Why don't providers of these office blocks understand the demands of the people who use them?' Yet both parties
in the equation need each other: the property world needs someone to pay rent and those in business need roofs over their heads
to carry out their operations. This mutual dependence makes for
a trying and testing relationship and is broadly the same all over
the world. Since dealings between these two players are generally adversarial, lacking in trust and with little understanding
between them, moreover this is not helped by the explosion of
intermediaries who are also involved in the mix.

Looking at these incommodious bedfellows often reminds
me of one of the great ABC TV sitcoms from the 1970s, *The
Odd Couple* – a spin-off of the equally brilliant Neil Simon film
starring Jack Lemmon as the obsessive neat-freak Felix opposite
Walter Matthau, the party-and-poker-loving slob Oscar. These
two seemingly incompatible, clashing characters end up sharing a small apartment in New York, providing endless hours of
superb comedy as they irritate and annoy each other with their
different lifestyles, while trying to find ways to co-exist within a
confined space.

The storyline mirrors the real-life interaction between how
commercial real estate, the enterprise and its consumers relate to
one another. Additionally, it is also a fair representation of how
management currently views its office portfolio. They are there
to operate a profitable business, but those in the 'office sector'
speak a different language – they are difficult to communicate
with and not very easy to understand; also, not particularly
customer-friendly. Moreover, the sector is expensive to run and
cuts into profit margins. Like 'fussy Felix', the occupier/enter-
prise and 'disorganized Oscar', representing the fragmented
property sector, they are mutually dependent on one another
and have to co-habit in the same environment, usually with
minimal trust, limited co-operation and lack of awareness.

These disparate Felix/Oscar sections have to find a rapprochement because both face a barrage of obstacles battering them at every turn. It is imperative that they understand and address these issues soon since the domino effect of twenty-first-century disruption encompasses both in a number of fundamental ways. In order for the enterprise to succeed and continue making profits, this problematic 'Odd Couple' have no option but to join forces to overcome these considerable challenges.

The Onslaught of Disruptive Forces Impacting the Enterprise, the Office and Society

When it comes to business, the certainties and rules of the past are no longer applicable and company chiefs are finding it very difficult to lead their enterprises by extrapolating from past experience in a world which is no longer controllable and is undergoing such dramatic social change. To paraphrase Charles Handy's assertion in his book *The Second Curve*, society and by extension business is not working as it should. People are increasingly questioning the inequality fuelled by corporations just satisfying profit margins and shareholders. In other words, 'the few' over the fairer distribution and creation of wealth for all.

Larry Fink, CEO of BlackRock, one of the world's largest asset management corporations, underlines this notion with the statement, 'Companies, investors, and governments must prepare for a significant reallocation of capital.' Slowly, we are all becoming more aware of rampant consumerism, the effects of the 'throwaway' society and its impact on our valuable resources and the way uncontrolled debt affects lives, our communities and even our countries. We are now entering the age of accountability and responsibility in both business and society and the property industry has to respond to the demands of this new era.

A corporation's real estate is now a vital physical manifestation of its worldwide standing: it reflects its strategy, reputation and brand, it is an effective indicator of an organization's competitive advantage, performance and its profitability, as well as its power to attract and retain the best people. At this juncture it is imperative that business leaders and managers master the opportunities and solutions presented to them by one of their largest and most important organizational assets.

The Value Chain: Linking Mindsets between Business Leaders and Real Estate

In the past management has been more reactive in managing the office as a profit/loss expense. However, business chiefs now have to take a more strategic and proactive perspective to be able to deal with the whirlwind of changes coming their way as well as making them better equipped to carry out the transformation to a more agile organization by optimizing the use of the built environment. This also gives the property industry an opportunity to step up to the mark, not only through bringing about innovation, but also by demonstrating the potential of dynamic and effective real estate management. This extends to both real estate tribes: the mainstream, which focuses on selling and leasing, as well as the internal side of CRE and FM. For many years the latter have been clamouring for the attention of the executive board and, in fact, some even go as far as wanting a seat at the table! Notwithstanding their ambitions, gaining C-Suite attention will give them a strategic business angle to prove their contribution in the organizational value chain.

The Relentless and Constant Change of the VUCA World
We ignore the perils of this unprecedented and unparalleled climate of volatility, uncertainty, change and ambiguity (often shortened by economists to the acronym VUCA) at our peril. Especially the disruptive and transformative impact of what is defined as the Fourth Industrial Revolution, which I see as a misnomer as I feel we are still in the midst of the initial surge of the First Digital Revolution, with more radical changes coming our way as the effects of technology gain an increasing stranglehold in our lives. Covid-19 only adds fuel to the fire.

As Klaus Schwab, Founder and Executive Chairman of the World Economic Forum noted: 'We stand on the brink of a technological revolution that will fundamentally alter the way we live, work, and relate to one another. In its scale, scope, and complexity, the transformation will be unlike anything humankind has experienced before.'

The current industrial or digital revolution is transforming entire systems in manufacturing, management and administration all at the same time, creating exponential rather than linear change. The internet has revolutionized our lives beyond measure in every aspect by linking billions of people worldwide, enabling all of us to be interconnected wherever we are, to manage everyday tasks in a few clicks or swipes and to share information and knowledge in an instant – and this is just the beginning of harnessing its enormous power.

Undoubtedly, it is not just technology, but many other factors at the macro level which are affecting enterprises, both private and public, all over the world and drives the impetus of why business leaders must sit up and take notice. At this point it is crucial that the 'Odd Couple' property and business world adjust their thinking and the way they view each other. As well as finding more complementary and purposeful ways to co-operate in order to survive, prosper and be more profitable.

The In-House Storm Brewing for Business Leaders

Despite the on-going march of the digital revolution and ensuing disruption in all sectors, there are still legacies from the twentieth century hanging around like a millstone in the twenty-first-century workplace. First, business leaders have to think the unthinkable and consider that the traditional Monday to Friday, 9–5 working day has had its day, but more importantly, the Taylorist approach to working is now obsolete.

This harks back to the early 1900s when American engineer Frederick Taylor pioneered office design akin to a factory production line. Office workers were packed into a large open central area, with their bosses observing from on high in private offices. However, this set-up suited the office work and hierarchical society of the early- to mid-twentieth century, which centred on repetitive tasks, paper processing and later on with typing pools, office memos, filing cabinets, etc. However, as a consequence of digitalization, the emphasis is now shifting away from merely processing – which is now undergoing automation – to one focusing on creativity, problem solving and collaboration. This means that traditional white-collar work is falling off the cliff, just as blue-collar work did since the 1980s, as the paper-pushing twentieth-century office drone is being forced out by the agile knowledge workers of the twenty-first-century digital revolution.

The Shift from Twentieth-century Stability to Twenty-first-century Agility

All in all, a combination of disruptive elements have upended the familiar characteristics which typified twentieth-century values: stability, conformity, mass-production, while the twenty-first century's mantra is constant change and customization. One of the best analogies is buses and taxis, and nowadays, we can add Uber to the transport mix. Buses are typical of many twentieth-century business models – they have a fixed route to a prescribed timetable and passengers are satisfied as long as they come on time. There is very little flexibility in the system, offering customers a limited, set and impersonal service, which does not veer even if the roads are jammed, but it is cheap and universal.

Taxis, on the other hand, aim to get their passengers to their destination in the quickest way possible, but at a premium price. They are adaptable to road conditions and customer demands, plus if you're lucky you can get a wealth of information and tips from the driver, with opinions on anything under the sun.

The arrival of Uber and others brought twenty-first-century customization to public transport, generally at lower fares than taxis; the convenience of ordering a cab on an app to pick you up on demand which you can track and the bonus of it being cashless, as payment is done automatically online. Uber cars range from budget to luxury and you can even ask for complete silence with no chatty driver! The business model is completely flexible and customer-focused to the extent that it now offers boats, helicopters and some other forms of transportation in some cities, as well as branching out to food delivery. This typically exemplifies the shift to agility, as well as showing how the gig economy is incorporated into an organization's structure, which naturally lends itself to a more agile workplace.

Uber is a prime example of the 'Shamrock Organization' as defined by Charles Handy in his 1989 book, *The Age of Unreason*. He describes these three-leaf organizational structures as a 'core of essential executives and workers supported by outside contractors and part-time help', the idea being that by contracting certain services, businesses could be made to work more productively and efficiently. Essentially turning away from the concept of 'jobs for life' and advocating for contracts or short-term jobs. The significance of this change is not confined to the transport industry and Uber but is happening across the board and affects every industry as the rise of the 'agile' or 'independent' workforce has driven the cultural shift of the 'work is a thing you do, not a place you go' mentality.

Since seeing my very first space utilization analysis by DEGW in 1998, which demonstrated the majority of office desks were only used 30–40 per cent of the working week, I agonized for years on how to find smart ways of improving on the rates of occupancy. However, I eventually learned that I was looking at the issue the wrong way round – the focus had to be on the people and their activities rather than the physical space. As Dr Paul Luciani, Executive Director for Real Estate at Ernst & Young in Asia, states, the 'digital revolution makes our love affair with spaces go out the window'. According to Luciani, business is moving very fast to the concept of 'the individual as the workplace'. The consequences of this notion and the impact it has, not just for CRE/FM, but for the wider real estate sector is momentous. The shift from fixed to fluid in terms of space consumption is compounded by the general societal move to using space on demand and via a subscription model, as per the alternative workplace business model.

This is another piece of evidence as to why both consumers and providers of commercial real estate need to get their heads together to figure out the implications of this paradigm shift, which is taking place under our noses. As one Head of Workplace for a well-known global sports brand observed, 'Maybe it is time for CRE and the business to redefine the notion of place?'

The Workplace Gets Smart

The concept of work being 'something you do' rather than 'somewhere you go to' is beginning to make an impact on working practices all over the world; which means that an organization's leaders and decision-makers are entering or are already in the midst of a maelstrom of uncharted managerial waters. In the US this debate has focused on whether 'telecommuting' is a good idea or not. I believe a more holistic approach is required beyond just whether your white-collar staff can work in the office or at home and this is due to the explosion of choice both in terms of workspace and actual working practices. For the first time ever, we are dealing with the convergence of multiple variations of employment and workplace environments likely to operate in a twenty-first-century enterprise, which could include:

Activity-Based Work or ABW was pioneered in the early 1980s by American architect Robert Luchetti and put into practice by Dutch architect Erik Veldhoen in the mid-1990s. ABW offers employees the choice of different types of workspaces, each designed to support the specific task they are working on. They are set up to include quiet zones or closed spaces for individual work, as well as open settings for meetings, collaborative work and team-based activities; this also extends to working remotely.

Agile Working provides employees with complete autonomy to work however, whenever and wherever they want, including from home, in a coffee shop and even behind a traditional desk in an office! There is maximum flexibility and minimum constraint in the way work is carried out. The onus is on employees to choose how and when they work in the most productive and efficient manner in order to drive long-term organizational success. Agile working environments often complement Activity-Based Work.

Flexible Working encompasses a full range of practices, listed below. In some countries, employees have statutory rights to apply for flexible working arrangements, although this is not a given everywhere. It is up to the employee to request this provision from their employer with both parties agreeing to a suitable consensus. It is interesting to note that a Lancaster University Work Foundation report published in 2016 predicted that 70 per cent of UK organizations would be adopting some form of flexible working by 2020.

- **Part-time Working** – Contracted to work less than standard full-time hours, with various permutations;
- **Flexi-time** – Freedom to work outside a pre-arranged set of hours;
- **Staggered hours** – Different start/finish times, meaning businesses can stay open longer;
- **Compressed working hours** – Working the normal contracted hours in fewer working days;
- **Job sharing** – A full-time job filled by two employees;
- **Home working/teleworking** – Remote working outside the office;
- **Shift work** – Work outside the normal 9–5 work schedule;
- **Shift swapping** – Employees trade shifts between themselves;
- **Self-rostering** – Employees design their own schedules matching individual preferences/skills;
- **Annualized hours** – Hours are worked out annually and any remaining are kept in reserve for busy periods;
- **Phased retirement** – Transitioning out of work with a reduced workload;
- **Term-time working** – Full-time work during school terms only;
- **V-time working** – Reducing hours for a fixed period.

Third-Space Disruption and Backlash

Pre-Covid-19 we saw the freeing up of the 'where' and 'how' we work options, in conjunction with the maturing of digital connectivity and the availability of a viable and secure cloud-based service. This means yet another dimension of flexibility has opened up. In the past it was a binary proposition when access to the internet was limited to the home and the office. In the last two decades we have seen an explosion of 'third spaces' where mobile workers can just plug, work and play. In fact, hotels, coffee shops and public spaces, such as libraries, have realized that they can provide solutions to those remote workers on the move.

Inevitably, with the rise of home, remote and 'third space' working, we are consuming space in a much broader manner than ever before – to the point where commentators speculate on the future (or even the demise) of the office itself! Covid-19 has just reinforced these calls. The most famous counter to working from home being Yahoo's former CEO Marissa Mayer, calling time on remote workers and bringing them back to the office in 2013. Mayer cited the fact that when she made the decision, she felt Yahoo staff would benefit more from face-to-face collaboration in an office environment. She commissioned a redesign of Yahoo's Sunnyvale HQ in California, but it did not stop a third of the tech giant's staff leaving in 2014.

To be fair, Mayer was landed with the impossible task of reversing Yahoo's downward spiral in the ultra-competitive world of Silicon Valley, which led to calls for her removal in 2015 by Yahoo shareholders and her eventual resignation in 2017. At the time of her reversal on Yahoo's telecommuting policies, she was criticized by a number of business leaders and Mayer herself conceded later that she 'had never meant to imply that remote working was wrong, just that it wasn't right for Yahoo, right then'.

IBM, one of the pioneers of the 'work-from-home' trend, cracked down on remote working in 2017, with a 'move back to the office or leave' policy. This was aimed primarily at their marketing departments, reiterating Marissa Mayer's view that working together as a team in an office has greater impact and inspires creativity. However, Global Workplace Analytics, a leading workplace research organization, has analysed 4,000 studies which indicate that remote working enables greater productivity, cultivates a happier workforce and encourages better employee retention.

On the flip side, Global Workplace Analytics also found that telecommuting did not necessarily suit everyone as some remote workers lacked motivation and self-discipline working on their own. It can also foster issues of mistrust between managers and their employees. So, in this light, the death of the office could be somewhat exaggerated! Since the first draft of this book was completed, pre-pandemic, many of my assertions have now taken on greater significance. Most of us have now experienced remote working and are really questioning the ways we used to work and the purpose of the office.

Sustainability – The New Competitive Environment

Another emerging factor that business leaders are becoming increasingly aware of is the importance of developing a better sustainability profile for their organizations. This encompasses the wider Corporate Social Responsibility (CSR) agenda, which is now morphing into areas of Environmental, Social and Governance (ESG). The concern over environmental and ethical issues is not a fad anymore, it is now viewed as a necessary and responsible obligation allied to good business practice. So much so that 20 years ago, Dow Jones introduced their Sustainability Index as a key reference for investors to track companies' performance in terms of economic, environmental and social benchmarks. Major multinational corporations like Blackstone the US-based financial group, launched their impact-investing platform in 2019. Goldman Sachs also aims to deliver investment advice in line with new ESG-related policies, 'because it makes sense from a business perspective', with BlackRock CEO Larry Fink stating, 'a company cannot achieve long-term profits without embracing purpose and considering the needs of a broad range of stakeholders'.

Transforming buildings to reduce emissions or the use of materials which are harmful both to health and the environment has now become a key consideration for management and the wider real estate industry. This means better use of materials and energy-efficient methods, including renewable energy sources, thermal and shading technologies, water recycling and natural ventilation systems, as well as thought going into the environmental impact across a building's life cycle, from construction to occupancy and beyond. This is reflected by the introduction of internationally recognized certification systems, including LEED in the US, BREEAM in the UK and Green Star in Australia, which asses and rate buildings' environmental credentials.

According to a 2019 Harvard University study, organizations with a more 'employee-centric' approach see a reduction in absenteeism and staff turnover, as well as a 16 per cent rise in productivity, an 18 per cent increase in retaining their talent and an increased 30 per cent attraction rate over their competitors. So, the importance of a well-laid-out, high-quality working environment, with ambient temperatures, workable noise levels, good lighting and air quality, together with easy access to local amenities and services cannot be underestimated. This is especially true now that Millennials and Generation Z make up more than half of the workforce. Interestingly, according to a CBRE worldwide survey of 13,000 Millennials, a remarkable 70 per cent of them rank a quality workplace above salary. More significantly, company review site Glassdoor found that 71 per cent of young workers would quit their jobs on a matter of principle and 74 per cent consider an organization's stand on political, social and ethical matters as crucial when assessing them as potential employers.

The Importance of Workplace Health and Wellbeing

Parallel to all these developments is the increasing understanding of the wellbeing dimension in the last five to ten years, both physical and more recently in mental health. Slowly, more companies are examining how the built environment is impacting on their employees and are adopting or incorporating Well Building standards into their workplaces.

No one can really afford to ignore the problem of health and wellbeing in the workplace anymore, as indicated by the findings of Integrated Benefits Institute, a research organization which focuses on health and employee productivity – an estimated $227 billion is lost in the US owing to employee absenteeism or presenteeism (when employees are at work, but are unproductive owing to health problems). The onset of the Coronavirus pandemic in 2020 particularly heightened organizations' concerns surrounding health and wellbeing in the workplace – and concurrently spurred a renewed interest in the dynamics and scope of remote working.

Moreover, a CBRE study found that work-related stress costs the UK 10.4 million working days per year in absences. A less obvious benefit is by improving workplace wellbeing, it could reduce pressure on health care services, especially public systems such as the NHS.

Dr Amanda Rischbieth, a current Visiting Scientist at the Harvard T.H. Chan School of Public Health, notes the leading work by Professor Tyler VanderWeele on wellbeing measurement. She sees the positive shift by organizations and individuals towards a broader notion of human wellbeing – that of flourishing – a broad range of states and outcomes, including mental and physical health, but also encompassing happiness and life satisfaction, meaning and purpose, character and virtue, and close social relationships. The emergent Flourishing Index from this work provides a modern and methodologically rigorous and useful approach to employee evaluation.

Sustaining the Value of Brand and Reputation

Sustainability now extends across many other spheres, however, including developing, as well as maintaining a company's brand and its reputation. Business leaders cannot afford to overlook the significance of their company brand and its reputation, as well as how it is perceived by the outside world. Every decision made in the boardroom can be curated and shared in an instant to millions of people and organizations have absolutely no control over how it is received and the ensuing reaction it causes. A brand or a company's reputation can easily suffer or even be 'killed' outright by negative social media.

The Generation Game: A Wider Dimension

The managing of the multi-generational workforce has become quite a major preoccupation for both HR departments and management. Each generation has its own characteristics, strengths and weaknesses, whose needs and demands must be accommodated and harnessed to enable them to perform at their best and above all, work together harmoniously.

+ **Baby Boomers – Born between 1946 and 1964**
  Increased life expectancy, coupled with rises in the age of retirement worldwide, as governments face a

pensions crisis means that 1960s-born Baby Boomers will retire nearer their 70th birthdays. This is an enormous demographic spanning those born after World War II through to the TV generation of the mid-1960s, incorporating both 'hippies' and 'yuppies'. They may have reached their peak but they will still be part of the workforce for the next 10 to 15 years.

+ **Generation X – Born between 1965 and 1984**

 More self-reliant and independent, since this age group were more likely to be brought up in households with both parents working. Their individuality and entrepreneurial spirit, coupled with a keenness to learn and explore, coincided with the onset of the internet and digital technology.

+ **Millennials/Generation Y – Born between 1985 and 1996**

 The first generation growing up with mobile phones and other personal tech gadgets on hand. This makes them natural networkers who happily share information, while thriving in collaborative environments. They certainly expect a positive workplace culture with a strong ethical/environmental stance and as 'digital natives' they champion flexible schedules and the remote working agenda since the work–life balance is key for them.

+ **Centennials/Generation Z – Born between 1997 and 2010**

 This iPhone/iPad generation is fully subsumed in technology, true 'digital natives' but they have grown up in a post-9/11 world, with the insecurity of the 2008

economic crash, the influence of social media and now
Covid-19. Economic worries fuel their ambitions and
they are very adept at multitasking; also, likely to have
a 'side hustle' or be part of the gig economy. They
also believe that technology and their smartphones
offer both a solution to a problem and an answer to
everything, yet they are also more aware of the risks
and complications of tech, than previous generations.

Looking at the Multi-Generational Workforce through a Broader Lens

For the most part, commentators have focused on the above
sweeping generalizations and stereotypes for each of these age
brackets and the workplace dilemma of four generations working
together at the same time being an unprecedented phenomenon. Then again, I think this is only part of the equation and
nobody has really seen the complete and holistic picture of the
multi-generational landscape.

Despite the workforce comprising these four age/genera-
tion-related segments, for the most part, the greatest focus has
been on the new entrants. Admittedly, they are the future and
will dominate the workplace in the next decade. However, I see
other nuances in the issues affecting the various age groups,
which adds a further layer of complexity for management:

+ The new entrants, Millennials and Generation Z, are
  generally more footloose in their approach to work.
  According to Deloitte's 2018 global Millennial Survey,
  only 28 per cent envisage staying beyond five years
  with their current employers. They are certainly the
  embodiment of the 'agile' workforce, as characterized
  by Charles Handy;

+ The middle Generation X tier – this is the 'hidden revolt' of middle-aged professionals, who now view the work–life balance as a priority and are voting with their feet to escape the 'rat race'. Their quest for autonomy and a more relaxed schedule means there has been an increased 'brain drain' of experienced talent in organizations;

+ The Baby Boomers/Silver Brigade – it is a given that the traditional age of retirement is not an option for this group. They are an untapped resource with a wealth of lifetime experience which could be used, albeit on a more flexible basis, with many willing to up their skill-sets, especially in technology;

+ Working Parents – Inadequate or expensive childcare facilities make it very difficult for working parents across the board. This is especially true in the case of new mothers wanting to return to work and not much consideration is given for the most part to maintaining access and facilitating this pool of talent.

The Critical Connection: Using the Workplace as a Tool for Organizational Change

Gregory Shea, Senior Fellow at the University of Pennsylvania's Wharton Center for Leadership and Change Management, is a noted academic and a consultant to numerous types of international organizations undergoing transformational change. He argues that although today's business leaders strive to transform a company's culture, they underrate woefully the value of the workplace in supporting the kind of change they wish to achieve.

Shea contends that without taking account of the working environment and its relation to people, it is virtually impossible to alter their behaviour. He proposes the only way to enable change successfully is to think of the behaviours you want to encourage in the workplace and then to construct a setting that promotes and supports them. Using the office, whether in a different configuration or actually moving to a completely new space, is still not a fully appreciated accelerator of organizational change. This underlines the key point here that most business leaders underestimate or fail to see the opportunity in using space as a strategic tool. It was recognized by the BBC's Director-General/CEO Mark Thompson during his tenure there and as a group, we soon realized that the estate transformation was much more than just a cost-saving programme – it became a key catalyst of change across the entire organization. My role as Head of CRE was to interpret, integrate and instigate turning an underfunded property portfolio which was not fit for purpose into a viable company resource.

Disruptive Forces in Commercial Real Estate Impacting on the Enterprise

On the surface the following factors affect commercial real estate directly, but the impact of these issues will eventually have implications for business leaders and decision makers through their organizational strategies and balance sheets.

Business Effectiveness Dimensions Come Home

People typically account for almost 80 per cent of an organization's operating costs when one factors in employee salaries, pensions and benefits. Conversely, occupancy/property expenses make up just 9 per cent and historically, these factors have always been treated as stand-alone issues. However, in recent years there is a growing awareness and overwhelming evidence demonstrating that a well-designed and well-run workplace has beneficial effects on the performance of its occupants.

The statistics bear this out since Gallup started polling US employees annually from the year 2000, measuring engagement, commitment to their work and workplace. The figures range from 26 per cent engagement at the beginning of the twenty-first century to an improved 34 per cent reported in 2018, although 53 per cent are still disengaged, with 16.5 per cent totally disengaged.

In his book, *The Elemental Workplace*, Neil Usher asserts, 'Everyone deserves a fantastic workplace in which to live, learn, grow, share and contribute. We know that a great workplace is motivating and uplifting and contributes to our sense of self-worth and wellbeing, and therefore benefits the organization in which we are employed.' Yet despite the figures and numerous studies done regarding the positive effects of a great workplace and the correlation to increased productivity and profitability, coupled with media attention focusing on the 'go-go' Google and Facebook offices with their bright colours, beanbags, slides and basketball hoops, the message has not really sunk in and the reality is that most workers are still stuck in usually uninspiring spaces of beige, grey or off-white. It is probably worse for American workers, who are often imprisoned in a sea of cubicles, cubes and corner offices. Indeed elsewhere in the world the cubicle also became the lingua franca of 'best in class' office design and layout. However, the tide is beginning to turn as corporations have come to terms with the realization that a great workplace can be a useful tool in the current war for attracting and retaining talent.

The Pitfalls of Measuring Workplace Productivity

This has led the CRE sector measuring and substantiating employee productivity in the workplace to the point of obsession. The leaders in this field are the Leesman Index, positioning themselves as the 'world's largest employee experience database' yet many commentators argue that demonstrating and measuring productivity has yet to be proved and is akin to searching for the 'Holy Grail', especially in the knowledge-based twenty-first-century workplace.

Maybe this is an example of how CRE and the wider workplace sector fails to grasp how business leaders view things and I also maintain that we are looking at this issue through the wrong end of the telescope in that quantifying productivity of any degree of percentage can have a huge impact on company profits – that is, say that regardless of whether it is a 5 or 10 per cent or even a 15 per cent improvement. These are all positive results which go straight to the bottom line. Therefore, my argument is we do not need to prove the quantum/percentage but merely demonstrate whether productivity has been achieved and this just requires a simple 'yes/no' test. It is the equivalent to the 'on/off' button in the digital world – either you have productivity or not!

The Key Link: A Well-Designed Workplace = A Well-Run Workspace

So far, most with some notable exceptions have focused on how a well-designed workplace has beneficial outcomes on the performance of its occupants but purely from the design aspect – agreeable architectural features of the building, the overall look and feel of its surroundings, the ergonomically-designed layouts of workspaces, offices, furniture and its aesthetics. However, it is all very well having a shiny new designer workplace but the crux of the matter is how it is operated to enable and facilitate work.

A truly effective workplace reduces the amount of friction and stress that a typical office worker endures in going about their day-to-day work and it is the result of a well-run and well-managed support organization, who can administer a work-place successfully. The crucial connection is linking the mindsets of the fragmented property industry, the people managing projects versus those in charge of its operational aspects, as well as those leading the enterprise.

Smashing the Shibboleths of Commercial Real Estate – The Customer is King!

The 'customer is king' approach might be a basic tenet in every other market sector and yet for the most part the real estate industry still seems to adhere to the old Henry Ford school of thought, that any customer could have any colour car they wanted 'so long as it is black!' – underpinned by its 'build it and they will come' mantra and mentality. The other driver for this is the major shift away from twentieth-century thinking: the obsession with owning and possessing property to one moving towards accessing and consuming space.

Other businesses have been grappling with changing customer needs for years, but it has now hit real estate in momentous fashion – giving consumers more choice in their workplace options for the first time. Guy Holden, Head of CBRE Enterprise Client Group EMEA, is quite forthright in stating, 'It's about time that the real estate industry woke up to the fact that we're here to bring to the market a product that the consumer actually wants, as opposed to an asset class that the developer wants.'

The Relentless March of the Flexible Workspace Disruptors

The emergence of alternative models for using office space accelerated back in 1989 with the arrival of Regus, now IWG. This was led by British entrepreneur Mark Dixon, who spotted a gap in the European market on a business trip to Brussels. He noticed that executives on the move had no place to work or hold meetings other than in hotels, so he had the simple idea of providing fully-staffed and maintained office space for companies to use as required. Similar ventures had started in the US earlier but were small-scale in nature. What Regus did was to 'weaponize' the concept and it expanded globally. His pioneering service reflects the view that, 'there will be winners and losers in the real estate industry like any other business, if you don't start giving the customer what they want' – a factor that sees IWG, together with its associated brands/franchise partners, as the workplace market leader, spanning 3,300 locations in 1,100 towns and cities across more than 110 countries.

Over the last 20 years multiple new entrants have expanded the 'serviced office' market offering various ways to consume working space flexibly. Certainly the dominant 'new kid on the block' as previously discussed is WeWork, with 625 locations in over 127 cities in 33 countries (2020 figures) riding on a blitzkrieg strategy of marketing, promotion and 'do what you love'. Their basic business model works on the premise of buying properties on a long-lease contract before refitting the premises and then subletting on shorter leases at a profit. In addition, they also woke up landlords to the fact that office tenants want shorter-term leases and no upfront capital.

Undoubtedly, they are giving their clients an appealing, attractive, flexible proposition but it has rapidly become a crowded market with many players, such as Convene, Offices iQ, Instant Offices, LiquidSpace, Knotel, Serendipity Labs, The Office Group, among others, all jostling to get a piece of the flexible space sector action. It has also prompted, or one might say provoked, a few of the property world's 'old guard', such as Land Securities, British Land in the UK, as well as Boston Properties, Tischman Speyer in the US and Australia's Lend

Lease and Dexus to dip their toes into introducing flexible workplace brands, with catchy names such as Myo, Storey, Studio and Dexus Place. These non-core flexible space products are offered alongside their mainstream traditional leasing operations. Although early days, it is expected that market forces will push these and other major players to think seriously about their role in flexible space.

The Penetration of Proptech

Another disrupting factor for the property industry as a whole has been the explosion of new easily accessible digital tools, which have boosted the service-side of the market in recent years. Similar to the impact Fintech had on banking, Proptech could end up being the real estate equivalent of bitcoin. The property world is finally facing 'a wave of tech-enabled innovation that is reshaping the way real estate is transacted, designed, built and marketed'. For the most part, the well-known companies such as Opendoor, Zillow, Trulia, etc. in the US and UK online platforms Purplebricks, Rightmove and Zoopla among others operate mainly within the residential marketplace although it is interesting to note that many of these Proptech initiatives have a mission to replace 'real-life' estate agents/realtors completely.

Proptech has had positive effects on the industry in two ways since it has driven the increased availability to information. Meaning that the property world's major players have lost their long-established power to control data and the way it was used in the past. Their position has been usurped, since transparency and accessibility are now the order of the day and Proptech companies are interpreting, curating and sharing information openly. The creation of international property databases offers a more reliable and accurate set of figures with a clearer picture of the value of real estate, rather than when individual groups or one organization produced their own set of numbers. The other plus point is that by digitizing the US Land Records and the UK's Land Registry, enhanced by data platforms like CoStar, the process of property transactions is being speeded up considerably.

Impact on Commercial Real Estate

Real estate strategist Dror Poleg, author of *Rethinking Real Estate*, asserts that 'technology undermines the inherent value of real estate assets' and this fundamental shift means that 'many of the assumptions that make real estate attractive to institutional investors are being challenged'. As Poleg explains, in his dissection of the world of real estate investment, there is tangible evidence of a big market shift. There is now a growing realization that consumers are less likely to take on long-term lease commitments, while also demanding greater operational-type services based around user experience and wellbeing. Thus, the predictable 'bond-like' income of a lease will diminish. In his book, Poleg lays out ten plagues, which describe the factors forcing real estate owners to consider shifting their business model to B2C. Or, as he puts it, 'shifting from a model that thrives on well-run assets to an industry that thrives on well-run businesses'. These real estate businesses will focus more on service than on the asset itself.

This shift is also coupled with the expectation that according to JLL, 30 per cent of corporate portfolios will be taken up by flexible office space by 2030. The key distinction being that this type of product does not require a formal lease and all the trappings that go with the leasing process and this includes transaction costs. In this context, commercial real estate companies, like JLL, have already seen the vital role Proptech will play in the future and their venture capital arm has already invested in digital commercial property advisor Hubble. This

UK-based tech group operates an online platform which matches companies needing flexible office space with landlords and commercial space providers – their ultimate ambition is to offer this service worldwide.

Canadian-owned Breather offers 'on-demand' private workspaces in North America and London booked through an app, by the hour, the day or longer in a wide range of locations to tailor every need. These customer-focused digital services are not confined to property players alone. Restaurant chains are getting in on the act by offering app services to reserve tables in their premises, with access to electric sockets, unlimited Wi-Fi and coffee, plus the added bonus of hosting clients/colleagues for a working lunch, all in one place. This all fits into the narrative of the 'Uberization' of the workplace, DEGW alumnus. WeWork SVP Ronen Journo points out that the future of the flexible office will be, 'The go somewhere and use it as a consumption-based model. Uber did it. And it is coming for the flex workspace.' In addition, these Proptech developments also intensify the debate of what will happen to the army of advisors/consultants/brokers who have been churning the supply side of the commercial property market for years.

Efficiency Has Hit the Buffers

The last decade has seen incessant effort on driving down occupancy costs and it has been particularly relentless in FM. However, from 2015 onwards, industry commentators including CoreNet Global started a refocusing exercise looking into real estate as a driver of value not just as an overhead cost. This is a concept which I had promoted for many years and was the linchpin of the transformation at the BBC, which proved the theory that it is not just about the buildings, but about the value chain beyond merely bricks and mortar.

✦ Space Standards

One area which has become a bastion of the efficiency drive everywhere is space standards – however, Covid-19 will be a game-changer in this factor now. Over the last decade there has been an extensive drive in allocating less space per person within office buildings. Typically, in the UK and Europe the traditional rule of thumb was one person for every 10m² of space; this is now reducing to one person for every 8m² and sometimes as low as one person for every 6m².

Over the years the US has based space allocations on one person for every 20m² or higher, but this is changing slowly. CoreNet Global estimates the average in 2017 to be 14m². (In the US, this would be calculated in square feet, with 20m² being 225sq ft and 14m² equalling 151sq ft.) Corporate America's love affair with cubicles in their workplace design means they have lagged behind in shrinking space per person, although they are now catching up;

✦ Questioning Headcount Forecasting Viability

Headcount forecasting is an essential business tool. A company needs to have data for staff planning to put their strategic priorities and budgets in place. They are key for the HR department since they are in charge of position requirements and hiring, as well as the training, development and general welfare of employees. It is also useful for the accommodation planning framework, especially given the complex and inflexible real estate systems that exists today. Still, like all measuring methods, the results can only be as accurate as the information submitted and now headcount forecasting can be considered to be fairly useless in the face of changing labour market dynamics.

Business leaders would probably find it more useful to have data on the actual needs of their enterprise, as opposed to simple headcounts. This would be in addition to comprehensive real-time information on their organization's real estate portfolio in terms of corporate and competitive realities, which also impacts on their strategic planning, budgeting, cash flows, etc. It was interesting to note that the CRE leaders of global organizations who attended my US workshop were regularly approached by the C-Suite to provide headcount and occupancy reports rather than HR;

+ **Outsourcing Corporate Real Estate/Facilities Management**

Over the last 10 to 15 years many companies have been outsourcing these functions, which were traditionally kept in-house. For example, BBC Property had upwards of 120 people at the beginning of 2004 and eventually reduced their staff down to 32 in 2019.

Contracting out these functions has both pros and cons: namely outsourcing companies are usually seen to offer a better service in terms of having more experience in specific areas, access to better resources and advanced processes, as well as specialized training and people beyond in-house teams. This certainly saves money, especially since the contractor also absorbs employee costs.

The cons are a lack of understanding and in-depth knowledge on the part of the outsourcing company of an organization's culture, its strategy, its people and its operations, since they do not have the same level of loyalty and affiliation as an in-house team. A further drawback is when organizations do not clearly articulate their service expectations or the contracting model has not been thought out thoroughly, inevitably causing dissatisfaction in the outcome for both parties.

Another factor in the UK was the collapse of outsourcing giants Carillion in 2018, followed by service providers Interserve in 2019, which have damaged the industry greatly. Resulting in an approximate 30 per cent decline in the number of contracts awarded to outsourcing companies in 2018, according to an analysis report carried out by *Facilitate Magazine* in 2019.

The Commoditizing of Facilities Management

As a result of this trend in outsourcing and the huge success of the procurement departments, the FM offering by third parties is rapidly approaching a commodity service. Not only that but it is fragmented, since its chief function is to co-ordinate a thin layer of management over the many services (maintenance, cleaning, security, waste management, etc.) and professional silos within an organization. In other words, providing 'service bundling', which is not quite the same as delivering a truly integrated, value-added service.

✦ The Decline of Public/Private Financing Models

An associated aspect of the efficiency drive especially in the UK has been public/private finance initiative types of outsourcing, known as PFIs, although recently some of these partnerships have suffered reversals and have subsequently fallen out of favour. However, back in 1999, there was a great swathe of large-scale outsourcing involving various government departments and their entire real estate portfolios under the two biggest schemes, PRIME and STEPS.

In 2001, the publicly owned BBC entered a joint venture partnership with Land Securities Trillium to the tune of £2.5 billion, which involved a series of building and renovation projects over a 30-year period. This came to a premature end in 2005, when the BBC recognized that it could obtain alternative financing by raising money on the bond market for its redevelopment at a cheaper rate than Land Securities. At that point it was felt that the BBC needed to rethink the agreement and perhaps outsourcing was not the right option, so the contract with Land Securities was cancelled. At the time it was perceived as hugely embarrassing, but it saved the BBC and the licence payer the tidy sum of £60 million.

Standing back and taking a strategic view of the situation may not result in certain parties seeing eye-to-eye, but the reality of the situation is that cost-cutting has achieved its goal and there is no more fat on the bone. In fact, there is now a significant risk that core service delivery can be compromised owing to the pressure on outsourced providers to deliver a service which is not profitable and this has implications for an organization's management and their balance sheet.

Implications of Shifting Regulations on Property Market Dynamics

+ **The FASB/IFRS 16 Accounting Standard**
  Endorsed by the Finance Accounting Standards Board (FASB) and the International Accounting Standards Board (IASB), its introduction in January 2019 concerns the leasing and renting of assets, which

is an important and widely used financing solution for many companies. This includes offices, power plants, retail spaces, warehousing and other high-value items and it enables companies to access and use property or high-price equipment without incurring large cash outflows at the start. The new requirements eliminate nearly all off-balance sheet accounting for lessees/tenants and redefines many commonly used financial metrics, such as the gearing ratio and EBITDA (earnings before interest, tax, depreciation and amortization). In a nutshell, leases will now be treated as a liability, not an expense item, which will have a great impact on demand and will also have implications on an organization's balance sheet. This might affect the economics of leases/rentals and put pressure on pricing, with real estate landlords finding it more difficult to demand higher rents, especially in tough economic times.

As a consequence of shifting developments in the property sector the question is: how will business managers and the commercial real estate world reach an equilibrium vis à vis the workplace and make a profit? Navigating this balance will be crucial to how organizations operate and thrive in the twenty-first-century.

How Will the Odd Couple Enterprise and Office Come Together?

So how is the business world to make sense of all these drivers for change and above all to find the missing link between making money and the workplace? Part of the difficulty is that old habits die hard, especially if they are aligned with vested interests and profits in both the business and the property sectors. However, we have now reached an inflection point and since everyone is living in a world full of change, complexity and ambiguity, we must act now!

Most importantly, it is time to build bridges with other players before it is too late. This message has to be hammered home and it applies to all parties. The Odd Couple of enterprise leaders and the wider real estate industry – all of them have to broaden their outlook, look over the parapet into each other's worlds to understand how they function. For corporate real estate departments, allied with FM, it is time to shift their thinking beyond cost control and efficiency and take responsibility for workplace effectiveness. Everyone needs to work together to build a deeper and more holistic understanding of how a smart and effective workplace can deliver tangible business value; not just reduced occupancy costs and this applies not only to the enterprise but also to the wider real estate world.

Business Leaders' Remit to Effect Change

Leaders have to understand how they can tap into an underutilized tool – their corporate real estate – and see how it can be used to their competitive advantage. There has to be a shift in focus from looking at their real estate on a cost centre basis and to accept that it is an intrinsic part of the corporation's value chain. Most managers see their real estate holdings purely as an expense line item and in some cases as an organizational millstone which eats into their profit margins, especially when they have far too much space.

As previously mentioned, the workplace now conveys an organization's purpose and its corporate values more than ever before. Enterprise leaders have to consider how the workplace can become part of a corporation's arsenal of competitive weaponry in this increasingly connected world, where brand and reputation are crucial factors. Therefore, harnessing the unlocked potential of the workplace has to be a serious consideration. Serial entrepreneur and former banker Kate Lister, President of Global Analytics in San Diego, is an internationally recognized authority on emerging workplace strategies. A long-time proponent of flexible working, she asserts that there has to be a 'shift from a return on cost mindset to a return on people one'. After all, people are a business's most valuable resource and ultimately, their engagement with their working environment is paramount to an organization's success. The important question here is: How many business leaders have made the connection between productive staff and a productive workplace?

Management has to recognize that an effective and efficient workplace contributes to the attraction and retention of its talent. A 2018 Gallup estimated that staff turnover costs US companies $1 trillion per year.[3] At a conservative estimate, the cost of replacing an individual employee can range from one-half to two times that person's annual salary. These expenses are never registered directly on a company balance sheet, yet they are phenomenal! Moreover, this is a fixable problem and business leaders must focus on commissioning work environments which engage people while creating a meaningful workplace culture. They have to understand and build new models of effective management, while also broadening and deepening their leadership capabilities – shaping them around a network of empowered teams composed of skilled people whose abilities they can develop, nurture and retain for the benefit of their organizations.

Creating a meaningful work environment and an effective workplace is a complex process, but business leaders have the

---

[3] McFeely, S. and Wigert, B. 'This fixable problem costs U.S. businesses $1 trillion'. Gallup Workplace, 2019. https://www.gallup.com/workplace/247391/fixable-problem-costs-businesses-trillion.aspx

resources on hand and probably in-house – provided they realize that by effectively leveraging and co-ordinating the skill sets
and perspectives provided by their CRE, FM, HR and IT teams.
In this way savvy leaders can achieve their goal and gain an
advantage over their competitors – finding themselves attracting the best talent.

Shifting Paradigms in Real Estate

Looking at the wider world of real estate, there seem to be
budding shoots of a fresh approach in how to supply buildings.
In part this change in starting to think about operating differently
has been forced on many property companies and investors by
the various disruptive factors, whose impact has already been
analysed.

This is certainly the view of Sir Stuart Lipton, founder of
Stanhope Plc, now Partner at Lipton Rogers LLP. Since the
1980s he has masterminded the development of many iconic sites
and buildings across the UK. Sir Stuart is considered the doyen
of the British developer cadre and father of its commercial real
estate. He might be the patrician veteran of the property world
but his 'call to arms' to the real estate sector is both progressive and succinct: 'Let's focus on the consumer. We have, as an
industry, to stop building buildings for ourselves and start building buildings for our occupiers.'

While I support Sir Stuart's point of view, I suggest that one
other positive step would be to consider the TI or fit-out process,
which in most cases is both time-consuming and complicated.
Given the speed to market business imperative that is the
norm nowadays, perhaps some thought needs to be applied to
streamlining a process which usually takes six to nine months to
execute – another reason why businesses are opting for taking
spaces in the flexible market.

Real estate needs to accept that the occupier is the customer as opposed to the property, investment or finance groups backing them financially and that the needs and demands of the occupier/customer come first. Consequently, the commercial property sector has to engage in a more meaningful manner with businesses, who after all are their customers and these business people now have a real choice in how they consume space.

Additionally, progress in effecting organizational change in enterprises occupying commercial spaces can only be achieved if both the 'older real estate siblings' can align with CRE/FM to support them to focus on making more effective use of offices. Accordingly, they also have a role to play in helping business leaders understand the link of how a corporate property portfolio delivers better business performance through better workplace performance, therefore maximizing the return on their investment.

Corporate Real Estate and Facilities Management Have to Shift Gears

An organization's internal CRE/FM still struggles to figure out how they can become enablers in providing solutions for the needs of the businesses they serve. While many believe they are hampered by the constraints imposed by the wider real estate world and thus have no options to progress, these internal teams actually have great potential in enabling real estate solutions.

First, and this is especially true in the case of FM, they have to overcome the perception management has of them as the 'people who do stuff' and transform this assessment into becoming a company's 'problem solvers'. Both CRE and FM must expand their remit to include not only the visible features of design and workplace functions, but also the less visible organizational factors such as strategy, structure, process, incentives and talent – that is, they must engage proactively with corporate executives if they want to receive the recognition they deserve and be seen as much more than mere 'order takers'.

Dr Barry Varcoe, former Global Head of FM/CRE at the Zurich Insurance Group and currently Global Director of Real Estate & Facilities at George Soros's Open Society Foundations, highlights, 'The core issue is no longer about buildings or services but about enabling productivity that delivers competitive advantage for an organization.'

The main objective of FM and CRE is to change mindsets from just managing their supply chains to delivering a coherent 'value for money' service and not just at the lowest cost. In order to accomplish that, they must understand and learn to speak the 'language' of the business their organization operates and become better aligned to an enterprise's objectives and business aims.

Up to now FM and CRE practitioners have not been required to learn about the wider demands of running a business, since they are anchored in measures which are purely real estate focused, such as improving occupancy levels and reducing cost per rentable square foot. Mainly because the wider industry itself is structured in such a way that it sees no real reason to concern itself with matters outside the commercial real estate and internal facilities silo. There are some examples of good practice such as programmes run by CoreNet Global, but mainstream participation is what is needed to change mindsets across the board. This also extends to business leaders, who have to realize that they too can direct change in the status quo and co-opt CRE/FM to add value to their enterprise. Plus, they could expand the way CRE/FM people are rewarded beyond the narrow definition of managing occupancy costs and doing good real estate deals to include how these functions enable productive work and create business value.

The Odd Couple and Other Stakeholders Must Join Forces

Having considered all the various players in isolation could there be untapped benefits from taking a more joined-up approach? By understanding the views and perspectives of all the stakeholders involved in the provision and consumption of real estate, could such an approach produce some fresh perspectives and insights?

The critical point here is that all the stakeholders – the consumer/tenant/ business, the real estate industry, together with the CRE/FM sub-sector – all have to engage at the same time and at the same pace. They could build a fresh perspective in creating a renewed approach to how we produce and operate workplaces and offices. To this end there has to be a shift in the dial on a three-way basis to change mindsets and adapt to new and innovative ways of thinking in order to generate both entrepreneurial and social value. No doubt the Covid-19 crisis of 2020 may well influence this aspect and if this can be managed, it can be mutually beneficial and a 'win-win' for all parties concerned. It will certainly generate significant dividends in the wider context of creating real social value, together with leaving a more sustainable legacy for future generations.

Six Steps for Businesses to Build Benefits from Fresh Perspectives

- ✦ Change the traditional workplace/real estate focus from being 'building-centric' to one that is 'people-centric';
- ✦ Recognize the potential of multiple workplace dimensions rather than just that of the traditional office set-up; we can now do office work anywhere, anytime, anyhow;

+ Pursuing a concerted effort in sustainability and carbon reduction solutions. The real estate sector could partner with corporate occupiers to make really meaningful contributions to the climate challenge. Thereby demonstrating tangible Social Value and compliance with investor ESG criteria;

+ Framing an alliance of CRE/FM and HR to join the dots between people and place has to be an essential ingredient of organizational success, as well as not ignoring the contribution of IT and Procurement; As part of the re-alignment, these support functions need to adopt a different form of leadership, which requires a wider business lens rather than just looking at it from their current respective professional and siloed points of view;

+ Use the combined influence of all the stakeholders with academia to include workplace strategy on MBAs and Senior Executive programmes to educate and build awareness into making better use of the built environment;

+ Consider broadening the current finance-driven bond-like model for real estate and evaluate options to take account of the growing flexible space sector.

Sources

1. 'Companies, investors, and governments must prepare for a significant reallocation of capital.'
   Fink, L. 'A Fundamental Reshaping of Finance'. BlackRock CEO Letter, 2020 https://www.blackrock.com/us/individual/|larry-fink-ceo-letter

2. 'We stand on the brink of a technological revolution that will fundamentally alter the way we live, work, and relate to one another. In its scale, scope, and complexity, the transformation will be unlike anything humankind has experienced before.'

Schwab, K. 'The Fourth Industrial Revolution: what it means, how to respond'. Global Agenda, 2016.

3. 'core of essential executives and workers supported by outside contractors and part-time help'.
Handy, C. 'The Shamrock Organization'. *The Age of Unreason* (revised ed.), London: Arrow, 2002. (First published Random House Business Books, 1989; reprint. 1991.) Chapter 4. p. 70.

4. 'had never meant to imply that remote working was wrong, just that it wasn't right for Yahoo, right then'.
Bort, J. 'Marissa Mayer defends her famous ban on remote work'. *Business Insider*, 2015. https://www.businessinsider.com/mayer-still-defends-remote-work-ban-2015.

5. 'because it makes sense from a business perspective'.
Stevens, P. 'Goldman pledges $750 billion for "large opportunities" in sustainable finance'. CNBC.com, 2019. https://www-cnbc-com.cdn.ampproject.org/c/s/www.cnbc.com/amp/2019/12/19/goldman-pledges-750-billion-for-opportunities-in-sustainable-finance.html

6. 'a company cannot achieve long-term profits without embracing purpose and considering the needs of a broad range of stakeholders'.
Fink, L. 'A Fundamental Reshaping of Finance'. Ibid.

7. 'Everyone deserves a fantastic workplace in which to live, learn, grow, share and contribute… We know that a great workplace is motivating and uplifting and contributes to our sense of self-worth and wellbeing, and therefore benefits the organization in which we are employed.'
Usher, N. *The Elemental Workplace: The 12 Elements for Creating a Fantastic Workplace for Everyone*. London: Lid Publishing, 2018, p. 5.

8. 'world's largest employee experience database'.
Leesman Index Website. 'How we do it'. https://www.leesmanindex.com/

9. 'so long as it is black!'
Ford, H. in collaboration with Crowther, S. *My Life and Work*. New York: Doubleday, Page & Company, 1922, p. 72.

10. 'a wave of tech-enabled innovation that is reshaping the way real estate is transacted, designed, built and marketed'.
Block, A. & Aarons, Z. *Proptech 101: Turning Chaos Into Cash Through Real Estate Innovation*, Charleston: Advantage, 2019, p. 3.

11. 'technology undermines the inherent value of real estate assets'.

12. 'many of the assumptions that make real estate attractive to institutional investors are being challenged'.

13. 'shifting from a model that thrives on well-run assets to an industry that thrives on well-run businesses'.
Poleg, D. *Rethinking Real Estate: A Roadmap to Technology's Impact on the World's Largest Asset Class.* Cham: Palgrave Macmillan/Springer Nature, 2019. Preface IX. p.240, p.97

Epigraph
Burke, E. (ed. E.J. Payne) 'Conciliation with America'. Select Work, Vol. 1., New Jersey: The Lawbook Exchange, Ltd., 1881, 2005, p. 222.

People and Place: Joining the Dots

Purpose, pattern, and people, the three Ps at the heart of life.
Charles Handy

'The only purpose of space is to help the performance of the business.' I almost fell off my chair when I heard that sentence and even more surprisingly, this was being articulated by an HR person! However, this was no ordinary HR person but someone who had a reputation for really 'thinking out of the box' in terms of how agility in the workplace could shape transformational change in a global corporation.

Caroline Waters held various managerial roles at the British Telecom Group (BT) during her 33-year career there, giving her a very rounded view of the organization, which culminated in becoming its Director of People and Policy. She was an intrinsic part of the team which pioneered BT's move in the 1990s to becoming one of the world's leading exponents of flexible working practices; the multinational telecommunications holding company is now one of the top 40 digital groups globally and attracted a revenue of £23.4 billion, with £2.2 billion profits before tax in 2018.

That initial conversation and a tour of BT's central HQ in London laid the seeds for a learning partnership which has endured over the years. I met Caroline at a critical juncture in

2006, while facing the enormous challenges of the BBC's organizational transformation, and I needed to define case studies of other large global institutions who had embraced flexible and agile working successfully, in order to promote the concept to the BBC. Caroline's innovative strategies provided me with insights into agile working but also helped me to appreciate the challenges my colleagues in BBC People were facing at the time and to see how important it was to align the workings of the business and its people to effect change.

I must admit I was also taken aback when Caroline bemoaned the fact that most HR practitioners were too narrow with a 'short-term' focus and how they were not trained or conditioned to think broadly. Adding that although HR had already 'made it' to the boardroom, this was just an illusion. The reality was that HR was not really seen as a fully paid-up member of the C-Suite, but as the company 'people's champion' and therefore rarely perceived as a strategic asset in the corporate world. Those were precisely the frustrations I encountered in CRE/FM.

In Caroline I found a kindred advocate from HR, with a broad viewpoint to appreciate that there has to be a better understanding between fellow workplace travellers to form a holistic approach across IT, property and HR. This ultimately creates a stronger and more impactful delivery system for the organization and its people. For those dealing with the physical aspect of the workplace it is essential to look over the parapet beyond the confines of the property sector in order to move forward to engage in a different manner with the worlds of HR and IT.

The first step is to evolve from the narrow, disjointed focus which is based on the 'three tribes' of the asset/transaction, facility and design construction management. There has to be an adjustment from a purely 'building-centric' focus to a wider 'people-centric', one which enables people to work anywhere and anytime, invariably with the support of technology. Teamwork and co-operation are what drives the formation of twenty-first-century business models and these have little bearing with the Taylorist-inspired models of the past. Since collaboration is now key in modern business practices, there is no option but to bust the silos which keep CRE/FM, HR and IT divided in organizations. Support professionals now have to accept that it is no longer just about servicing buildings, employee contracts or systems performance and that people and the workplace are a company's most valuable assets. Only by developing them both in tandem and as an integrated whole, rather than the sum of their discrete parts, can their true value be unlocked to become an asset for the enterprise.

Boards and management must move to a business model where engagement, flexibility, authenticity and sustainability are evident and without making this transition, they will fail to attract and retain the talent they require to meet the demands of twenty-first-century business. They need to find and harness the enablers of creativity, the knowledge management experts and leaders who have the ability to cope with the ongoing changes of the VUCA world.

For the most part the established modus operandi is building showpiece warehouses to house a whole load of disengaged departmental silos of office drones, where information and intelligence is kept under lock and key within each sector. However, there has to be a collective change in mindset from the boardroom, through the support sectors, all the way down to the newest apprentice regarding the perception of the workplace.

It is not just a place which contains the people who merely work there, but a dynamic ecosystem where individuals can deliver greater creativity and innovation, which drives improved business performance. The challenge is to create workspaces which enable knowledge and information to be communicated effectively in an open and collaborative environment. As BP's

Special Senior Advisor Helmut Schuster, the company's HR director for nine years, points out, 'We need to create an organization where work doesn't feel like work.'

Caution: People at Work!

Taking a leaf out of Caroline and BT's holistic approach to the workplace helped me see how crucial a people-driven agile working environment was in navigating organizational change. Even though I was head of the BBC's corporate property division their integrated approach became my lodestar in steering the BBC's workplace strategy.

The connection between people and place sometimes does get 'lost in translation' for those working in real estate. Perhaps not enough attention is paid to the variety of ways people use buildings and also to the requirements and functionality of their workplaces. This 'different strokes for different folks' approach to how diverse people and cultures use their offices was brought home to me at Disney and made me very aware that joining the dots between people and place was hugely important.

As part of my brief at Disney, I worked on setting up the company's international TV channels in their London, Milan, Munich, Madrid, Paris and Tokyo offices. Of course it was all heavily influenced by what was done in the US in terms of how much space was required for the new offices, space standards per employee, allowances for meeting rooms, etc. A key characteristic of the model was that most staff were allocated open-plan desks, with managers in offices, which worked reasonably well in London but was totally unsuitable for Munich. Disney could deliver the space as per the US corporate standard, but they would not be able to hire anyone to work for Mickey Mouse in Munich since culturally this type of workplace was unacceptable in Bavaria in the 1990s. This was an early salutary lesson in how relevant the working environment is in terms of how people view it and the significance of the 'right' workplace culture.

At the BBC I was also facing issues regarding the cultural aspects of space and I realized this as I was being guided around BT Centre by Caroline. As I looked around at all the open-plan offices, shared desks and communal working spaces it dawned on me that BBC folk tended to be very territorial over office space and proprietorial over their personal desks – could they possibly be persuaded to share workspaces or even go for hot desking?

Certainly over the years Caroline and I have heard numerous arguments from various business leaders, the C-Suite and even colleagues who were very wary of getting into the strange world of agile and/or flexible work practices. They were mainly about how complicated or difficult it would be to implement and manage 'open' systems, their concerns for security/privacy in agile environments and even that workplace 'hot potato' hot desking, but if approached properly, even 15 or so years ago there were ways of managing all these issues. Here are some examples of pioneering workplace practices introduced back then and some of their outcomes:

+ **Making space fluid**

Back in 2006, when I was doing my research at BT, I was struck by Caroline's rather smart office with her name on the door and how it functioned with a personal barcode which denoted it was hers while she was working there. When she was away or travelling, that space was available for someone else to use as long as they had booked it in advance and the system switched to their name on the door.

This was the perfect example of using a static space as fluid and how it can add value by being reusable and this approach has now been adopted in most places. It is interesting to see other methods implemented, such as how UniCredit utilize vacant executive offices in Milan. They operate a clean desk policy, so people working there can automatically use an empty office with ease;

+ **Tech is the workplace's best friend**

During my time at BT, Caroline also pointed out a colleague who had just come in from Germany; he had booked a workspace at BT Centre in London from Dusseldorf. It took just three simple steps and he was furnished with a map of the building, the location of the desk and how to find it. All digitized and updated in both the BT system and on his phone. With the arrival of smartphones and apps this process can be made available readily and yet it is remarkable how many organizations still stick to the traditional paper pass and laborious sign-in process;

+ **The DIY flexible workspace**

BT had introduced some innovative systems where flexible workers could 'design' their workspaces virtually – choosing the type of desk, chair, filing system, etc. that suited them and placing it the way they preferred within their space. They could order their specific choices through their line manager, who would ensure that it would be passed on to the company's supply and accounts department.

This would also apply to senior management or sales teams dealing with BT's other corporate clients, who needed high-end boardrooms or high-spec meeting rooms set up for them. Departmental files and dossiers were transferrable in smart mobile cabinets, with everything on hand for carrying out high-level executive meetings. Everything was fluid, flexible and changeable to the particular need and environment required for the type of business conducted;

+ **Security and privacy fears**

It is quite understandable that in a large corporation security and privacy are of paramount concern, so different strategies and systems have to be adopted for each sector to administer this aspect effectively.

In shared working environments confidential information or sensitive emails can be sent to specific addresses or computers, which are accessed by personal codes to be seen privately and then deleted. The onus of keeping things secure or private is up to the owner of the information and falls on them to correct the system if it fails;

+ **Hot desking – is it hot or not?**

Probably one of the most divisive trends in the twenty-first-century workplace and one which is loved or loathed in equal measure. First, I am not particularly keen on the term 'hot desking' with its implication of burning and danger ('touch-down' is another term for this nomadic workstation hopping). Understandably, management see it as a solution to save space and money although employees often find it frustrating scrambling around to find a free desk, which is not particularly conducive to creating a happy and productive workplace.

Aside from the common complaints of desk shortages and the inability to personalize workspaces, this is not just about personal mementos marking out 'your' territory. This is more about time-wasting and general irritation at having to set up a computer at a different desk, adjusting a random office chair for comfort, while figuring out where other team members and relevant colleagues are located, before any real work can actually begin – and this scenario plays out every time they hit the office. However, if managed properly, it can work well. One solution BT came up with in the early 2000s was to provide an in-house 'hot desk concierge'. They were responsible for dealing with all the problems people have in a hot-desking environment. This could mean supplying them with stationery, helping with printing and generally overseeing the process so it ran smoothly. In those days, the concierge would log all the various workstation bookings and workplace arrangements on a paper list and transfer the information to a large electronic monitor, so everyone could see what was going on, who was where and at what time.

Now all these functions can be easily done on an app; a state-of-the art example being Deloitte's HQ in Amsterdam, housed in The Edge – described as the 'Most Intelligent Building in the World'. The building's digital network is connected to an app on every employees' smartphone, which assesses their schedule in the morning and allocates the best desk or workspace to suit that particular person and the work they are undertaking that day. As well as configuring their preferred lighting and temperature settings, the app also facilitates finding their team members and relevant work colleagues.

As managers tend to view hot desking as a panacea to cutting costs and solving the issue of space, they must also be aware that there has to be an element of support to ensure hot desking operates efficiently for employees;

+ **Open-plan: Opening a can of workplace worms**

The debate over open-plan offices has raged for years and is also another very emotive workplace topic. This feature has also attracted plenty of media attention and legions of etiquette rules and 'survival guides' as to how to work in open-plan offices. Some see them as promoters of collaboration, flexibility, sociability and upping the workplace 'buzz', while others view them as noisy, cluttered, too distracting, even 'toxic'.

My view on the subject is that one size does not fit all and provision can be made within workplaces for quiet areas, break-out zones and private-seating areas or booths to alleviate open-plan stress.

This 'either/or' mindset of the rights and wrongs of open-plan offices and hot desking versus personal work-stations is a classic case of 'bipolar thinking'. This is a term which organizational theorist Fons Trompenaar has coined to describe our propensity to think about decisions as 'mutually exclusive polarities'. As a leading expert in the field of cross-cultural communication, Fons is of the opinion that dilemmas like this can be reconciled by fostering diversity, respect, collaboration within the workplace and by using innovation to solve challenges.

Workplaces need to be designed to support the wellbeing and productivity of employees, but they also have to enable the different ways people work and the jobs they have to do, which does require a considered and more nuanced approach. However, it does strike me as odd that we are still making analogue-type decisions in the digital era when it should all be about choice of how and where we work.

Unleashing the Potential of People and Place
The basic questions that company leaders, together with CRE/FM, HR, IT and Procurement, should ask themselves is how their organization is run – its structure, procedures, controls,

systems, functions, hierarchy and goals – as well as understanding the needs and demands of the business, together with the objectives of its people. First, it requires a merger of all these skills to put together a viable solution. Second, by answering these fundamental questions collectively boundaries should break down and enable all sectors to collaborate as high-performance teams.

There also has to be a mutual view of the workplace with a more 'people-centric' approach. Rather than concentrating on space standards, fitting in more people per square foot and cost efficiency, the emphasis should shift on how the workplace can become an effective tool in enabling people to work in the best way possible. To create a productive and innovative working environment people require diverse work settings for the different functions they perform, as well as areas to collaborate with colleagues, socialize with them or spaces just to take time out for some quiet work, to think or relax. In a nutshell, 'a great workplace must be an investment in space and an investment in people in equal parts'.

Additionally, business leaders and the support sectors also need to take a much more holistic view in engaging their people as part of their business strategy. Companies normally employ annual staff surveys to monitor employees' engagement and commitment to the organization, but these are seen as 'box-ticking' exercises which rarely give a true picture or insight into what is actually going on in the workplace. Given that staff and potential hires can now check out and report on corporations independently using sites such as Glassdoor. Therefore, it is vital that communication channels are kept open with regular and continuous feedback and not just the yearly assessment.

This should not just be about paying lip-service but should offer a genuine platform where employees' thoughts about their working environment are considered, together with an understanding of their work. This would be underpinned by the long-established feedback loop principle – 'you said, we did'. Alternatively one could look to a benchmarking tool, such as the Leesman Index which has established itself as a major provider of insights based on a world-wide 700,000 strong database of office worker insights – as Leesman CEO Tim Oldman points out, 'it's the people stuff, time and time again'.

With better and more open communication, management, both executive and those in corporate real estate or facilities, together with HR and IT, can take remedial action sooner rather than later if problems arise in the workplace. Conversely, this dialogue should be a 'two-way street' with any new company policies, working practices, significant business decisions and progress on relevant projects being shared with personnel, be it through webcasts, blogs or the company's intranet. With any good ideas or suggestions heeded, implemented if appropriate and duly rewarded.

Another element to consider is the extent to which business leaders empower employees to make decisions and how they interact and support the people within their organizations. Many managers insist on being able to see their staff and have them physically present in the same office. This is a misguided approach since no one can actively manage people on an individual basis at all times, especially if a team grows in size and projects get bigger and more complex. No doubt the enforced home-working brought about by the Coronavirus crisis will provide fresh impetus for business leaders to review this type of approach.

Caroline suggests that it would be more beneficial for managers to foster 'trust-based relationships' with their employees. This should leave leaders free to concentrate on the constructive management of the factors which add to the business's productivity, through engaging the workforce in a better way. Ultimately, this builds up the case for agile or flexible working practices, where it is irrelevant whether your people are three minutes away down the corridor or 300 miles working from their own home – the premise being that you will get the best out of people by freeing them up and they achieve more when they feel in control of their work.

Flexing the Workplace

Giving people the autonomy to work when and where they wanted was a giant pioneering leap forward for BT. Especially since the telecommunication giant made the radical decision to go with flexible working when it was going through a particularly tumultuous time in the early 2000s, saddled with a debt of £30 billion. Analysing the business showed that both their infrastructure and operating costs were high. One solution was to encourage BT employees to work remotely from home: this saved the company at least £6,000 with each home worker it created. By 2005, BT had 11,000 home-based staff, which saved them over £60 million.

BT's 2019 Annual Report states that 80 per cent of their 106,700 employees worldwide work on either a flexible or agile basis, with a notable 30 per cent surge in productivity, proving that investing in a flexible approach that works best for people reaps the rewards in terms of engagement and productivity. However, the biggest benefits of flexible employment, aside from recognizing that everyone has different ways of working, is putting people in control of their work–life balance. This is of paramount importance for those with children or carers responsible for elderly or sick relatives. It also affects those returning to work after parental leave or approaching retirement, who wish to stagger their exit from working life, but crucially, it also impacts on overall health and wellbeing.

Long, inflexible working hours coupled with unsustainable extended commuting times are obstacles in accommodating work–life needs. According to data released from the US Bureau of Labor Statistics in 2019, 57 per cent of employees have some form of flexible work arrangement, with a further 29 per cent working remotely. A *State of Remote Work 2019* report found that 20 per cent of the US workforce admitted that they were willing to take a pay cut of more than 10 per cent in order to be able to work from home. Furthermore, a study carried out by insurance company Aviva revealed that work–life balance was behind 22 per cent of British workers quitting their jobs in 2019 in search of more flexible employment – equivalent to more than 7 million people across the UK's working population.

Globally, working remotely or from home has grown exponentially as efficient, high-speed internet and mobile data connectivity, effective cloud-based services and improved cyber-security revolutionize the way people work. This has certainly been accelerated by the uptake of remote working during the pandemic which also aligns with changing social attitudes.

Even before Covid-19, statistics from IWG's annual Global Workplace Study had already indicated that 85 per cent of over 15,000 global businesses confirm what BT also discovered, that greater flexibility leads to an increase in productivity and a happier workforce.

+ In the US alone, forecasts predict that an estimated $4.5 trillion will be saved per year as a direct result of remote working and increased workplace agility;
+ Flexible workers are 13 per cent more productive overall and take less days off due to stress or illness;
+ Flexible workers are better motivated, show a greater level of engagement and a higher degree of commitment to employers who consider their work–life balance. People do go that extra mile and contribute more to an organization that values and cares about them.

However, getting the board and management to accept flexible working as the norm is not without its challenges. First, business leaders have to be convinced that organizations who implement flexible working practices produce better bottom-line results than those who stick to traditional office methods.

In 2016 one of the largest global surveys of its kind interviewed 8,000 employers and employees across ten countries, assessing the impact of flexible working on their businesses. Sixty-one per cent of companies worldwide reported an increase in profits and 83 per cent saw an improvement in productivity.

One example of effective and productive flexible working happened quite inadvertently at the BBC during the run-up to the UK's 2010 General Election. At the time the Deputy Director-General Mark Byford, who was also Head of BBC Journalism, found himself laid up with a badly broken leg for three months after an unfortunate accident. This made it difficult for him to make the daily commute from his home in Winchester, 60 miles out of London, to the BBC's studios. Despite the obvious inconvenience of not being able to get to the BBC, Mark was determined to lead the overall co-ordination of the all-important election coverage.

Armed with just a laptop, BlackBerry, TV and radio, Mark probably watched and listened to more output than anyone else at the BBC from the comfort of his home while also managing the BBC's election team effectively throughout the campaign, chairing daily phone conferences and giving regular feedback. No one could have guessed that the BBC's 2010 General Election coverage was run from Mark Byford's front room! For me this is the perfect illustration of the well-known adage that 'work is something you do, not a place you go to'.

Fast forward ten years and our ability to work differently has developed at great pace. This has all been made possible by enormous strides in connectivity and the acceptance of the smartphone as a core business tool. The last decade has seen the emergence of many tech companies such as Automat (the WordPress Company); whose staff work remotely. Plus, there are a growing number of organizations who are experimenting with a mix of office-based and remote working, with many more now re-thinking their Covid-19-impacted workplace strategies.. Companies, such as Ernst & Young, have been in the vanguard of this development. Their Asia Pacific Executive Director of Real Estate, Dr Paul Luciani sees a shift to the individual 'being' the actual workplace, or as he puts it, 'the digital revolution makes the love affair with spaces go out the window'.

Undoubtedly strong relationships between management and team members are vital as this improves communication for flexible working arrangements to be carried out successfully. Collaboration across every sector and all employees is crucial in enabling the integration of flexible working into an organization's culture. Line managers should always be asking themselves, 'How do I make people happier and more productive?' This is also determined by the support managers receive from HR to develop their people management skills, combined with their IT department providing a sound technological infrastructure, reinforced by an effective workplace strategy and a conducive working environment.

Putting People at the Heart of the Workplace

People-centric working environments value their employees' wellbeing, which in turn translates into 'organizational health' and subsequently business success. A FlexJobs annual study showed that 86 per cent of US professionals reported that flexible work practices would mean less stress, while 77 per cent admitted that being able to manage their own work–life schedules would also encourage them to adopt a healthier lifestyle.

If the workplace can play an active role in supporting people to live a better life, the benefits to the individual, business and society as a whole are self-evident.

In order to build a labour force of engaged, healthy people who are fulfilled at work, senior management must respond to the shift in the needs of their employees by investing in workplace strategies which, together with promoting their health and wellbeing, enable and encourage people's development, career prospects and their skills for the future.

Commercial real estate transformation and technology strategist Anthony Slumbers contends there has been 'so much focus on being able to embrace technology by developing programming skills, etcetera. What is really needed is to focus on the human aspects skills such as empathy, design, imagination and social intelligence.'

With a younger generation who are hitting management level rising in the ranks, there will have to be a reshaping of the workforce as careers in general are becoming more flexible, primarily since young people want to learn a variety of skills and try different lines of work. In any case 'jobs for life' are a thing of the past in both economic and social terms, especially now that the age of retirement is going up worldwide and working lives will be extended.

Many people want portfolio careers to fit in with the various phases of their lives. This encompasses the whole gamut from parents coping with a new baby and sleepless nights to employees of all ages dealing with childcare, caring for elderly parents or the health needs of their partners/relatives, but who still have to continue working.

In the main, companies and HR tend to look at the entire employment journey from the perspective of the employee life cycle within an organization. However, enterprises which truly value their workforce must rethink this model and get a holistic view of where their employees are in their life cycle beyond the workplace. It makes it much easier for managers to make the necessary adjustments enabling employees to work more effectively if they understand the 'real' life cycle of their people. In this way they can formulate strategies for them to be able to work better and smarter by shifting the focus to a recognition of the quality of their output and contribution to the business rather than where and at what time it was done.

The Fusion of People and Place

In the last century there was hardly any connection made between the workforce and the workspace. Offices were commissioned and operated using headcount numbers on spreadsheets. Over the last 20 years the changing workforce dynamics have compelled employers to grapple with the challenge of different approaches. However, there is also a hidden consequence in that the emerging new order is impacting the demand for space and also how organizations consume this space.

By coming to terms with these changing factors and by applying a holistic perspective, business leaders can provide workplaces fit for twenty-first-century enterprises which are not only efficient but effective too. Furthermore, they are also people-friendly, as well as being productive places to work in. This framework also applies to the supply side as understanding these changes can help them provide solutions which are fit for purpose for the twenty-first-century. Therefore, it is incumbent on both demand and supply sides to understand how the new paradigm is evolving. Figure 4.1 below describes a series of six factors which in combination are going to drive a big change in how we consume office space.

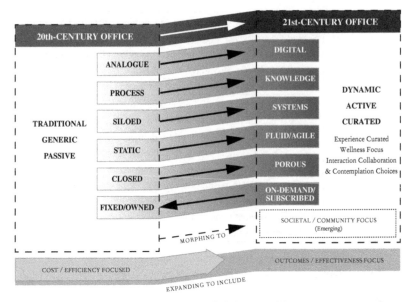

FIGURE 4.1: The Hidden Paradigm Shift from Building-centric to People-centric

The Shifts	Features
Analogue to Digital	✦ Cloud-based systems have enabled dynamic working; ✦ Self-service and bring/use your own devices are game-changers; ✦ Endless possibilities are available through smartphones.
Process to Knowledge	✦ Shift to automation/self-service is now getting into gear and altering the working landscape; ✦ Focus on different types of workforce and what knowledge/ experience they can bring to the workplace; ✦ Transparency in knowledge impacts on organization, hierarchy, procedures, controls, etc.
Siloed to Converged Systems	✦ Traditional twentieth-century mindset of focusing on 'my patch, my territory' is changing for twenty-first-century agility. It is now all about collaboration, curation and sharing; ✦ Thanks to digital technology everything is converging; ✦ Systems thinking is a daily necessity.
Static to Fluid	✦ Business cycles have sped up, with five- to ten-year planning sidelined; ✦ Office work is now untethered/multi-dimensional; ✦ VUCA world demands agility and speed for organizations to survive.

Closed to Porous	✦ The ascendancy of freelancers, independent or contract workers and the emergence of the gig economy; ✦ Twentieth-century work mindsets struggle with implementing and managing agility in the workplace; ✦ Collaboration, co-operation and partnerships are now key.
Fixed/Owned to On-demand/ Subscribed	✦ The quickening pace of life and ubiquitous choice are driving the twenty-first-century mindset shift; ✦ Amazon, Uber, Airbnb, Netflix and other twenty-first-century businesses like them exemplify putting consumer demand, convenience and choice first; ✦ Needs of VUCA business to access space now – not in six to eighteen months' time – is leading the shift from a purely building-centric focus to a wider portfolio relationship with landlords/providers.

Six Steps for Harnessing the Links between People and Place

In order to generate greater competitive advantage:

+ Ensure that everyone on the team understands that the only purpose of space is to enhance the performance of the business;
+ Understanding the difference between 'Agile' and 'agility'. In other words, knowing that organizational agility means adaptability, rapid change and speedy renewal versus Agile working practices;
+ Identifying where the misalignments or chasms of misunderstandings are in your organization;
+ Driving a more genuine collaboration across the support functions of an organization by encouraging convergence;
+ Giving a balanced hearing to those who propose effectiveness as well as those who focus on efficiency, since cost should only be part of the picture;
+ Making the connection between people and place is dependent on good leadership and unequivocal commitment to drive a change in mindset.

116

Sources

1. 'a great workplace must be an investment in space and an investment in people in equal parts'.
   Graham, R. 'Delivering Great Places to Work: Optimising the User Experience in Our Buildings'. The Cabinet Office, 2019, p. 11.

Epigraph

Handy, C. *The Age of Unreason*. London: Random House Arrow, 1989 (2nd edition 2002), p. 143.

The Twenty-first-century Workplace Navigator

We all want progress, but if you're on the wrong road, progress means
doing an about-turn and walking back to the right road.
C.S. Lewis

Coming from an island-nation, I have always been fascinated by the sea and seafaring and have admired the men and women who embark on long sea voyages across the oceans or circumnavigate the globe. The sheer tenacity they display negotiating extreme challenges by using their wits and skills to battle the elements and the determination they show by overcoming every difficulty to reach the safety of their final destination is awe-inspiring.

I was fortunate enough to work with Nick O'Donnell, who not only sailed around the world, but was also another fellow traveller in helping me translate the property strategy for the BBC's White City campus. Nick had also done stints as EMEA Head of Corporate Real Estate & Facilities at Microsoft and is currently at the helm of the University of London's King's College estate. Working with Nick and hearing about his adventures on the high seas, where he faced and coped with obstacles on board, certainly inspired me to view my journey at the BBC in nautical terms.

Being in that leadership role, in which I was figuratively the captain of the BBC's property transformation, I felt like I was steering a ship, especially the moments of self-doubt and outright frustration when the team struggled with the relentless pressure and were unable to perform to their utmost ability. It also taught me that it is lonely being at the top and having to skipper the course through some pretty ugly storms; when the terrain was tough, the maps let me down and the incessant pressure felt like a constant downpour. Yes, at times I did feel like I was very close to a *Titanic* iceberg! However, the sense of fulfilment, achievement and pride I felt for all the crew when the sale of Television Centre in West London was complete was tremendous, once this mega-project had reached its ultimate destination – it also marked the end of my ten-year BBC journey.

With Nick's input into shaping the nautical narrative, I hope to help leaders and decision-makers in their journeys across the treacherous waters of today's unpredictable business environment. The solutions I am proposing may not be a panacea to every problem, but at the very least they should provoke management to consider taking a fresh view in how their organizations use offices. A view that is more holistic in its approach, underpinned by the human dimension and conscious that it can add value to the business, while also becoming more sustainable.

Developing this set of tools prompted me to extend my thinking to consider life beyond the status quo of the existing model for providing and consuming real estate. The results of my analysis 'New Horizons' conclude this chapter as a challenge to both sides of the equation to think 'outside the box' as I believe this could well lead to better outcomes for all parties.

Charting the Route to a Great Workplace
In developing this framework I have worked with my workplace 'partners in crime', HR supremo Caroline Waters and Max Luff

from Six Ideas, plus a range of collaborators in this somewhat rarefied field. We belong to a very small group of thinkers who can transcend the rigid and formulaic world of real estate, design and facilities to connect with the world of business, the workforce and indeed the wider community, which extends to the economy.

Figure 5.1 below proposes a five-step process which provides some suggestions as to how to create great places to work. It charts the broad bones of a process that could help organizations benefit from harnessing an effective workplace, one that meets the demands of operating in today's business world of volatility, uncertainty, complexity and ambiguity.

I have found that most leaders need a highly tailored approach, which can be customized to suit their particular set of challenges, which have to be dealt with at a specific point in time. One also has to keep other factors in mind too, such as the particular organization's life cycle, the composition of its leadership cadre and the appetite of the CEO to personally drive change.

What this route provides is a set of charts for organizations to follow either in their entirety or just by dipping in and using some elements. This is not a detailed step-by-step manual nor is it a specification, but a guide to be adapted by management to fit in with their particular enterprise and its demands. One important lesson I have learned from my experience at the sharp end

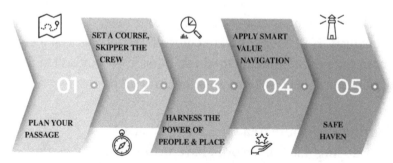

FIGURE 5.1: The Journey to Great Places to Work

is that there is no fixed recipe for success so beware of those who proffer cookie-cutter-type solutions!

Plan Your Passage

A savvy skipper pays careful attention to planning before setting out on a voyage. Apart from the seaworthiness of the vessel and the weather forecast, there are many aspects to consider, such as tides, currents, supplies and number of crew required. So before setting sail to create that great workplace, the savvy leader can be better equipped and better informed of the risks associated with the change voyage.

One might argue that a similar approach is applied when an enterprise contemplates an organizational change or workplace project. However, I wonder how much consideration leaders give to 'how' they will achieve these changes? Do many leaders ask themselves questions such as:

+ How will we ensure it is successful?
+ How are we covering off the risks?
+ How will the project deliver the required outcomes?

This is not about examining the 'the nuts and bolts' of a project delivery mechanism; what I am advocating is a more contrarian approach. Maybe leaders should ask the project sponsor(s) why things are being done in a certain way? The majority of answers will probably be 'because that's how we've always done it'.

There is fundamentally nothing wrong with pursuing tried-and-tested methods which have worked in the past. However, if leaders are prepared to build a better understanding of the behaviours, components, factors and practices which form part and parcel of a workplace project they may unlock some hidden benefits such as ways of mitigating risk, avoiding waste and reducing costs.

Having successfully navigated organizational transformation journeys at the BBC and Disney, I have learned that it is very important to have a good grasp of what roles the diverse elements play in the overall structure of the business. By taking a holistic view, I was able to see the big gulfs that exist between the perspectives of the various stakeholders involved in the operation of its facilities and its people. However, when it comes to projects which involve work, the workforce and workplaces, there are a host of variables which are poorly understood by one or more of the stakeholders. Many leaders are unaware of the gaps of understanding that exist in the system which produces and operates today's workplaces. Understandably, management also place their reliance on the views of their team, who may also be unaware of these gaps. Then, when things go awry or fail to deliver the required benefits, everyone is left wondering why.

When it comes to these gaps in understanding, they always remind me of the warning announcements on the London Underground – mind the gap! – alerting travellers to the gaping hazardous space between the platform's end and the entrance to the train. So alerting business leaders to 'mind the workplace gap', I have pinpointed the six areas in the ecosystem of real estate and the workplace which impair and negatively impact projects, increase friction within their operation and incubate risks that cause significant problems to the extent that these gaps of understanding are a lost opportunity. I have labelled them 'The Chasm of Misunderstanding' in Figure 5.2, below.

As I discussed earlier, I contend that due to the fragmented nature of the real estate ecosystem all the key stakeholders have different perspectives on the situation. Currently all the players have as their primary focus the twin factors of cost and efficiency. To cite EQ Office CEO/President Lisa Picard, 'We are still managing business and real estate using metrics from the machine age when we thought about humans in the same way

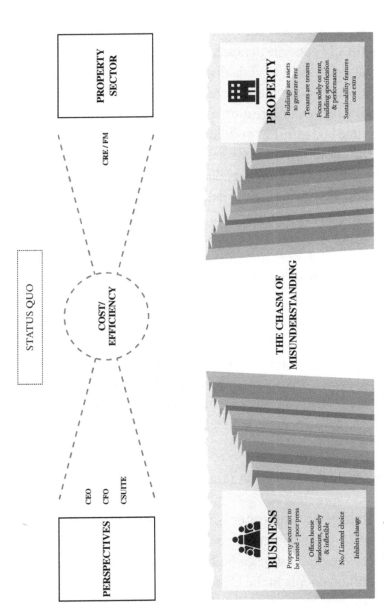

FIGURE 5.2: Six Bridges

as machines who needed to be housed efficiently in order to be productive. The arrival of knowledge work has changed all this.' Plus, we have the two sides of the supply–demand equation with diametrically opposite perspectives. For example, business views the real estate sector with disdain while the supply side sees business as just another tenant who pays the rent. Therefore, I suggest the key to creating a great place to work is to invest some time and effort in building 'Bridges of Understanding' to span the chasms in these six areas (see Figure 5.3, below). This can be achieved by understanding the overall context of how the system works, including the delivery process for the workplace, the silos that exist and, above all, the differing mindsets involved.

Building a bridge of understanding between each of these six areas will deliver a range of benefits not only for an organization's leaders, but for all the stakeholders involved in the provision, operation and support functions of the workplace. However, it is pivotal to expand the discussion beyond just cost and efficiency to business value and effectiveness. The first step is recognizing the nature of the link between the two sides of the chasm and why there is a gulf between the two entities. It is also worth analysing the potential benefits of bridging the gap between these disconnected features.

The Six Bridges Spanning the Chasm of Misunderstanding

+ **Bridge 1: Customer – Landlord/Developer**
   When one comes to consider the production and consumption of office buildings, a place which 61.5 million people in the US alone use on a daily basis; it is incredible to think that for the most part there is no direct relationship with the occupiers apart from the lease contract. This lack of a connection between the

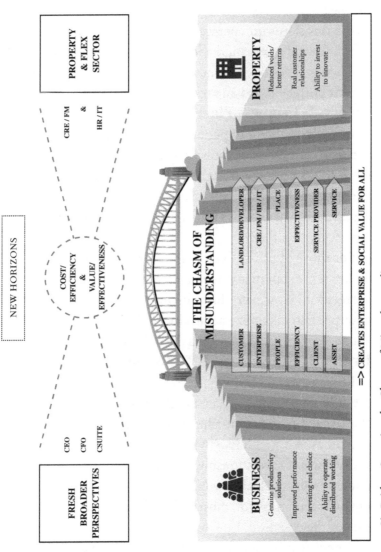

FIGURE 5.3: Six Bridges Spanning the Chasm of Misunderstanding

landlord and tenant prohibits the creation of a true relationship with the customer/end-user.

There are exceptions to this state of affairs, but for the vast majority of real estate markets around the world this status quo persists. There are ways and ideas which the industry could adopt to try and build new and better types of customer relationships, which could benefit both landlord and tenant;

+ **Bridge 2: People – Place**

It really is all about people and their ability to access their choice of tools and spaces, which allows them to do a good job in the best way possible. People need to feel that they can be productive, but the organization also needs to believe that the workplace has motivated them.

For those of us involved in the workplace sector this makes sense, but many people do not understand this correlation. However, this thinking should enable the enterprise to maximize creativity, collaboration and engagement while fostering a desire to learn and grow;

+ **Bridge 3: Efficiency – Effectiveness**

Efficiency and effectiveness reflect two sides of a set of 'terrible twins'. They are inextricably linked, share many common attributes, yet generate different outcomes. Although like twins they seem similar in many ways, the relationship between them is not well understood. As efficiency is the easier of the two to quantify and measure, most stakeholders focus on that side of the equation. I have also seen evidence where efficiency is mistaken for effectiveness. Yet overall, it is the effectiveness aspect that is more valuable and what few people realize is that both sides are required in tandem to navigate towards a great workplace. One needs to facilitate both the efficiency and effectiveness factors to steer your crew;

✦ Bridge 4: Enterprise – CRE/FM/HR

The way organizations engage with their internal support teams, who are responsible for their real estate portfolio, facilities, technology and human resources, is crucial to bridging this particular gulf. These groups, whether unified or disconnected, need to be challenged or encouraged to move from being mere order takers, process managers and dealmakers to provide much greater strategic support for the enterprise.

On the flip side, senior management need to empower and equip these teams to operate strategic-ally to add value to their business. As discussed earlier, facilities services have seen justifiable cost-cutting over the last few decades. This has resulted in a downwards spiral into providing mediocre and fragmented services.

These three groups, CRE, FM and HR, need to be challenged to shift their focus to demonstrate a 'value for money' service and to become better enablers of work within twenty-first-century organizations. In parallel, there are also benefits to be had from partner-ing with Procurement to help them understand how to support the strategic aspects of workplace provision. Overall, the key outcome is to reduce 'friction' in the workplace, thereby improving productivity;

✦ Bridge 5: Client – Service Provider

Over the last 20 years businesses have been outsourcing and off-shoring services extensively. The prevailing mantra of any savvy enterprise seems to be retaining its core activities and subcontracting the rest. When it comes to the workplace sector this has been central to the way most companies have been operating, whereas it is not a bad development in itself – organizations would be better served if there was a rapprochement in terms of the relationships. For the most part they are still based on a 'master/slave' arrangement, even though some of these contracts are labelled as partnerships or alliances. I sometimes question if these arrangements are mere window dressing, with both sides paying lip service to partnering.

It would be better all-round if senior management invests time to establish 'principle-to-principle' relationships with key supply chain leaders to build a real understanding of stakeholders' priorities in order to become a truly intelligent client. This is a role for the Procurement team to participate in and help build better understanding and it would also shift the focus to value creation rather than pure cost;

+ **Bridge 6: Asset – Service**

There is no denying the workplace sector is undergoing real change and this is proving really challenging for many players. Therefore, a better understanding of respective priorities and the potential for alternatives should be a way to generate benefits.

It is dawning for some on the supply side that they will have to adjust the model to consider the needs of their customers. However, this does require a two-way dialogue to define a new model which produces gains for both sides.

Benefits Derived from Bridging the Chasm of Misunderstanding

Shrewd leaders should therefore develop a stronger understanding of the discrepancies between these six areas concerning work, the workforce and the workplace. In bridging these gulfs they can derive a range of benefits for their enterprise, while potentially unlocking some innovative opportunities and improving its competitive advantage in the marketplace:

+ Higher probability of a successful project outcome;
+ Significant increase in staff engagement levels;
+ Enhanced ability to mitigate project and enterprise risk;
+ Support functions that add to enterprise value, not just cost controls;
+ Improved value for money from knowing how to make the best use of an organization's physical resources;
+ Tangible demonstration to the outside world that their enterprise has a coherent grasp of the sustainability and social value agenda.

Set Course and Skipper the Crew

A smart CEO understands the lie of the land of their particular organization as this will inform them of the overall capabilities, appetite and appreciation of what they are trying to achieve. Just like a skipper planning for an ocean racing event, shrewd leaders should consider setting a course that harnesses all the favourable currents, avoids reefs and ensures the crew can set the sails that catch the fastest winds. This not only requires adept leadership but a team which is committed, fit and capable of delivering the task and reaching the eventual goal.

I once watched a sailboat race in the English Channel from the vantage point of a pleasure boat, with yachts similar to the types that compete in the America's Cup. The sight of these remarkable craft speeding across the waves using only wind power was quite incredible, but what also struck me was how the crews worked together to manoeuvre the vessels. They all worked in complete synchronicity and harmony following directions from their skipper as they adjusted the sails and rigging to take advantage of the direction of the wind. As I watched the race through my binoculars, a phrase I once read sprang to mind, 'We cannot direct the wind but we can adjust the sails.' Certainly a useful metaphor for business leaders, no one can control events but how to manage them is well within our power and this can also be applied to adjusting to the winds of change.

Undoubtedly, it is not just adapting to change which is difficult, but also implementing it is even harder. Whether that is effecting transformation in the workplace or in any other generic change initiative, the same challenges exist – how to affect change and make it work. Unfortunately, many are doomed to fail and the business world is littered with numerous examples of unsuccessful transformation projects. According to a much-cited McKinsey report,[4] as many as 70 per cent flounder en route and there has been much debate about how to mitigate the risks of failure.

The Key Reasons for Change Projects Failing

+ Insufficient executive sponsorship or lack of senior management support;
+ Underestimating the complexity of the transformation;
+ Employees not involved in the change process;
+ Lack of a key person to champion/drive change;
+ Not adopting a rigorous and structured approach to the change programme;
+ Not breaking down the change process into clearly defined segmented initiatives.

---

[4] McKinsey Survey. 'What successful transformations share', McKinsey & Co., 2010. https://www.mckinsey.com/business-functions/organization/our-insights/what-successful-transformations-share-mckinsey-global-survey-results

Effecting Organizational Change the Waters Way

When the board of an enterprise sets out a change programme for the CEO to champion, it is presumed that the intent will be delivered. Key Performance Indicators (KPIs) will be put in place to measure results and the best project/change management strategies will be applied. This is followed by an appropriate announcement of the transformation initiative to great fanfare, by way of encouraging everyone's enthusiasm to adopt it. Yet so many of these programmes run out of steam and I often wonder why and what happens since they seem to be set up in 'textbook' fashion and yet something goes awry...

The answer to this conundrum came from my friend Caroline Waters, former director of People and Policy at British Telecom, who introduced me to her solution for 'operationalising strategy' – the development of a project's functional strategies and the establishment of its objectives. Her approach – which I call the 'Waters Model' – is based on her experience at BT and came from the enormous challenges faced by the organization in the late 1990s. This required the root-and-branch transformation of the ailing telecommunications giant, while reducing its workforce from 265,000 down to around 80,000, while expanding to into 176 countries as it globalized its business.

On his arrival as the CEO in 2002, Ben Verwaayen set the company on course for nothing short of a total transformation. Ben's aspiration was to break the command and control labour-intensive siloed patterns and build an increasingly collaborative operating model with increased flexibility and responsiveness factored in, by improving communication skills, external awareness and knowledge sharing.

Caroline's method considers the complexities of a large enterprise and is based on securing traction for a particular initiative among its multi-layered ranks. It centres on the principle that, aside from the usual delegation routes through the existing organizational hierarchy, there needs to be additional oversight from the person at the helm. They should be responsible for skippering their team on precisely what each member is required to do, to maintain control of the project.

In this way management needs to apply leadership to drive context down into the operating divisions and in one way it is an extension of the long-established practice of 'Management By Walking About' (MBWA) so it involves direct participation and a high level of familiarity with organizational practices and the enterprise's employees, but with an additional dimension.

The model in Figure 5.4 sets out a way of navigating the various silos which exist in a large organization:

+ **The pyramids** describe a typical organization with a series of divisional silos;
+ **The gaps between each pyramid** represent the vacuums between each division.

Each has its own characteristics informed by its function and purpose, as well as its custom and practice. They also have divisional systems – career, paths and processes. Underpinning these will be the people-related aspects such as culture, politics and egos.

Take, for example, the typical career journey of an individual employee in an organization. On joining, they will encounter the compelling experience of belonging to a department or a team. As they progress up the leadership ladder they will focus more on their own personal agenda and that of their particular area, which limits their scope to their specific professional 'turf' or silo. What motivation do they have in going beyond their field and familiarizing themselves with other aspects of their organization?

Very few managers encourage their people to take time out to look over the parapet and scan what is a rapidly changing external

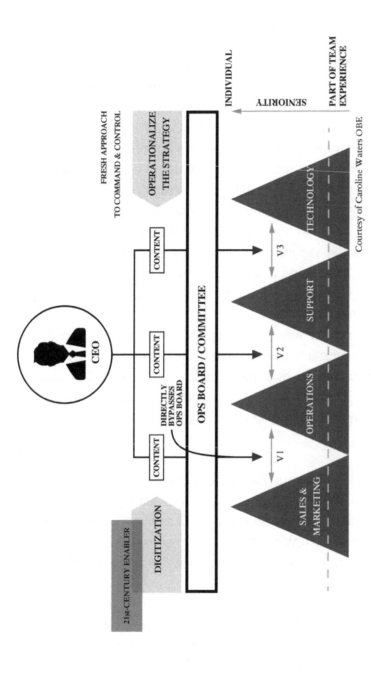

FIGURE 5.4: The Waters Model for Driving Organizational Change

(Reproduced by kind permission of Caroline Waters.)

environment. Many would argue that organizations are joined up at the top by management committees and operational boards and this is the appropriate forum for broader views to be discussed. In reality, how much of this is actually acted on subsequently? There is value to be had from co-opting a wider range of people to look at issues. Given their relative position, they may have different perspectives, which might even lead to better solutions.

In this context, the role for business leaders is to take a fresh approach to the traditional 'command and control' model. In addition to the normal management structures of administrating day-to-day functions via operational boards, etc., the CEO must take personal and visible responsibility to drive context down into the vacuums between the divisions in providing a clear unequivocal and physical direction, which demonstrates a consistent journey by joining up the functions of the enterprise on a common roadmap.

By filling these inter-divisional vacuums, the CEO creates a genuine organizational ecosystem, which is much more resilient and self-supportive than the traditional hierarchical or matrix approach. It also gives out an unequivocal message to employees that this organization values their input and is worth working for.

Harness the Power of People and Place

The importance of connecting people and place has been explored earlier in Chapter 4, as well as how business leaders could profit from linking the two together for the benefit of their organization. This section extends the theme to include three further ingredients:

+ Understanding the total operating costs of the people working in your organization, including the space they consume and the value they add;

+ Recognizing that the workplace now operates differently;
+ Applying the Workplace Management Framework to transform the workplace.

People-related Operating Costs

A great deal of time and effort has been expended on understanding occupancy costs in relation to leasing office space. They are usually articulated as cost per square metre or per square foot, yet I suspect that many business leaders are quite baffled as to what cost per square metre/foot actually entails.

As the world of work is changing and the idea of how the twenty-first-century workplace is evolving alongside it, the emphasis has to shift from being solely about office leasing and operating costs. Since a company's greatest asset and expenditure is its staff, then perhaps it is time to factor people into the occupancy cost equation. So, what about using a system based on total operating cost per person rather than per square metre or square foot? Furthermore, the definition of 'person' would include the entire spectrum of people who work for the enterprise, including not only full-time employees but also remote workers.

This holistic approach was undertaken by BT to address the issue of the amount it was paying for its employee labour, together with what BT provided to its staff and the associated costs. This facilitated understanding the people costs of running the business; in parallel, it also enabled BT to start seeing how each sector added value to the business.

By applying this fresh perspective, the company was able to build a much broader concept of managing its people by turning BT into a porous organization. This is described as 'one in which the boundaries are highly permeable across functional interest areas within the organization, as well as between the organization and the external environment'. A porous set-up can also be defined as one that evolves over time as circumstances change and the activities, demands and roles of those working there develop at different stages.

By figuring out the total 'worth' of their employees and developing a workforce management approach based on a porous organization mindset, BT took out approximately £1.5 billion of costs. Figure 5.5 is the result of BT's journey into developing the People Related Occupancy Costs (PROC) System.

In directing a fairly dramatic and drastic downsizing, BT had to be careful in considering how it would impact its people, most of whom had been lifelong employees who started off as civil servants since BT was originally a department of the UK's public post office service. They enjoyed generous public sector pension packages, but more importantly, had amassed a tremendous pool

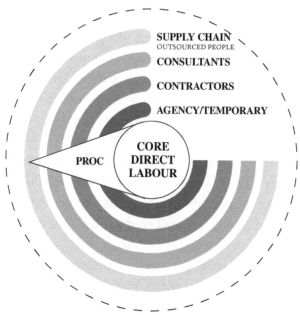

(Reproduced by kind permission of Caroline Waters.)

FIGURE 5.5: People Related Occupancy Costs (PROC)

of skills, experience and knowledge, in addition to being part of the organization's history. Aside from providing generous severance payments, BT also wanted to find a way to retain their resources.

The PROC model has a core of in-house full-time personnel and the concentric circles emanating from the centre include free-lancing/temporary workers, contractors, consultants, service providers, who are paid a fee for their work. This system provided a useful frame of reference and formed the premise of finding opportunities to move BT staff, especially long-standing experienced employees, to the outer rings. A key aspect was actively encouraging those wishing to leave BT to become entrepreneurs or 'intrapreneurs' and populate them into BT's supply chain.

In many ways, PROC is a practical interpretation of Charles Handy's Shamrock organization (*see* pp. 64–5). It recognizes that most enterprises now have a diverse range of ways of engaging with labour. The model defines the various components of the 'new look' workforce. The question is whether the total operating cost of each section is adequately captured and understood, especially the quantum of space the various categories consume. For the most part the add-on costs are reduced to just applying a percentage to core salary/payroll.

As one cannot look at real estate, technology, HR and other costs in isolation, applying this strategy might help to eliminate both inefficiency and fragmentation, plus improve the performance of a highly capital-intensive resource – an organization's people. The benefits are two-fold for business leaders: in becoming informed clients they can drive for more sustainable construction and operational solutions, which would significantly impact their bottom line.

Applying the Workplace Management Framework

Who is best placed to deliver change in an organization can be a moot point. The received wisdom is that it usually falls to the HR division. While there are many methodologies and change models available to map out the journey and define what needs to be accomplished, I have seen little reference as to how to achieve change management involving a real estate move. I found the simple framework adopted by the International Facilities Management Association (IFMA) and Workplace Evolutionaries (WE) to be the best roadmap in understanding the various constituents involved when it comes to workplace transformation. This was formulated by Andrew Mawson and Dr Graham Jarvis of Advanced Workplace Associates (AWA) – see Figure 5.6, below.

Underlying this framework is AWA's belief that effective change management is all about 'preparing and supporting people to adopt new thinking, behaviours, practices, understandings and competences'. It also encompasses the physical, technological

reproduced with the courtesy of AWA

(Reproduced by kind permission of AWA.)

FIGURE 5.6: The Workplace Transition Management Framework

138

and social environment in which work is performed, which can be done anytime, anyplace and anywhere.

This framework comprises of ten management capabilities which determine how the organization achieves workplace change in the best possible way:

+ **Strategic Management** is the core element which has to align all the assets and service management programmes to those of the organization's business. It must engage with the C-Suite to interpret the demands of the enterprise and drive them down to the services;

+ **Client Relationship Management** develops an understanding of the demand for the assets and services provided by the workplace through their relationship with the organization's internal clients and its consumers;

+ **Performance Management** measures the effectiveness of the operational delivery and quality implementation of improvement plans;

+ **Supply Change Management** ensures that services are provided so that they support the strategic needs of the enterprise;

+ **Capacity Management** provides services, technology and physical assets in the most economical way to benefit the organization;

+ **Resource Management** – the day-to-day management of resources, encompassing the physical, utilities and employees, which ensures the effective running of the workplace;

+ **Improvement Management** ensures that the workplace experience and the service performance is improved in a cost-effective way;

+ **Risk Management** identifies and analyses the sources of risk which could impact employees and minimize the effectiveness of the workplace. Also, how malfunctions will be managed and how recovery from disasters is handled;

+ **Change Management** endorses and supports the way the changing services/assets are used in the workplace;

+ **Project Management** – primarily aimed at CRE/ FM to plan, organize and put procedures into place to complete projects on time and on budget.

Apply Smart Value Navigation: The Background Behind Smart Value

In exploring new ways of helping the BBC to make the best use of its real estate while supporting its ambition to produce great broadcast content, it struck me that the relentless drive to cut occupancy costs was only part of the equation. It was through listening to the advice from the creative side of the Corporation such as the then Director of Drama and Entertainment, Alan Yentob, Peter Salmon who was the Director of BBC Studios, and the Controller of Operations, Sally Debonnair, that it became clear that it was also very much about creativity too.

This revelation led me to commission a piece of research into what makes a creative working environment. It was inspired by my collaboration with Philip Ross, a leading authority on new ways of working, and architect Clive Wilkinson – the designer of Chiat/ Day Building in Los Angeles, known as the 'Binoculars Building' – who has been at the forefront of introducing alternative ways of using office spaces. Their 'Creative Spaces' advice helped steer my team to gain a much better appreciation of how other organizations across the globe view their places of work as enablers of creativity.

This was the springboard for Smart Value and the BBC's workplace department used the concept in its most elementary form to roll out the Corporation's new real estate strategy – 'The

Creative Workplace'. One based on massive consolidation and rationalization, which centred on driving down costs by being efficient and providing an effective, agile workplace which could enable great content production. Yet at the heart of this was the constant focus on supporting the BBC's creativity. Additionally, the basic Smart Value framework was used to sell this large-scale estate transformation to win the hearts and minds of sceptical BBC divisional leaders. Plus, persuading nervous and apprehensive executives to come to terms with the overwhelming notion of the BBC's moving out of London to other hubs around the country.

Given the huge amount of change taking place across the BBC's portfolio throughout the UK and considering the BBC's unique role in the fabric of the nation, I recommended to the board that we get some external strategic advice on an ongoing basis. This gave birth to a group with the unwieldy title of the BBC Architectural Design and Workplace Advisory Council (ADWAC), chaired by pioneering workplace strategist Frank Duffy. This high-profile creative group helped ensure that the masterplan for MediaCityUK in Salford and White City in West London worked for the BBC and for its other stakeholders.

Through the ADWAC discussions I framed my views on spaces and places, plus I saw the potential for the consumer to influence the direction of the master-plan design. After all, for the most part regeneration and development projects are mostly designed on what architects and developers perceive as being the best solution. This undoubtedly means both a certain degree of uncertainty and a great deal of risk as to the outcome of the scheme.

Solving the seemingly intractable problem of selling Television Centre in White City provoked me to take Smart Value thinking to the next level. Having been advised that the market would not pay much for the property in a run-down neighbourhood at the height of the financial crisis was bad enough. This was compounded by the BBC piling on added constraints, such as ensuring the legacy of the BBC's historic television studios and maximizing its value, which spurred me to re-evaluate Smart Value.

The impetus for Smart Value was sparked by a 'Eureka' moment standing on the roof of the BBC's Television Centre in 2008. From that vantage point I could see the potential of linking the BBC brand with that of its White City neighbour, the newly-opened Westfield London shopping mall, then one of the largest shopping complexes in the city. Additionally, in 2009, Imperial College, a world-renowned centre of scientific excellence, bought a former BBC vacant lot to house its new innovation hub. So, by allying three premier 'brands', value was added to the land, which attracted developers, investors and other leading companies to this once-neglected area. How

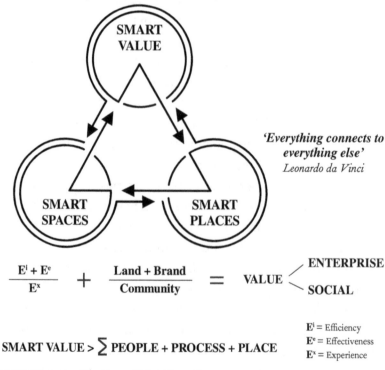

'*Everything connects to everything else*'
Leonardo da Vinci

$$\frac{E^i + E^e}{E^x} + \frac{Land + Brand}{Community} = VALUE \begin{array}{l} ENTERPRISE \\ SOCIAL \end{array}$$

SMART VALUE > $\sum$ PEOPLE + PROCESS + PLACE

E^i = Efficiency
E^e = Effectiveness
E^x = Experience

FIGURE 5.7: The Smart Value Formula

Smart Value impacted on the evolution of White City will be discussed further in Part 2 – The BBC Story (*see* p. 175).

The model is not a formula in the traditional mathematical sense. It has been designed to be easily understood, since most people find numbers and figures simpler to digest. Essentially, it is a framework dressed up as an equation to help stakeholders appreciate a complex topic, albeit through a different more strategic lens. Put simply, it is all about joining the dots, reiterated by Leonardo da Vinci's quote, 'Learn how to see. Realize that everything connects to everything else', which I find is true about most things in life. I was also influenced by another thought-provoking piece by da Vinci – his drawing of the Vitruvian Man, which is described as 'seeing the world upside down and back to front… as a way to understand reality better'.

I have attempted to create a graphic depiction of how to take a realistic view in making the best use of the workplace. All stakeholders have a different perspective on the office, the Smart Value framework attempts to help everyone see the workplace in a holistic manner.

Smart Value has two interdependent components: Spaces and Places. Regardless on which side of the supply/demand one sits, spaces and places cannot be looked at in isolation anymore.

For Smart Spaces – this part of the model was informed by the two elements, Efficiency (E_i) and Effectiveness (E_e), and these are extended to include (the workplace) Experience – which comprises both wellbeing and engagement (E_x).

For Smart Places – this takes the perspective of the consumer, as opposed to the supply-side, urban planners, architects and developers.

In the case of an enterprise they would normally be concerned with the cost/value, the technical characteristics of the site or the piece of land they occupy. However, now they would also consider the impact their brand has on the location. This is not only about having a logo on the building, but incorporates the much wider field of brand appreciation, such as engagement with the surrounding neighbourhood and improving amenities for all.

Underpinning all of this is how the location fits in with the local community and the emerging importance of sustainability. The days of anonymous non-porous office campuses are coming to an end and it is no longer just a matter of paying the zoning fees or making contributions to a local event. Neighbours demand much greater engagement, especially as some of them may be customers of the organization or even part of the workforce. By partnering with a developer effectively, the true value can be created and it can be easier to demonstrate in a transparent manner.

Value – When it comes to assessing value, there can be tangible and intangible benefits for both Enterprise and Society.

Value for Enterprise – Bottom line is that such an approach must generate business value. Taking my experience at the BBC as a case in point, using the Smart Value approach to sell Television Centre produced over £200 million for the Corporation, which far exceeded the £90 million originally offered through the conventional route of a developer purchasing the former BBC site, as well as delivering a range of business benefits.

Social Value – In recent years the community aspect and social value agenda has widened owing to the challenges felt globally from environmental issues, traffic congestion and workers' inability to access affordable housing. So, the Smart Value formula also considers the emerging importance of the social value aspect. As a spin-off, this also helps the supply side substantiate its contribution to the ESG performance criteria required by its investors.

Reach Safe Haven – A Great Place to Work

After making a sea crossing, seafarers breathe a sigh of relief when land is in sight, yet they recognize that the journey is not quite over. There is one more obstacle to navigate: getting into port and docking safely. Larger commercial vessels are usually aided by pilot tugs, but smaller boats use a pilot's book or a set of charts to reach their intended berths. So like a skipper who is almost in sight of the journey's end and has to manoeuvre into port, business leaders who are navigating the transformation of their workplace also need to be steered to reach the end product – in their case, a Great Place to Work!

Overall, a 'Great Place to Work' is one which enables people to work productively, where they are content with the purpose of the organization who employs them and makes them feel part of an organic community of workers. It also has to be one where there is minimal friction in getting work done.

Additionally, a first-class workplace should:

+ actively support employees to carry out the job they have been hired to do;
+ meet the diverse needs of the various roles people carry out at work;
+ engender a sense of pride;
+ help create a strong sense of community.

So, to help leaders create the vision of what they would like the twenty-first-century workplace to be for their particular organization and one that is suitable for the needs and demands of their business, I would refer them to the thinking of my friend and fellow traveller in workplace strategy Neil Usher, who has been behind many workplace change programmes all over the world for the past 25 years, as well as being the author of *The Elemental Workplace*.

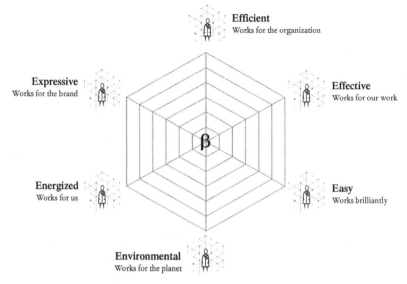

reproduced with the courtesy of Neil Usher

(Reproduced with kind permission of Neil Usher.)

FIGURE 5.8: Neil's Diamond – The Six Es

This thought-provoking guide provides many tips to pilot executives into port in order to realize their ideal workplace – and it cannot be stressed enough that 'one size' does not fit all. Neil has also set out six ingredients to make the finished product a great place to work. These are set out in Figure 5.8 above, which has become known as 'Neil's Diamond'!

The model is an extension of Frank Duffy's original framework of the three Es – Efficiency, Effectiveness and Expression. They all add up to create a workplace which is conducive to the performance, productivity and wellbeing of the people who work there. In summary, here are some key points of Neil's six-sided diamond:

+ **Efficiency (for the organization)**
  Reduces overall space required. Allows for flexibility of size within working teams. Enables learning and growth;

146

+ **Effectiveness (for work)**

   Brings out the best in people. Enables choice. Allows people to work their way, whether in a team or independently. Creates workplaces which inspire and motivate;

+ **Expression (for the brand)**

   Employees feel valued and appreciated. Promotes the attraction and retention of talent. Supports social responsibility;

+ **Environment (for the planet/society)**

   Fosters a caring culture. Cultivates a commitment to the local community. Engenders responsibility for sustainability. Creates awareness of energy resources/ethical issues;

+ **Energy (for people)**

   Supports employee wellbeing. Reduces absence and illness;

+ **Easy**

   A great workplace should just work brilliantly!

Discovering New Horizons

The impact of the various disruptive forces in the form of enabling technology and a host of new players coming into the very conservative real estate industry means that at the moment it is in a state of flux. The current status quo needs to be explored with an alternative approach looking at the two key dimensions of supply and demand.

Over the last 20 years there has been much discussion about the agile workplace, as well as flexible and agile working. These are examples of a range of generic labels which emerged to reconcile the range of choices people now have in terms of how they work. Initially, the option was a binary one – you either worked in the office or at home. The advance of technology saw the emergence of third spaces such as coffee shops and the like, made possible by the expansion of better connectivity, which opened up a whole host of alternatives as to where and when people work. This was coupled with the arrival of a herd of flexible space providers mixed in with the birth of 'Workplace Strategy' as a standalone advisory function, its purpose being to advise occupiers on the best use of space. So how have the providers of offices responded to this shift in demand?

The real estate sector is notoriously introspective as it has never really had to go out and seek customers – encapsulated by the business model of 'build it and they will come'. As indicated, this is a sector whose approach is notoriously singular, siloed and self-centred. However, a hidden paradigm shift to a more people-centric workplace has reshaped how business can consume office space. Nowadays, from large multinationals such as Unilever to traditional SMEs and new start-ups, all focus on flexibility when it comes to offices.

To paint a picture of what this all means Figure 5.9 below demonstrates the emerging new pattern, where consumer demand will give rise to a significant re-balancing of the traditional offer, which was dominated by long-term leases or buying a freehold or

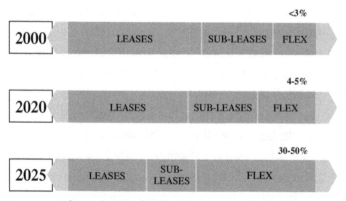

FIGURE 5.9: The Evolution of Office Consumption in the Twenty-first Century

taking a sublease. As indicated, the alternative flexible office market will explode to become much more significant. It is estimated to be 30 per cent although some commentators predict an even bigger percentage. This opens up a completely different range of possibilities for innovation and entrepreneurs – for example, what new products are there to run alongside the traditional leasing model?

The growth of flexible solutions has now created a multiplicity of work settings for the 'liquid workforce'. Each of the options where people can work, be it office, home, remotely or in a third space, has providers offering solutions. The other elements one has to consider are not 'place-related', such as working across time zones and engaging with work outside of the traditional days or hours of the working week and even work which is done via a job share arrangement.

This concept needed a label and the clichéd multi-dimensioned workplace did not quite fit the bill since it was anchored in the 'place' aspect and does not factor in 'activity'. DEGW alumna Despina Katsikakis, now International Partner and Head of Occupier Business Performance at Cushman & Wakefield, pointed out, 'We need to recognize demand is dynamic whilst buildings are static. The only way to reconcile the two is through embracing a dynamic portfolio flexibility and on-demand spaces.'

The Omnichannel Workplace

The inspiration behind integrating the multi-layered twenty-first-century workplace offerings came from former BBC colleague Dave Crocker, now CIO of US care-plan provider AllyAlign Health. He suggested that I look at what happened in the retail world with the emergence of omnichannel marketing. The concept being both traditional and digital channels are used in-store, online and at point-of-sale so a seamless, integrated and consistent customer experience is orchestrated across all platforms. This resonated with me as a way of explaining this paradigm shift to a twenty-first-century workplace based on providing and consuming offices across to a much-wider spectrum and creating an explosion of optionality in the context of an ecosystem.

Figure 5.10 below describes the new spectrum for consuming offices from fixed to fluid. It includes what are status quo options which will remain but are no longer the sole choice of the consumer. This is now recognized by a growing number of players on the supply side, as John Duckworth, MD of Instant Group, points out, 'the real estate industry is at a crossroads, as it has been operating on a 150-year-old blueprint, which is now outdated.'

Whether or not the traditional gatekeeper role played by the broking community is sustainable is a moot point. Will it be threatened by disintermediation? Clearly there are plenty of new entrants to the market operating under the Proptech umbrella who are seeking a share of the lucrative broking commission pie. While transaction costs of this nature have always been the bane of the CRE leader's life, conversely there is also growing discomfort among the property sector concerning broking fees. Certainly, this unease over vast fees should be a subject for concern for the leaders of the major property advisory and transaction houses.

The schematic in Figure 5.10 aims to demonstrate that it is now possible to take a more holistic view of the entire system for consuming space. There has been much comment on the flex-sector and all its component parts, but has anyone taken a 360-degree view of workplace offerings. According to organizational management specialist Fons Trompenaar (*see also* p. 106) we all have 'a bipolar view of office work' – one that involves either working in your own office or an open-plan to one that comprises working in an office building or at home.

The schematic describes a variety of working modes, more than ever before. While the Covid-19 crisis of 2020 focused attention on working from home, the truth is that it is now possible to consider a much wider permutation of options. Especially as managers are becoming more comfortable with the shift of large numbers of office staff working in different ways. The reason being that this shift actually runs on two parallel dimensions – not only where work is done, but when it gets done – and this defines the move from fixed to fluid. It is one which retains traditional core office structures, such as headquarters which will be leased, but can also be expanded to include the emergent range of flex sector options; including working from home, in cafés, on the move and in a plethora of flex-space options. I believe this emergent sector will become more significant, as was discussed in Chapter 3.

However as technology progresses it is also important to include virtual options into the mix. AI, avatars, chatbots and digital twins[5] have come out of the realms of science-fiction and into the workplace, with many forward-thinking global companies already using these computer-generated devices for training purposes or to test out organizational structures, change management scenarios and the effects of ideas virtually, before implementing them for real. When it comes to defining space needs, the potential of these virtual tools working alongside people needs to be considered, as in the case for chatbots potentially replacing call-centres. These factors should be considered when businesses craft distributed workforce strategies.

All this indicates that the time has come to wake up to the opportunities presented by the shift from an analogue way of

---

[5] Avatars – virtual workplace aliases. Chatbots – computer programs designed to communicate with people virtually. Digital twins – a virtual copy of a living or non-living physical entity.

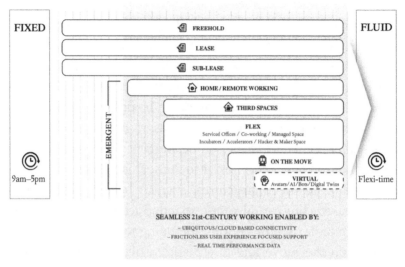

FIGURE 5.10: Omnichannel Working – The Workplace Redefined

providing and consuming space to one based on the new reality of digitally enabled working, where the emerging wider range of choice offers consumers what they have been lacking for years. As part of this shift in thinking we need to consign the building-centric twentieth-century mindset to history and think about a more people-centric twenty-first-century ecosystem of work based on a distributed workforce approach and economically viable for all. Additionally, it also generates real social value and takes account of environmental factors.

The Twenty-first-century Workplace Ecosystem

It never ceases to amaze me how the real estate industry functions, given its fragmented nature. However, there are 'green shoots' as we are on the verge of seeing the paradigm shift become reality. At this point it makes sense to consider how all the various stakeholders might adjust to the disruption to our existing analogue system.

Debating this with my Six Ideas business partner Max Luff, who specializes in systems thinking, we landed on the concept of thinking about the situation in terms of a twenty-first-century digital omnichannel ecosystem. This system advocates for a workplace which is dynamic, active and curated. One where all the existing stakeholders can either continue to operate as they have always done or they can explore new opportunities. The principal difference being that all parties are freed of the existing analogue constraints, where the transaction of space is the sole preserve of the broking community and transacted via a complex, costly and convoluted lease contract. Exploring this nascent omnichannel approach to support the multi-faceted demands of the twenty-first-century workplace, it makes sense to also consider the roles of the key stakeholders. Figure 5.11 below sets out the prototype of this new framework.

To harness the potential of having much greater choice there has to be a significant adjustment on the parts of both the demand and supply side of the old equation. It also involves reimagining the roles of the intermediaries and brokers.

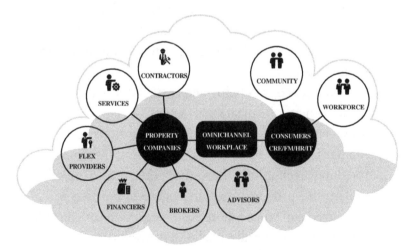

FIGURE 5.11: The Twenty-first-century Workplace Ecosystem

The new look office supply model recognizes that the best results emerge from having the benefit of multiple inputs. A big idea and not one designed by committee, it also calls for a variety of involvement from across a wide spectrum of stakeholders. This is not an easy process and since it is not straightforward, it will require perseverance. First, it envisages a fluid and flexible system for the provision of offices which is underpinned by the concepts of a distributed workforce.

The New Look Supply Model

These are some of the potential characteristics of what the supply side might look like:

+ The traditional leasing system would continue, but not as the dominant component of the market;
+ Property owners could develop portfolio wide propositions for customers as an alternative/extension to the core long lease offer;
+ There will be a focus on the whole life cycle of the building and not just on the construction phase. Providers will really have to get their heads around how the building enables people to work and the nature of that experience;
+ User experience, wellbeing and sustainability matters will be seen as critical success factors;
+ Design and construction providers get serious about modular and fully embrace BIM (Building Information Modelling) technology throughout the entire life cycle;
+ Similarly, the property/asset management function will be digitized and will be more customer service orientated;
+ Reward systems for all stakeholders need to be overhauled;

+ There will be multiple new players and new offers in the advisory segment;
+ The current raft of flexible providers will continue to expand and offer a more coherent value-for-money service based on true 'plug-and-play' offerings[6];
+ The FM model should expand to include not only the experience and wellbeing dimension, but the entire omnichannel working experience;
+ The Proptech sector will provide a wide array of initiatives that facilitate the rapid roll out of change;
+ All parties will need to consider the true impact of AI/ avatars/bots/ digital twin technology in both how we work and how we support work.

A New Look Consumer Model

If the purpose of a workplace is to enable business performance, then this system considers the premise that business leaders review how their internal support functions enable work and productivity in the twenty-first century. Underpinning this thinking is the concept of redefining place according to the omnichannel model. This entails considering how their enterprise goes about delivering change, procuring assets, operating real estate, undertaking capital projects and delivering technology solutions. However, the following factors have to be considered:

---

[6] A alternative take on the original technology-based view of Plug-and-Play which describes computer equipment, for example, a printer which is ready to use immediately when it is connected to a computer. So a Plug-and-Play workspace is one which is available on demand, rather than having to negotiate a lease, prepare the space, add furniture etc.

- There is no single point of leadership in how an enterprise enables its staff to work in an efficient and effective manner;
- Technology is now a commodity and has effectively 'left the building' so the need for large help desks and IT support teams has diminished. Furthermore, 'Bring Your Own Device' is the order of the day for a large part of today's workforce;
- The world of HR is rapidly automating;
- The schism between FM and CRE is inefficient and the two groups need to be fully integrated, including becoming better consumers (intelligent client) of the supply chain;
- Procurement in the main struggles to deal with anything complex, intangible and people orientated;
- The turf wars and the chasm of misunderstanding between all these groups reduces speed to market, focuses effort on non-strategic priorities and is not outcomes based.

Intermediaries

The current arrangement of the brokers as the single conduit between supply and demand changes to a multi-dimensioned one. The increasing developments in Proptech will only accelerate the disruption of the old order. For example, the leasing transaction procedure would be digitized, requiring the broking community to re-invent themselves.

In order to progress with the development of this prototype, there are six features which are necessary to foster the 'green shoots' of progress, enabling them to sprout into something worthwhile. This would make the model useful to all parties, as well as being economically and environmentally sustainable:

+ Respond to the huge changes taking place in how we work and use offices, made possible by technology;
+ Recognize that the system of providing, supplying and operating offices is undergoing dramatic change;
+ Rapprochement between the principals involved in the supply and consumption of offices, creating a different type of customer-focused relationship and not one anchored by landlord and tenant mindsets;
+ Reinvention of the intermediary (broker) to provide their clients with real value-added services fit for twenty-first-century purposes;
+ Revisit the way corporations lead and manage their support functions and refocusing them on enabling work – reviewing how the traditional support functions of HR, IT, Procurement and Real Estate/FM can be unified with fresh leadership;
+ Reduce the environmental impact on our planet by using infrastructure and buildings in a smarter way, while building real engagement with the emerging ESG/Social Value agenda.

Reap the Rewards

Together with the frameworks and guides in this chapter provided by those who have piloted successful workplace transformation projects, I hope that business leaders will have a better understanding of how to navigate change by harnessing their workplace to better advantage, whether the journey is one that makes better use of existing offices or one that requires moving to a new facility and using it as a catalyst for organizational change. Of course it is up to the leaders of organizations to use the suggested guidelines or even opt for a 'pick and mix' approach depending on their needs and goals, as well as those of their particular enterprise. I hope at the very least that the ideas and guidance offered will be 'food for thought' and might encourage people to view the workplace through a different lens. Even if that just means positioning yourself in the shoes of other stakeholders, which might alter long-held precepts and processes.

One common thread underpinning my thinking is the need for an improved relationship between customer and supplier. Building stronger links opens a wider range of possibilities. More importantly, each group just needs to see that by taking a different approach, they can harness wider value and greater benefits.

In the case of business leaders, the advantages could be as follows:

+ A much easier and more transparent decision-making process;
+ A variety of improvements to the underlying perform-ance of the business based on:
  ○ superior competitive advantage;
  ○ faster speed to market;
  ○ brand awareness and standing;
  ○ better employee engagement;
  ○ improved staff attraction and retention;
  ○ demonstrable contribution to the sustainability agenda and carbon footprint reduction;
+ By having a better understanding of the associated enterprise and project risk profiles leaders can make better informed decisions on how to mitigate exposure.

There are also positive gains to be made by the supply side, whether they are providers of buildings or services, as UK developer and REIT The Peel Group has discovered. As one of the creators of MediaCityUK, Executive Director Stephen Wild views placemaking and stakeholder engagement as equally important to the company's success as its finance and management departments so by closing the emotional connection between tenant and landlord, the supply-side could:

+ reduce voids;
+ increase returns owing to better-informed client needs;
+ create an opportunity to streamline/automate the process;
+ improve levels of customer relationships, leading to more repeat business.

One of the most overlooked or misrepresented stakeholders in a business yet one of the most important is the actual workforce. Henry Ford recognized their value when he said: 'You can take my factories, burn up my buildings, but give me my people and I'll build the business right back again.' The average office worker can derive many benefits from having an enlightened management apply principles, such as:

+ better working conditions;
+ encouraging their employees' sense of self-worth;
+ improving staff engagement with the business.

Finally, organizations have to consider the wider community and society as a whole. Professor Franklin Becker, Director of the International Workplace Studies Programme at Cornell University, asserts that there has to be a more 'joined-up approach' and 'a shift of focus from the "built environment" to a "community ecosystem" way of thinking'. At present this is at a very rudimentary stage, but these factors could deliver the following benefits:

+ better engagement between the corporate office and the local community;
+ opening up opportunities for collaboration through connections with local people;
+ creating better amenities, which serve both the workforce and the neighbouring community.

All in all, it is difficult to see why employing some or all of these ideas would not yield positive outcomes. They are not all that radical but could help savvy management to navigate their enterprise successfully through the storms of the VUCA world into calmer waters. English Historian Edward Gibbon wrote 'the winds and waves are always on the side of the ablest navigators' – as long as leaders understand how to steer their organization to a safe harbour.

Sources

1. 'We cannot direct the wind but we can adjust the sails.' Bertha Calloway.
   Clark Hine, D. & Thompson, K. *A Shining Thread of Hope: The History of Black Women in America*. New York: Broadway Books, 1998, p.240.
2. 'one in which the boundaries are highly permeable across functional interest areas within the organization, as well as between the organization and the external environment'.
   Bartone, T. & Wells II, L. 'Understanding and leading porous network organizations: An analysis based on the 7-S model', Center for Technology and National Security Policy National Defense University, 2009, p.1.
3. 'preparing and supporting people to adopt new thinking, behaviours, practices, understandings and competences'.
   Keller, S. & Aiken, C. 'The inconvenient truth about change management'. McKinsey & Co., (2008), p.3.

4. 'You can take my factories, burn up my buildings, but give me my people and I'll build the business right back again'. Henry Ford. Boone, L.E & Kurtz, D.L. *Management*. New York: Random House, 1987, p. 138.
5. 'The winds and waves are always on the side of the ablest navigators'. Gibbon, E. *The History of The Decline and Fall of the Roman Empire*. London: J.F. Dove (1825). Vol. VIII, Chapter LXVIII, p. 235. (1787)

Epigraph

Lewis, C.S. *Mere Christianity*. London: Geoffrey Bles/Macmillan Group, 1952.
© copyright C.S. Lewis Pte Ltd., 1942, 1943, 1944, 1952. Used with permission.

6

The Future Now

The future is not inevitable. We can influence it,
if we know what we want it to be.
Charles Handy

W hat comes to mind when you pass by an office building? Those ubiquitous concrete, steel and glass monuments built to service commerce and Mammon; commanding the skyline of the modern cityscape and dominating the lives of the millions of people who work in them. Most people hurrying past these monoliths do not pay them much attention. For the workers themselves, one office building is pretty much the same as all the others: it is just the place you go to work. Pre-Covid-19, many employees were unaware of the different work options now available which do not necessarily involve commuting into an office every day. Business leaders, and especially CFOs, view the office building as an expensive, inflexible liability, especially when coupled with complex leasing systems – making it difficult for them to see how a cost centre can transform into value creator for their enterprise.

Again it is down to how one perceives work, the workplace and how one relates to office buildings, but it is becoming more evident that they are no longer seen as edifices providing shelter for those working in them. As has been demonstrated, the way that many organizations function and the very nature of work has now changed. Covid-19 has certainly provoked a wider debate about what the office of the future might look like, with some even proclaiming the demise of the office itself.

What should be discussed is: what is the purpose of the office and the workplace in today's business environment? This is a question I asked many interviewees while doing my research for this book and for the most part they confirmed my long-held view that the workplace in all its guises, is there to support the enterprise – that the buildings are not just an asset, but that they should also enable business performance and productivity. I have always wondered what would happen if both sides of the landlord and tenant divide could align around this goal. It would require a shift in both the traditional landlord and tenant mindset to a more progressive and forward-looking standpoint. However, this is being influenced by the convergence of three key aspects:

- The way the use of offices has changed owing to the digital revolution, the maturing of flexible working options and the nature of demand;
- The impact of the 2020 pandemic and Proptech on the supply and demand side of the commercial real estate equation;
- The upsurge in sustainability and 'doing the right thing' agenda – in other words, what I call 'Smart Value'.

One has to also factor in the enormous changes taking place which are altering the working landscape. This is a landscape which is becoming more reliant on talent who wish to be agile and are more footloose. This 'liquid workforce' will drive real estate agility as the gig economy grows significantly over the next decade. Added to that, people are also becoming increasingly discerning about where they work and who they work for – reflected in global consciousness surrounding sustainability, the environment and ethical governance (ESG), plus the effects they have on business, society and by extension everyone's lives. This is a dilemma which enterprises and leaders are faced with, especially when major Wall Street CEOs make bold statements such as 'awareness is rapidly changing' or that the business world is 'on the edge of a fundamental reshaping of finance', – businesspeople are sitting up and taking note.

The events of 2020 may well add to their focus as the impact of the Coronavirus pandemic has yet to be understood at the time of writing. One thing that is certain is that the crisis forced us all to consider different ways of doing office work at scale. Having experienced different ways of working and seen how well it operates, both employers and employees will recognize that there are in fact alternatives which are feasible and practical – but will the effects of the pandemic bring about a significant change in perspective into how we use offices?

Furthermore how does commercial real estate fit into this 'new reality'? Many involved in the supply side of the equation would point out that the last ten years have been very profitable, with low voids, high rents and better still, they enjoyed good personal bonuses. After all, in their view tenants will always exist and they will always have to rent or buy buildings so there is no reason for them to concern themselves in helping the business or ESG performance of their tenants. After all, who wants to rock a boat on a very smooth, profitable journey? Unless the boat is about to hit a typhoon, which might be a distinct possibility, given that the Covid-19 crisis may well prove to be the 'accelerant' for other forms of disruption in the pipeline. Coping with the need to adapt to remote working at scale has demonstrated to many leaders that distributed working is feasible and it has now totally discredited the long-held fears of managers that no work gets done unless they can see their staff at their desks. As Dr Marie Puybaraud, Global Head of Research at JLL commented; 'once people have moved to remote working there is no reason to go back to the old ways'.

Covid-19 apart, it would be commercial suicide for the property world to ignore the all-pervasive impact of technology. Coupled with the events of 2020, it would be wise to adopt a positive approach and harness the dividend made possible by developments in digital capability. The other aspect is Social Value and the ESG factors, which are still relatively new, but will provide significant gains if the supply side helps the performance of its tenants and their businesses.

The broader impact on society and the community experience will become an important factor for both organizations seeking to attract talent and for building owners/landlords wanting to attract corporate tenancies. There needs to be a combined effort from the providers, operators and consumers of real estate embracing Social Value for the benefit of the wider environment and society as a whole.

Harnessing the Digital Dividend

One of the main imperatives of regenerating the BBC's property portfolio was the broadcasting industry's switch from analogue to digital. This was something I witnessed first-hand as the UK's national broadcaster struggled to come to terms with what was a new order powered by technology.

It was not merely a case of installing new digital equipment, but even the way programmes were being made was changing right in front of our eyes. For example, producers could edit content on an Apple Mac at home rather than book time in an edit suite. However, the real disruption came with the explosion of choice in programming and the shift in putting the viewer in control of what they wanted to watch.

If we look back on how we grew up with TV, in the UK it was just three channels, with a fourth joining in the 1980s. Over in the US, TV viewing was dominated by the 'Big Three' – NBC, CBS and ABC – with independents, including Fox and cable-TV networks such as CNN, jumping into the fray in the mid-1980s. Whichever side of the Pond you were on, the common denominator was that they ruled the airwaves, dictating programme selection and scheduling – it was their way, or no way!

The mass-marketing success of video cassette recorders in the 1980s gave the viewer a little leeway into the possibility of choice, despite the clunky system and remembering to record favourite programmes. Fast-forward 40 years and digital technology has enabled us to stream our favourite shows into our tablets/phones and watch them whenever and wherever we want – even binge-watching to entertain us on that long, boring commute! Our viewing pleasure is now on-demand at any time and place so broadcasters, whether 'old-school' BBC, ABC and their ilk, or 'newer kids' like Netflix, HBO, Sky and many others, are putting their customers/viewers in control of their personal schedules and really upping the ante by competing to make really watchable Hollywood-style content.

The key point here and the lesson for commercial real estate is that technological change will impact on workplace provision dramatically by disrupting the system as it did for TV, particularly in the last 20 years. The question is how will the property world adapt to it, especially the nascent inroads being made by Proptech in developing more customer-focused tools such as office space sourcing apps, which will inevitably lead to the much-vaunted 'Uberization' of the workplace?

Established commercial real estate providers, either from fear of stagnation and decline or through recognition of the necessity to progress, are taking the venture capital route and investing or partnering up strategically with tech companies, either in the Proptech sector itself or developing their own tech in-house tools to deliver solutions for their own enterprise or for the wider-built environment. They have come to realize that technology and improved access to data enables real estate operatives to provide better advice for their tenants/clients. Some are looking into virtual and augmented reality to help sell a building or a space, making it possible to visualize its capacity as a workplace or even to demonstrate what a change-management programme will look like.

Leading US real estate operator/developer and landlord Tishman Speyer, who own the Rockefeller Center, used technology to improve the work–life balance of its tenants and staff by setting up an app and web portal offering a comprehensive concierge service, with other property players following suit. Tishman's platform extends to healthcare screening, personal grooming appointments, backup childcare, food deliveries, travel planning right through to organizing community volunteering for its more altruistic occupiers and employees. On launching the initiative, CEO Rob Speyer commented, 'Instead of defining ourselves by the square feet we own, we will define ourselves by the quarter million people who use the square feet and how well we tend to them.'

Undoubtedly there will be casualties in real estate with the onslaught of digital disruption. We only have to look at the way it has impacted accountancy and the legal sector, where many basic processes have been automated and are being simplified or integrated within digital systems. This is affecting paralegal and book-keeping jobs, just as the advance of Proptech will put pressure on the real estate brokers in the middle ground.

Many forecasters say that disintermediation will hit the broking world hard. However, I take a more positive view of how the cosy old world of traditional leasing will function, as the need for broking decreases. It will not disappear altogether, but companies offering this product will need to reinvent themselves; especially as other functions such as asset and property management face disruption. In my opinion, this reinvention of the intermediaries aligns with the 2018 World Economic Forum report on 'The Future of Jobs', which states, 'New technologies give rise to new job roles, occupations and industries, with wholly new types of jobs emerging to perform new work tasks related to new technologies.'

Nevertheless, the current reality is that for the most part commercial real estate is stuck in analogue, 'Big Three' channel mode. The appearance of serviced offices in the 1980s is commercial property's 'VCR moment' and co-working/flexible workplaces are its equivalent of multi-channel, on-demand digital broadcasting. Like the world of media, corporates will soon be able to have real multiple choice as the growth of flexible space options builds to industrial scale, leaving the traditional core leasing sector as its junior partner.

It is likely that the enforced largescale shift to remote office working brought about by the Covid-19 crisis will accelerate awareness in boardrooms of the widening range of choices available in ways of working. Also many of their doubts will be alleviated as to how it will work for their organization. As this is still at a rudimentary stage, maybe leaders need to direct their teams to start focusing not just on cost-cutting, but on how the office portfolio could help business performance, as more and more organizations shift increasingly to flexible work, which also includes more traditional companies such as Amex, BP, Cisco, Dell, JP Morgan Chase, Philips, among many other major international firms. Taken together with early-adopters like Google, Microsoft and Salesforce, who have already shifted their thinking away from real estate portfolio strategies to focus more on distributed workforce strategies, for the large number of their employees who will be working differently. This must be seen as a sign that just like the broadcasting world's migration into multi-channel viewing options, which provide choice for the consumer, commercial real estate's answer has to be multi-modal omnichannel working.

One important aspect of the omnichannel model is empowering both the real estate sector and the enterprises which use its spaces to develop a joint approach in building real engagement with the emerging ESG agenda, while demonstrating true Social Value.

Embracing Social Value

How might a more joined-up approach deliver significant social value is a topic that merits further consideration beyond this book. For me, it is all about figuring out how we make better use of the built environment, since social value cannot be created in a vacuum, it requires the co-operation of all the stakeholders.

Together, we can all create social value by considering the economic and environmental impacts on society, as well as how to increase the wellbeing and development of an organization's workforce and those of the neighbouring community around it. It is simply not enough to put lofty strategies in place if people, both on the consumer and supplier side, do not have the mindsets to address these issues in a cohesive way. On a basic level, which is well within the control of the two principals involved in the real estate equation, why not direct the industry to make a concerted effort to take waste out of the system of constructing and also operating offices? Some useful initiatives have been put in place but no one is talking about 'the absolute disgrace' of the tonnes of waste heading to landfill sites from commercial fit-outs or that offices continue to pump thousands of tonnes of carbon into the atmosphere. Andrew Mawson, founder of AWA, points out that a typical 50,000 square foot building generates the same CO_2 in a year, as 320 return trips from London to New York. Only by engaging with the occupiers of the buildings, the intermediaries and contractors – basically, the groups who write the million dollar/pound cheques – will any progress be made to improve matters. Old habits die hard in real estate, but the difference now is that the occupiers are calling the shots.

Unlocking social value is a process of collaboration between society, company leadership, investors, public opinion, local community and most of all, the workforce. The biggest challenge for real estate is to convince everyone that they are actually part of the solution rather than being part of the problem. Currently, developers and contractors do offer a range of Social Value initiatives such as job creation schemes, generous charitable donations or community outreach programmes, etc. Some cynics could claim that they could be tick box exercises to smooth over the planning permission process. Especially in the UK, where government introduced the Social Value Act back in 2012, which requires public sector bodies to consider economic, social and environmental wellbeing as part of the procurement procedure.

However, 'doing the right thing' has to go beyond an Act of Parliament and as the world of work is moving towards a truly agile distributed workforce and the adoption of the omnichannel workplace, it is time for some 'big picture' thinking. For example, along the lines of the entire occupier sector in partnership with the property industry, engineering a shift in commuting and working patterns. By adopting a 'plug and play' approach to how employees can use offices, this can enable individuals to move to a lifestyle with less commuting. Apart from the gains to the enterprise in terms of productivity and staff wellbeing, the secondary benefit is reduction in pollution from less car traffic and less pressure on public infrastructure such as roads and rail.

Many major world cities, such as London, Sydney, Paris, Rome, São Paulo, Istanbul and Moscow, along with the US hotspots – Los Angeles, Chicago, San Francisco, Boston, Washington DC and New York – suffer some of the heaviest traffic congestion in the world with inevitable long commutes. In San Francisco's Bay Area workers can spend an average three to four hours commuting every day, which is untenable. Additionally, the high cost of living in some of these cities, coupled with unaffordable housing, is pricing out the workforce, especially young people.

International Workplace Studies specialist Professor Frank Becker contends commercial real estate together with corporations could provide a solution by taking a leaf out of the academic world, which provides accommodation for both students, academics and visitors, as California's Stanford University had done in Silicon Valley, Cornell Tech doing the same in New York on the Hudson River and London's Imperial College offering reasonably-priced living in White City. Frank's proposal focuses on building new affordable communities not just for company employees but extended to locals as well as a means to attract and retain valued talent and engender a better and closer community spirit.

Regus's Mark Dixon is a firm believer that 'if you embrace the future, you will be a winner' and he certainly subscribes to the notion that if organizations want a happy and productive workforce, commuting times have to be reduced. The challenging question is how to provide a more localized workplace to the knowledge worker in order to give them more time to spend with their families or their leisure activities. His answer is to open up 2,500 alternative/flexible workplaces in locations away from the big city centres and provide facilities locally in most towns and villages across the UK. Maybe some public sector organizations could take a leaf out of Dixon's book and introduce community workspaces in their public spaces, such as libraries and civic buildings.

The time has come for the real estate world to realize its potential in the social value agenda and the beneficial role it could play in the surrounding communities where its buildings are located. This is all part of the wider remit of both supporting corporations in their ESG performance, as well as supporting the businesses which operate within their spaces and places.

Converting social value into 'hard numbers', a Bank of America Global Research study found that US companies with high ESG rankings in the S&P 500 Index have outperformed their counterparts with lower ESG rankings by at least 3 per cent every year from 2014 to 2019. Put simply, ESG derives value in the millions of dollars, but when an enterprise applies a holistic approach through using my Smart Value framework, then the potential can generate billions – undeniably a really great prize!

To help move to the next stage, here are six basic factors to achieve a Great Place to Work:

+ Becoming better informed about enabling workspaces that generate meaningful outcomes and measurable impact wherever people work. Ones that deliver not only Entrepreneurial Value but Social Value, which also satisfy the ESG criteria of investors;
+ Spaces and places can be used in a smarter, more sustainable way for all the stakeholders – providers, consumers and intermediaries – by adopting a fresh approach based on improved awareness and stronger relationships;
+ Recognizing that the provision of offices/workspaces has shifted irretrievably from fixed to fluid with the new dimensions in demand and this should be seized on as an opportunity for all parties;
+ Real estate providers/advisers need to create better relationships with their customers by educating occupiers on making the best use of real estate;

+ Enterprise recognizes the competitive advantage opportunity of harnessing the link between an engaged worker and a well-run productive workspace. This is now underpinned by distributed working;
+ Review how enterprises organize their internal support groups (HR, IT, CRE/FM and Procurement) to enable work and productivity, consolidate and empower fresh focus to support omnichannel working.

The vision is to create twenty-first-century workplaces which inspire employee engagement, foster creativity and increase productivity while also improving an enterprise's capacity to compete and create value in all its guises. By working together, both producers and consumers of real estate can create effective and engaging workplaces which play their part in leaving a more sustainable 'built' legacy for future generations.

In the words of social thinker, art critic and poet John Ruskin, 'When we build, let us think that we build for ever. Let it not be for present delight, nor for present use alone; let it be such work as our descendants will thank us for.'

Sources

1. 'awareness is rapidly changing' ... 'on the edge of a fundamental reshaping of finance'.
   Fink, L. 'A Fundamental Reshaping of Finance', BlackRock CEO letter, 2020. https://www.blackrock.com/us/individual/larry-fink-ceo-letter
2. 'Instead of defining ourselves by the square feet we own, we will define ourselves by the quarter million people who use the square feet and how well we tend to them.'
   Tishman Speyer News. 'Tishman Speyer Introduces Zo – a Comprehensive Suite of Wellness, Lifestyle and Corporate Services to Tenants', Tishman Speyer website, 2017. https://tishmanspeyer.com/news/announcements/tishman-speyer-introduces-zo-%E2%80%93-comprehensive-suite-wellness-lifestyle-and

3. 'new technologies give rise to new job roles, occupations and industries, with wholly new types of jobs emerging to perform new work tasks related to new technologies.'
Centre for the New Economy and Society. 'The future of jobs report 2018'. World Economic Forum, p 18

4. 'when we build, let us think that we build for ever. Let it not be for present delight, nor for present use alone; let it be such work as our descendants will thank us for.'
Ruskin, J. *The Seven Lamps of Architecture*. London: Smith, Elder & Co., 1849, p. 177.

Epigraph
Handy, C. *The Age of Unreason 2nd edition, 2002*. London: Random House, Arrow, 1989, p. 7.

Part Two

The BBC Story:
From Analogue to Digital

7

Introduction

All that is best in every department of human knowledge, endeavour
and achievement.
John Reith, First Director-General of the BBC

The BBC Story is my personal view of one of the UK's world-famous institutions, undergoing a once-in-a-lifetime, large-scale transformative property/business initiative. As Head of BBC Corporate Real Estate between 2004 and 2012 and then CEO of the BBC's Commercial Projects until 2015, I felt enormously privileged to be part of this extraordinary organization at a critical juncture in its long history. More importantly, it gave me the opportunity to work with so many inspiring, talented and creative people who supported me in the challenge to transform the Corporation's estate and make it fit for the demands of the twenty-first century. This is their story just as much as mine and it has never been told before through the lens of the BBC's regeneration programme, where the organization was, literally and figuratively, switched from analogue to digital.

My part in all this was developing, financing and implementing the BBC's £2-billion property strategy and realizing the organization's goal to consolidate and upgrade its fragmented estate after decades of under-investment. Additionally, my remit was to create better working environments for employees, both in London and other regional hubs all over the UK. Although one aspect of the project was the renovation of the BBC's historic central London HQ Broadcasting House, another aim for the regenerated BBC was to shift its mainly London-centric broadcasting production to other regions. This involved a new HQ for BBC Scotland, studios in Cardiff and many smaller schemes in Liverpool, Coventry, Leeds, Hull, Cambridge, Southampton and Birmingham. The centrepiece of this regional development was the creation of a brand-new centre of broadcasting excellence, MediaCityUK in Salford, near Manchester.

The final piece of the jigsaw was the rationalization of the BBC's West London campus in White City and the redevelopment of its historic Television Centre, home to so many well-known and well-loved BBC programmes.

When I departed there was some unfinished business, including completing the disposal of the remainder of the BBC's White City leases to real estate developer Stanhope Plc, which were completed under the steady guidance of the then Director of Workplace, Tim Cavanagh. Plus, providing the long-awaited new home for BBC Wales, which was stewarded by Alan Bainbridge, the current Director of Workplace, this concluded the property transformation. Now the BBC's real estate portfolio comprises about 140 properties and 4.4 million square feet of space across the UK and meets the objective of a 40 per cent reduction in its real estate footprint (*see* Figure 7.1).

+ It delivered over 20 projects, which together account for £2 billion of project investment;
+ Sixty per cent of the estate was refreshed;
+ BBC Workplace teams moved over 12,000 people;
+ The regeneration delivered £47 million annual savings in property expenditure by 2016–17.

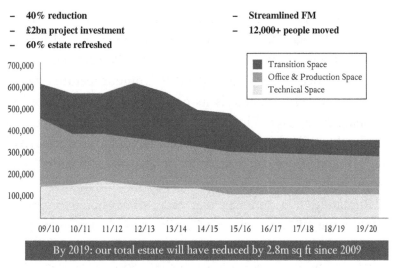

- 40% reduction
- £2bn project investment
- 60% estate refreshed

- Streamlined FM
- 12,000+ people moved

Transition Space
Office & Production Space
Technical Space

700,000
600,000
500,000
400,000
300,000
200,000
100,000

09/10 10/11 11/12 12/13 13/14 14/15 15/16 16/17 17/18 18/19 19/20

By 2019: our total estate will have reduced by 2.8m sq ft since 2009

FIGURE 7.1: The BBC Estate Transformation – In a Nutshell

My reflections of the BBC's transformation programme are not just a 'trip down memory lane' but a real-life guide highlighting insights and key learning points, which I have developed and analysed in Part 1 of the book. It also demonstrates the effectiveness of the Smart Value Concept and how it was applied by BBC Workplace, especially in the case of White City, which produced the desired results for the Corporation.

Focusing on the development of the BBC's four mega-projects as case studies – Pacific Quay in Scotland, MediaCityUK in Salford, New Broadcasting House and White City's Television Centre in London – business leaders and property professionals can evaluate how organizational transformation can be enabled through their corporation's real estate, while also adding both commercial and social value to their property portfolio.

The other key aspect of successful organizational change is aligning corporate property to the enterprise through understanding its culture and people. The importance of that significant factor is clearly demonstrated throughout the BBC Story. In this case it was enabling the production and broadcasting of an enormous variety of radio/TV programmes to global audiences 24/7. One of the BBC's unique features, which cannot be underestimated, is its position as the world's oldest national broadcaster. This legacy needed to be understood and respected by all of us working there, including those in CRE/FM/HR and IT – so there is plenty of historical and operational insight in my story to interest media folk and others too.

Ultimately, if a complex and multi-dimensional organization like the BBC can embrace agility and change, managing significant structural and administrative reorganization while incorporating new technology and working practices, then any business can be steered to accomplish this effectively and successfully too.

8

The Creative Workplace

'Oh my God! What have I let myself in for?' I thought to myself, as I looked around the room at the faces of various BBC executives and the then CEO or Director-General Greg Dyke congratulating me gregariously and welcoming me warmly as Director of Property/Head of Corporate Real Estate of this iconic British institution. This was back in January 2004 and I had swapped the roving life of Disney's Magic Kingdom for a once-in-a-lifetime chance to lead the world's oldest national broadcaster and one of the UK's most globally recognized brands in a £2 billion property expansion programme.

I could not help but be struck by the history and the cultural significance of the place as I wandered the warren of hallways and radio recording studios at the BBC's distinctive 1930s Art-Deco Broadcasting House in central London. Or around the maze of studios in Television Centre in Shepherd's Bush, West London with its unique circular question mark design, affectionately referred to as 'the doughnut' by BBC staff. The entire spirit and history of a nation's life seemed to echo from its walls: it was remarkable to think that George V, the present Queen's grandfather, first broadcast his Christmas address (scripted by Rudyard Kipling no less) through the BBC in 1932. As Queen Victoria's grandson he was effectively a direct link to the nineteenth century. During the war years the BBC transmitted Winston Churchill's rousing speeches which became integral in boosting the nation's morale during its darkest hours.

The new Elizabethan Age heralded the golden age of BBC TV as 3.2 million television sets were purchased in 1953 alone to watch a young Princess Elizabeth crowned Queen in flickering black and white; 15 years later, some equally grainy images were broadcast from a Space-Age designed Television Centre studio of 'one man's small step' on the moon, witnessed by 22 million in the British Isles. These images brought to us courtesy of the BBC were certainly an awe-inspiring and memorable moment for me as a young lad.

Growing up, the BBC provided the narrative of our lives, with much-loved children's programmes like *Blue Peter*, which is still going strong, featuring the nation's cherished pets along with friendly presenters who encouraged us to make models out of everyday items, went on daring adventures and fostered our involvement in numerous charity appeals. Whole generations have memories of cowering behind the sofa on a Saturday afternoon as terrifying Daleks threatened to exterminate the world in *Doctor Who*. Our teenage years were marked by the weekly rave of *Top of the Pops*, Led Zeppelin's 'Whole Lotta Love' riffs backing those all-important Top 10 charts. The BBC, both radio and TV, were integral to the success of British pop legends like The Beatles, The Rolling Stones, Pink Floyd, Queen, David Bowie and numerous other great bands and singers. Indeed, that global fame was harnessed for good when the world rocked together to raise money for famine relief in Africa – 1.9 billion people – 40 per cent of the world's population – watched Live Aid that day in 1985 – all triggered by a BBC news report on the catastrophic tragedy of the Ethiopian famine, which galvanized rock star Bob Geldof to act.

In fact, it is astonishing just thinking about the amount of talent launched by the BBC in terms of well-known entertainers, actors/actresses, presenters, writers, producers, directors in addition to their first-class, innovative dramas, comedies, factual programmes, news services and documentaries, which are viewed internationally and have become popular globally. Even now, with so much competition in broadcasting, we are still inspired and educated by BBC programmes like David Attenborough's groundbreaking documentaries on our planet and the natural world.

Another significant cultural aspect is the BBC World Service, which is still the world's largest international broadcaster, transmitting in more than 42 languages. The BBC's 'London calling' was a lifeline for occupied Europe and the Far East during World War II, with a certain George Orwell broadcasting on the Eastern Service. It was also a vital link to the West for those living under the Soviet-controlled Iron Curtain during the Cold War. Now, the rebranded World Service English and BBC World News reach 426 million international viewers per week, with an average of 38 million in the US.

Indeed, for many the BBC is a symbol of 'Britishness' and is woven into the psyche of the nation as 'Auntie Beeb'; additionally, another unique feature which distinguishes this broadcaster is that it is funded by the British public through an annual licence fee. It certainly plays a big part in the organization's decision-making and personally, I was very conscious of this during my time there. The fee is set by the British government and is classified as a tax; it also keeps the BBC free of advertising although commercial divisions have been added recently, which generate income through overseas sales of programmes and other profit-making ventures, which are returned back to its core production activities.

The other quaint factor is that the BBC is run by a Royal Charter, which outlines its constitution and sets out the public purposes of the Corporation while guaranteeing its independence. This agreement – presented by Royal Command to Parliament – is renewed every decade and inevitably when reviewed questions always arise over the increasing cost and validity of the BBC licence fee. Especially now in the age of digital TV with new competing networks offering their own subscription services. Another contentious point is the Corporation's impartiality in its programming, which forms a big part of the BBC's remit and is seen as fundamental to its principal values and maintaining the trust of its viewers. Nonetheless, this set-up means that the British public are truly invested in their national broadcaster, both financially and conceptually, and understandably they can get very vehement and opinionated at the way things are run at the BBC. It certainly attracts a fair amount of criticism from all quarters and depending on your outlook, it can be perceived to be too liberal, left-wing, politically correct, London-centric or right-wing, elitist, middle-class and a government mouthpiece.

Also, the question of the BBC's public funding often causes controversy; whether the cost of productions, staff salaries or any expenses pertaining to organizational policies, with accusations of wasting licence payers' money in 'out-of-touch' decisions – something I had to contend with quite often with our so-called 'pie in the sky' property strategies, which were viewed as profligate and unnecessary at the time.

Wallowing in BBC history and its past achievements, as well as reaping the rewards of the 2001 BBC/Land Securities Trillium Property Partnership, defined my initial 'honeymoon' period at the BBC. The real estate department had received great accolades, winning industry awards left, right and centre for this groundbreaking deal although I do recall that some of my peers remarked to me at the time that I was going to a 'non-job' since everything had been outsourced to Land Securities Trillium and there would not be that much for me to do!

Nonetheless, even back then in early 2004, a little over two years into the partnership, BBC Property seemed to be a bit like a swan streaming along, looking serene on the surface and furiously paddling underneath on a 'wing and a prayer' of substandard and outdated premises dotted all over the country. The estate's portfolio was woefully underfunded and certainly not fit for purpose for twentieth-century standards, let alone the demands of the twenty-first-century digital age. Working conditions were so shoddy in places, to the extent that female colleagues at BBC Radio Leicester had to leave their office on the 12th floor of an old building and go to the adjoining shopping centre to use the WC.

When I joined there were three major new buildings in the pipeline, with one almost ready to move into: a new 500,000 square foot complex, curiously titled Media Village in White City, near the 'doughnut' Television Centre in Shepherd's Bush. In the meantime, across in Central London the iconic Broadcasting House was in the somewhat painful throes of being rebuilt and in the regions a new lease had been taken on a spanking new space in downtown Birmingham, known as The Mailbox. The only element which remained constant throughout all this 'root and branch' transformation of the BBC's property was that broadcasting had to carry on, no matter what!

Personally, I landed to earth with a thud a month into what seemed to be both a plum job and a challenging one, attempting to makeover Auntie Beeb into a modern, fitter, leaner broadcasting machine. Enabling her to take on the cable and satellite disruptors like CNN, Discovery and Sky, whose broadcasting tentacles were spreading globally and ready to face the onset of digital and subscription TV. Nonetheless Auntie's cosy image took a real battering as a result of the Hutton Inquiry[7]

---

[7] The Hutton Inquiry was a judicial investigation into the death of biological weapons expert Dr David Kelly, who died in questionable circumstances, after he was exposed as the source of a BBC news report alleging that the then UK government, under Prime Minister Tony Blair, had 'sexed up' a dossier making the case for going

of 2003, which questioned the BBC's impartiality and led to the sudden resignations of both its Chairman Gavyn Davies and the Director-General Greg Dyke, within 48 hours of each other.

Effectively for six months the BBC was a rudderless organization in turmoil, while undergoing one of the most complex and complicated transitions in its 77-year history. I needed to adapt quickly to a role which I had to make my own in being part of a tightly knit executive team headed by the BBC's Chief Finance Officer, John Smith. It gave me some great insights into how events can come out of the blue and severely dent the confidence, morale and consequently the reputation of an organization.

The appointment of a former BBC2 Controller – Mark Thompson as Director-General – was perceived as a steadying influence after the resulting fallout of the Hutton Inquiry. Mark quickly grasped the potential in harnessing the regeneration of the BBC's property portfolio as a means to facilitate or act as the catalyst for his organizational change agenda. He saw it as a much-needed 'creative response to the amazing, bewildering, exciting and inspiring changes in both technology and expectations'.

BBC Property's State of Play

I did feel that I was on the cusp of doing something radical for the BBC in 2004, in terms of introducing new ways of working and how real estate could make its contribution in transforming this extraordinary organization. Obviously, a project of this

---

to war in Iraq. The inquiry cleared the government of wrongdoing and dealt a damaging blow to the BBC's journalistic integrity, criticizing the Corporation for failing to check the story adequately, which resulted in the resignation of the reporter who broadcast Dr Kelly's findings. This was swiftly followed by the departures of the Director-General and Chairman – the aftermath of the Hutton Inquiry was described as 'one of the worst in BBC history'. (Quote source: ITV).

magnitude required a good team of people who were all 'singing from the same song-sheet'. However, what I had inherited was a fragmented and disjointed in-house property function, who certainly did not have the capability to deal with the tsunami of work it was expected to deliver.

BBC Property had recently merged to bring together the traditional asset side and facility management teams under one roof. It was evident at the time that these two groups were uncomfortable with each other – in fact, they were like chalk and cheese. FM were trying hard to deliver a great customer service, while Real Estate's function was deeply rooted in its traditional view that they were the BBC's in-house landlords. Delving deeper into BBC Property, I discovered a culture of inadequate decision-making, limited accountability, poor levels of capability and a 'master/slave' approach to working with the supply chain. Despite these drawbacks, I also found plenty of capable people and team players, who just needed a bit of clear direction and leadership support to harness their potential so that they could take on the mammoth challenge facing them.

The whole department needed a complete overhaul and I needed a solid framework to help me map out how we might go about achieving the stated aims – the primary focus being helping the BBC move into the digital era, the other one being turning BBC Property into a strategic function within the organization. In the process I had to change my own organization totalling 2,200 people of in-house and service provider partners by going through a series of organizational changes to match our strategic journey. Thankfully, I received strong sponsorship from my boss, CFO John Smith and looking back it set the foundations for my views on organizational development and change – especially in evolving how to align property or the CRE function to the goals of the enterprise it serves. More importantly, as a property man, so to speak, the BBC's organizational change taught me about people and how to lead teams across boundaries, cultures and processes that perhaps they would not otherwise have attempted to cross.

The Learning Curve

Despite the challenging circumstances facing me, I viewed my time at the BBC as a tremendous learning opportunity. Not only did I get to use the strategic analysis and leadership skills I had learned from my MBA, but I also got the chance to experiment and test a framework developed by my American friends, workplace specialists Professor Frank Becker from Cornell University and MIT's Professor Mike Joroff.

Both Frank and Mike proposed that CRE professionals in any organization can move up the value chain from being mere 'order takers' to trusted strategic advisers. However, they will need to get to grips with understanding finance, technology, managing talent/people, planning, integration and other skills beyond real estate to add real business value to the enterprise they serve. This guidance was invaluable to me as a leader setting up the strategic direction for our group to help the BBC switch from analogue to digital. Being my own 'boss' so to speak as Director of Property certainly helped since the BBC treated its real estate division as a separate company, complete with its own finance director, the very capable Gerry Murphy. So, in this capacity it was up to me to 'write' the CRE rule book, my principal guidelines being:

+ It is essential to align with the business;
+ In delivering 'best in class' CRE/FM services, one has to operate as an 'Intelligent Client' – meaning there has to be commercial awareness and capability to effectively harness an outsourced supply chain;

188

✦ To achieve organizational change, it is vital to secure C-Suite support and sponsorship;

✦ Leverage existing tools and as many resources available to be used, as there is no point in reinventing the wheel;

✦ Another truism is to invest in one's team as nothing can be achieved without their commitment and engagement. Personally, I found the 'High Performing Team' framework[8] of great value. I used this to help the team to focus on their goals through sharing a common vision.

Navigating the BBC's Ocean of Uncertainty

Looking around the BBC at the beginning of my ten-year roller-coaster journey, it was evident that many people regarded it as a very stuffy, civil-service driven organization and steering it successfully to a modern, twenty-first-century technology-enabled, flexible open-plan inevitably required perseverance and persistence. Undoubtedly, it could not have been done without a colossal team effort, made possible by the contributions of numerous fellow travellers in every area of the organization. We certainly had an enormous amount of novel and challenging work, which was fairly problematic, coupled with a suspicious set of BBC Governors (supervisory board), an executive team in transition, plus a non-existent relationship with our customers – the wider BBC who used our buildings and facilities.

Additionally, there were two goals to achieve: the primary focus being switching analogue Auntie Beeb over to digital broadcasting by 2012. Mark Thompson's arrival as Director-General in 2004 really accelerated the BBC's shift to digital and

---

[8] A high-performing team is one which shares a common vision and goals by collaborating, challenging and holding each member of the team accountable. Thus generating greater commitment, in order to achieve outstanding results.

at that time, little was known about its implication, especially in terms of how audiences would react.

Mark talked a lot about 'Martini media' and the move to 'an on-demand world' – it was difficult enough for me coming from Disney and as a 'newbie' to come to terms with all this. I can only imagine what it must have been like for those BBC veterans who had been around for some time. Watching from the sidelines as broadcasting and production colleagues got to grips with some traumatic shifts in how things have been done across the BBC since 1922, three things stood out for me:

+ Seeing how digital exploded, providing audiences with such enormous and varied range in programming after decades of the old analogue world of two TV channels and four radio stations. Now it is hard to imagine that today's choice of 70-plus Freeview TV channels, plus more than 30 radio stations in the UK and over 200 channels across the US's digital network, were but a gleam in our eyes about 15 years ago;
+ Conversely, the big concern then was how would these rapid changes impact BBC audiences and how would they navigate this new digital world;
+ Witnessing the birth of 'citizen journalism' and the impact of social media on broadcasting. This happened as a result of the July 2005 London terrorist attacks. These atrocities marked a turning point in how the BBC covered news. At the time hard-pressed colleagues in the newsroom talked of the tidal wave of hundreds of emails and texts arriving at Television Centre, along with hundreds of photos and videos pouring in from the public and the way they used this influx of information.

The other goal, which was my responsibility as Head of BBC Corporate Real Estate, was dealing with 500 buildings spanning approximately 7.5 million square feet, spread around the UK, most of which were in fairly bad shape. The property portfolio had suffered from over 30 years of underinvestment.

Most of the buildings could not physically accommodate the additional requirements of transitioning to digital broadcasting operations – even the basics, such as having the capacity for extra cabling. This was not surprising given that in 2000, less than 2 per cent of the entire portfolio of more than 500 properties was under 15 years old. To add to the problems, key leases were due to expire on some of the BBC's larger buildings in central London.

The combination of all these factors was the impetus for the 1998 announcement of the 'BBC 2020' property vision. This aimed not only to address significant shortcomings in the estate, but to prepare the BBC for a period of tumultuous change, driven by new technology, increased competition and budget constraints. Nevertheless, through this major estate upgrade the BBC recognized it was essential to 'open itself up' to its audiences and stakeholders, increasing the imperative of securing new 'fit for purpose' buildings as soon as possible.

It was the far-sighted leadership of financial director John Smith at the time and his aspiration for 'decent quality architecture across the whole estate', which set up the framework for the Corporation's property vision. John's thinking was greatly influenced by his visits to open-plan environments in California, where he saw the cultural benefits they could bring to the workplace. He acted in conjunction with creatives Alan Yentob, then Director of Drama, Entertainment and Children's BBC, and Tony Hall, who was Director of BBC News and eventually became Director-General. They also supported John's appreciation for stimulating working environments in well-designed, functional buildings.

As part of this initiative they engaged the services of DEGW in the form of its founder Frank Duffy and then Head of Consulting/Chairperson Despina Katsikakis. They were tasked to take the first tentative steps in moving the BBC to open-plan workspaces, which was to be a physical signal of the Corporation's desire to open up as an organization. Back in the late 1990s this was revolutionary for the BBC as it set up a test floor in Broadcasting House, where John took himself out of his Director's office to sit at a team table. It was a far cry from the isolated offices/cubbyholes at the end of labyrinthine corridors occupied by the rest of the BBC.

This inspired test case in Broadcasting House led to the framing of the five key themes underpinning the 2020 vision:

1 *Flexibility:* Property must not restrict the BBC's freedom to evolve its operations.
2 *Technology:* All BBC space must support future technological requirements without incurring costly reconstruction.
3 *Talent:* BBC buildings must be showcase sites of technology and innovation in order to attract and retain the best talent.
4 *Audience:* New competition would test public sympathy on the cost of the licence fee, so the BBC must demonstrate value by engaging local communities with opportunities to experience the BBC in action through live broadcasts and open access to buildings.
5 *Cost:* BBC Property's role is to help the Corporation save money rather than spend it.

To achieve these aims I relied heavily on the framework provided by my friends, workplace specialists Professors Frank Becker and Mike Joroff at the then International Development Research Council (IDRC), the precursor to CoreNet Global. Their five-step process gave me the inspiration to look at the real estate/FM function and adapt it to incorporate the BBC's property vision, see Figure 8.1. In this way everyone could visualize how the process of transition could add value to the BBC and how the CRE department could move from 'order taker' to a much more strategic role.

In addition, it was also imperative that old-fashioned organizational silos must be broken down and different professionals had to learn to think and work out of their particular specialist boxes. I also realized that most workplace projects of this scale and magnitude fail because they focus on driving property efficiency at the expense of encouraging people effectiveness – driving down cost had to become an important, yet secondary

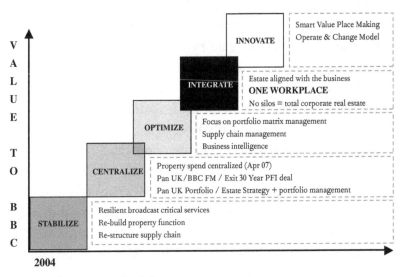

FIGURE 8.1: Framework for BBC Property 2004–12

factor. The key to success is creating a workspace that enables people to be more creative and productive. If that can be achieved, cost reduction and value generation will naturally follow.

Shifting the Focus to a Creative Workplace

Taking on all of this additional responsibility and learning by experience, plus dealing with all the ongoing project challenges, the property and facilities team I inherited in 2004 had been swept away in a tidal wave of intense activity. The group not only had to cope with enormous transformation on a massive scale over a few short years and in rapid succession, they also had to shift gears from dealing with run-of-the-mill estate activities to cope with a vast array of new construction projects all being developed concurrently: Central London's W1 Broadcasting House, BBC Norwich, Birmingham's Mailbox and the new campus at London's W12 White City. The latter project was managed by the BBC's Major Developments team under the very capable leadership of Tony Wilson. So, I decided we needed to reinvent the property, facilities and construction team by turning it into a more 'business-like' and coherent team and re-named it BBC Workplace.

Having kicked off a major team transformation within the old BBC real estate division, for me it reinforced that the property function itself would really have to step up to the plate and become much more strategic in its approach. This required some reimagining of the scope and reach of its role within the organization to enable the new look BBC Workplace to act as a trusted advisor to the Corporation, while collaborating more effectively in cross-functional teams, with both internal and external partners. In doing so, BBC Workplace adopted a mission whose stated aim was to 'deliver the right workplace for the most creative organization in the world'. This all had to be accomplished with an eye to public value which required us, as property facilities and construction professionals, to really broaden our understanding of what this meant. To give it a business or corporate definition, it is a public-sector version of shareholder value. For me personally and all those in real estate, public value is an unfamiliar term, but it enabled us to see another perspective: that it was not just about rents per square foot or building values.

Aside from these factors, however, there was one serious obstacle remaining in our mission and that was demonstrating to the BBC Executive how real estate could positively contribute to the BBC change agenda by taking advantage of the slew of new spaces coming on stream, which could act as catalysts for transformation.

Crucially, Director-General Mark Thompson could see that regenerating the property portfolio could help facilitate organizational change so he stepped into the breach in September 2006 by calling all senior management involved to a meeting at Broadcasting House in London and tasked them to push the boundaries and take the risk in supporting our initiative. It proved to be a seminal moment, both for the rebranded real estate team, BBC Workplace and for me personally; looking back, it ensured these projects were delivered successfully.

BBC Workplace worked hard to define its contribution to the Creative Future business plan. We created a schematic to demonstrate how we would go about producing a truly creative workplace based on agile working, see figure 8.2. Our manifesto was to deliver business and public value in partnership with HR and IT at minimum cost and at maximum effectiveness. The proposal went down well because for the first time the BBC executives, embattled by constant and unrelenting demands for cost-cutting and efficiency, could now see an alternative, one which focused on matters closer to their hearts – creativity and collaboration.

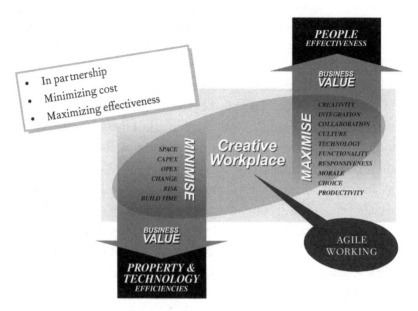

FIGURE 8.2: Delivering Business Value through Agile Working

Undoubtedly it was difficult building bridges of understanding between the BBC's HR group (people), its IT department and BBC Workplace. It required an enormous amount of effort to build trust between all the teams and get them on board with our common aims for the BBC's new-look working environment. Shifting the focus was also not easy as the creative world, like many other industries, is full of egos and idiosyncrasies. A pragmatic approach was required, especially in attempting to roll out agile or alternative workplace strategies as part of the new generation of facilities. However, I did learn an important lesson: even if you provide a great new workplace, it is very difficult to harness the hearts and minds dividend if you try to introduce desk sharing in an existing space!

Another useful and new exercise BBC Workplace employed was to use Customer Relationship Management tools to engage with our stakeholders and also to demonstrate to external auditors, the BBC Executive, Governors and others how things were developing on the property and workplace front. A by-product of such was the publication of an annual report called the 'State of the Estate' – a comprehensive analysis of how the BBC used its real estate portfolio and how it benchmarked against the outside world. It was useful to have evidence such as this to contribute to the regular assessments of the BBC by the National Audit Office (NAO), the UK's public spending auditor and watchdog.

The 2013/14 NAO report which came out in 2015 – a year after I had left the BBC and 11 years after I had taken over as its Head of Property – stated that it was 'generally supportive' of the BBC's estate management and that it found despite large initial costs 'the organization had made good progress in rationalising (by almost a third) and upgrading its estate. It had also improved its use of available space'. This was a great affirmation for BBC Workplace and its many years of trials, tears and tribulations.

Stabilizing the Good Ship BBC

It certainly helped me that the BBC had already started its major estate upgrade when I joined in 2004 and more importantly, it had charted its course with the 'BBC 2020' property vision. What was lacking was a clearly defined roadmap and delivery strategy and my job during 2004–06 was to figure this out and craft a plan which took the following parameters into account:

+ Maximize space utilization to drive reduction in BBC costs and footprint;
+ Leverage partnerships or other major occupiers, local communities, the supply chain and others;

197

- Ensure flexibility in order that the property portfolio could meet the needs of the business;
- Drive cultural transformation.

A pretty tall order! I recall visiting the BBC's then Chairman, Lord Grade – now Baron Grade of Yarmouth – at his Marylebone High Street office off London's West End to explain how we intended to get the BBC's property ship back on course. Michael Grade has British popular entertainment and TV coursing through his veins, having served as Controller and Chairman of the BBC, as well as CEO of the UK's main independent broadcasters ITV and Channel 4.

Being a highly experienced career-long broadcaster, Lord Grade hammered home to me the importance of getting under the skin of broadcasters and creatives if I was to make any headway with steering the BBC vessel on course. It was a great tip and reinforced what I had learned at Disney: it is all about the show, not the building! In short, it was the 'missing link' aligning the business with its real estate, which left me in no doubt that I had to drive an intelligent real estate strategy that enabled the BBC to deliver high-quality original content, inspire innovation, support new technologies and engage a global audience.

Taking Care of BBC Business

Lord Grade's advice about really understanding the 'business' of the BBC was a message reiterated by Caroline Thomson, the newly-created Chief Operating Officer and my new boss from 2006, during her weekly senior team meetings. She religiously hosted these meetings at 8.45 a.m. every Monday, gathering the heads of all the BBC's support and strategic units together, where we discussed any hot topics and set priorities for the week ahead. In this way, I found myself right in the epicentre of how the BBC functioned and it gave me enormous insight into the workings of a complex and highly politicized organization. Especially as it was going through some testing times following the announcement in 2005 that London had won the race to host the Olympics in 2012 – the same year the major switchover to digital technology was due to take place, as well as the BBC's migration across to the renovated New Broadcasting House and up north to Salford.

To really get into the underbelly of understanding this multi-layered and multi-faceted national institution, I certainly wanted to try and do something different. One way was giving everyone in my team of over 2,000 people across all the BBC regions and at every level the opportunity to get involved and have a say in how we as a team could support the Creative Future initiative.

Bearing in mind that one criticism of the BBC was that it was too London-centric, rather than having one big 'impersonal' meeting in London, a member of BBC Workplace would hold a series of sessions and debates in London (in the main Central London W1 and West London W12 sites), Glasgow, Birmingham and Manchester. This certainly proved a valuable exercise because the comments made by my colleagues provided a pretty fair insight of how the wider BBC – a 25,000-strong workforce – felt about their working environment, their requirements and demands. To this end the Workplace Management team narrowed the points made to three main priorities which needed to be tackled first:

+ *Improve up and down communications:* To find ways to improve communication across ONE Workplace team in all locations and reduce London-centricity;
+ *Simplify processes*: To identify ways to improve the processes for initiating and managing jobs and projects;

+ *Focus on how to make the big picture small:* To improve
  awareness of strategy at ground level, so staff know
  what is expected of them and how wider workplace
  aims are relevant to them in their everyday work.

The other key factor for me was that we ensured that everyone at
BBC Workplace and the external supply chain understood 'the
show must go on' and had to be kept on air – a challenge given
the legacy of the old 'master/slave' mindset. Good progress
was only achieved on this agenda as the leaders of our principal partner – Johnson Controls – responsible for FM grasped
the importance of workplace services aligning themselves to
the business of the enterprise. I was extremely grateful for the
broad-minded attitude of Vice-President and General Manager
at the time, Rick Bertasi, who was followed by Steve Quick,
currently CEO of Cushman & Wakefield.

It was essential to the success factor for the new-look BBC
Workplace team that it not only understood the business of
broadcasting, but also spoke its language in conjunction with
listening to the needs and requirements of the organization's
workforce. To build on our 'One Team' game plan we lever-
aged the BBC's annual fundraising telethon *Children in Need* as a
team-building initiative. Taking over the *Children in Need* studio
the night before the main event allowed the entire team to put
'its money where its mouth was' in order to generate hundreds
of thousands of pounds for this charitable appeal. All of this
resonated with creative and operational colleagues across the
broadcasting world and showed them that the property/work-
place division was on their side.

The most important piece of advice, however, came from
Tim Cavanagh, then Director of Workplace Operations: 'stay
on air and don't kill anyone!' To this day, I still marvel at how
the BBC achieved putting out high-quality content to a global

audience on a 24/7 basis with hardly a glitch despite all the troubles and turmoil involved during its decade-long transformation. In fact, during the six-year period of construction work on Central London's Broadcasting House only eight minutes of broadcast outages were recorded. Hiring Dave Ronchetti, whose experience in overseeing the relocation of the UK's air traffic control facilities, proved a wise decision. Especially since I discovered that six months before I joined the BBC, there had been major power problems at Television Centre, causing a series of unprecedented blackouts, when either television went dark or radio went silent. The most significant being the inexplicable loss of 20 minutes from the *Today* programme, BBC Radio 4's flagship news and current affairs show, which has been transmitted live from 1957 – all the more embarrassing as during that time Tessa Jowell, the then Minister for Culture, who is also responsible for broadcasting, was being interviewed!

According to BBC folklore such an event is not merely an inconvenience to audiences, it has an even more sinister implication to do with Britain's nuclear deterrent. A submarine commander, serving on one of the four Trident nuclear submarines, which for the most part are submerged, goes through certain protocols to determine if the UK continues to function. One of them is to check whether the BBC's daily *Today* programme is still broadcasting – it would be interesting to note what the commander thought was going on when it went quiet that day in November 2003!

It was inevitable that something had to be done about Television Centre as broadcasters were tearing their hair out and demanding solutions fast. This also provided me with another key learning point: leaders need to step in and sort out situations which are business critical. It was essential to find a way of preventing Television Centre going 'off-air' again and it required the BBC's governing board approving £10 million to secure effective and continuous transmission.

Looking back, it was the fastest capital approval I had ever secured from a board and it demonstrated to me the importance of really understanding what is critical to the business, not what our CAPEX limits are or what technical considerations need to be considered – the problem just needed to get sorted! After all, 'the show must go on' and part of the workplace team's remit was to demonstrate to broadcast colleagues that we understood them and their requirements.

To this end we brought in experienced BBC veteran Jim Brown to help us understand the nature of TV studios and how they worked. Jim had been Chief Operating Officer (COO) of BBC Resources, which includes delivering studio services, outside broadcasting and post-production. As part of a multi-national team, he also led the resources and IT rebuilding of broadcasting infrastructure in Sarajevo after the Balkan War so I figured if he could manage bombed-out TV studios in a war-torn region, there was some hope he could help us with the tough journey of rebuilding trust among the BBC's broadcasting community.

It's All About the Money!

In order to deliver 'BBC 2020' property vision the Corporation had to figure out how to deliver all their goals in a world where it was not possible to use capital markets to fund the upgrade. Since 1991, the UK Treasury had imposed a borrowing limit of £200 million on the organization. Furthermore, these funds were prioritized as general working capital to finance programme-making. Also, part of the BBC's '2020 vision' aside from upgrading its buildings was to find the optimum way to work as an organization and to change how it related to its audiences.

The BBC took a novel corporate finance approach and some highly creative thinking to secure investment for their property transformation. The solution was found by establishing a public/private partnership in which the Corporation could transfer its property portfolio into a partnership, while retaining a 50 per cent interest. The partnership would raise funds for the capital investment and, as part of the arrangement, the BBC would not incur any additional expense above current property costs.

In 2001, following an options appraisal, the BBC agreed to a £2.5 billion partnership with Land Security Trillium. Under the scope of the joint venture, Land Securities Trillium would be responsible for managing the BBC's property redevelopment programme across the UK, provide finance for new construction and undertake FM and other property services for the Corporation over a 30-year period.

The BBC, along with other public service organizations at the time, was at the forefront of large-scale public/private finance schemes. These schemes, known as the Strategic Transfer of the Estate to the Private Sector (STEPS) and the Private Sector Resource Initiative for Management of the Estate (PRIME), meant that accommodation and its management transferred to the private sector. Other major projects such as the Channel Tunnel rail link linking the UK to France and British Intelligence's GCHQ building among others were also funded this way. However, in contrast to the other deals, the BBC opted for a significantly different approach, which involved a phased agreement to transfer the freehold estate on a piecemeal basis.

This proved to be a very useful move for the Corporation and the initial project for Phase 1 of the BBC/Land Security Trillium's Property Partnership was the new White City campus in West London, known as the Media Village. During these early days of the partnership, the BBC learned that it could secure cheaper finance by taking advantage of the bond market and the historic low rate of interest being charged. When the funding for Broadcasting House, the BBC's Central London HQ, was presented for review in 2003, the BBC had two options: finance via Land Securities Trillium or through the bond markets. While the latter proved to be cheaper, such a decision challenged the reason for having the property partnership.

In removing the need for a partner to finance and own new buildings, the BBC found that the scope of the partnership was reduced to FM and construction management services. It sowed the seeds for a fundamental review of the entire contract in 2005, just four years into its 30-year contract period. As the BBC had invested so much effort in this deal and had 26 years unexpired, I set about trying to find ways to salvage what was truly a sinking ship. 'Project Prospect' was set up in a genuine effort to try to find common ground, led by procurement expert Andrew Thornton. As I suspected, hearts had hardened when Land Securities Trillium lost out on taking on big money-making development deals which were more profitable versus run-of-the-mill facilities and construction management. Quite honestly, who could blame them for not taking advantage of better, more lucrative propositions? But for the BBC it did mean that its FM services had to be re-tendered – with the added complication of unravelling a business relationship, envisaged to last for 30 years, in an extraordinarily tight timescale.

Of course, changing course particularly given the nature of the contract, the public procurement constraints and the need to refinance the £341 million 500,000 square feet, the Media Village scheme was not straightforward. The exit negotiations were further exacerbated by the changing rules for financing transactions and increased costs associated with such matters. In the end, White City was re-financed through a bond issue. It all certainly took plenty of juggling, especially since my next adventure consisted of bringing about the BBC's new mega-projects and aligning the '2020 Property Vision' with its emerging Public Value strategy.

Securing the Delivery of Public Value

Public Value formed the key platform in the manifesto of the newly arrived Director-General Mark Thompson, back in 2004. I imagined that it was a major concern for him in 2005 when he mentioned to me that it was 'one of the three things that kept him awake at night' – the other serious one being a whole raft of construction and property-related issues he had inherited.

The run-up to the 2006 Charter Renewal certainly piled political pressure on the BBC, its significance being that the Corporation needs to secure a renewal of its franchise (the publicly-funded licence fee) from the British government. In addition, another layer of scrutiny is added by the external audits carried out by the National Audit Office (NAO), which I generally found very useful, but were hugely time-consuming and fraught with political challenges. Especially as the NAO reports were scrutinized by British Parliament. On a number of occasions, I found myself supporting Mark Thompson and financial director John Smith as we faced some thorough cross-examination from the Public Accounts Committee to account for our decisions and their subsequent expenditure. To my mind, these experiences were akin to what a grilling from the Inquisition must have been like!

Another aspect of working for a publicly funded organization like the BBC is 'trial by UK press' and of course there were instances when their blazing headlines about the Corporation's excesses, inefficiencies and extravagance are justified, but when it came to my particular world, they had a field day. Damning reports abounded on the over-the-top costs of the BBC's new headquarters, describing it as a 'citadel of profligacy', how millions were being squandered on new buildings up north and in Scotland, as well as the wilful misuse of licence payers' money on moving personnel up and down the country.

I would like to think that it was mostly based on a lack of understanding of what the real estate regeneration was aiming to achieve and the acute problems it was trying to solve. Also, press reports ignored the fact that this was a long-term strategy requiring an enormous initial outlay, which would reap benefits in the future. In fact, by 2016–17, the BBC's redevelopment project delivered a £47 million annual saving in property expenditure. Nevertheless, back in 2005–06, it was a struggle to find a way to supply and operate a fit-for-purpose portfolio of broadcasting and production facilities, which were functional and safe to work in, plus deliver value for money. Also, they had to meet the expectations of the BBC Board, the BBC Trust (the then supervisory body), under the watchful eyes of its chairman Lord Grade, followed by Sir Michael Lyons in 2006. The following summarizes some of the factors we had to take into consideration:

+ Ensure 'elastic' or flexible building design which could incorporate the production team's requirements to steer the constant evolution of new styles and technologies;
+ Provide attractive spaces which are available and accessible to the public;
+ Keep 'on trend' within a highly creative workplace environment in order to retain valuable skills and attract new talent;
+ Fulfil the commitments of the BBC Charter to support urban regeneration programmes across the UK.

One of the best decisions I took at the time was to establish a comprehensive portfolio management framework and the formulation of a 'corporate property plan'. It became the cornerstone of the transformation and an overall roadmap to help us navigate through what seemed at the time an ocean of stormy waters, made all the more difficult by the relentless spotlight of public scrutiny that we encountered along the way.

The BBC also launched its 'Creative Futures' project in 2005–06, which aimed to streamline its operations and prepare the Corporation with the right resources and technology for the digital age. This effectively shifted the project emphasis from being focused purely on the buildings to being aimed at delivering major business transformation in support of the 'Creative Futures' strategic agenda.

The 'Creative Futures' initiative did encourage me to persist with my efforts for a better alignment with the business of broadcasting: by securing an adjustment to the 2020 estate strategy by linking it more coherently with the BBC's 'Creative Futures' produced by Mark Thompson as his strategy to deliver public value. The physical manifestation of this was a corporate property plan based on streamlining the entire estate into eight major hubs. This made sense to me, given that BBC technology had just invested in creating high-speed fibre links between the eight hub locations in Belfast, Birmingham, Bristol, Cardiff, Glasgow, Salford, London's Broadcasting House and White City.

Sources

1. 'decent quality architecture across the whole estate'.
   Jackson, N. *Building the BBC, A Return to Form*, BBC London, 2003. p.14.
2. 'the organization had made good progress in rationalising (by almost a third) and upgrading its estate. It had also improved its use of available space'.
   NAO Report. 'Managing the BBC's estate'. Report by the Comptroller and Auditor General, 2014, p 10.

3. 'citadel of profligacy'.
   Scott, P. (2013) 'The citadel of profligacy... or how the BBC flushed another £200m of your money down the drain'. *Daily Mail* https://www.dailymail.co.uk/news/article-2337744/The-citadel-profligacy--BBC-flushed-200m-YOUR-money-drain.html

Epigraph to Introduction
Reith, J.C.W. *Broadcast over Britain*. London: Hodder and Stoughton, 1924, p. 24.

Delivering Agile Workplaces
Across the Nation

*You must try to do something that really works for the people who are
going to be in the building, and for the community who are going to
have to live around it.*
Kevin Roche, Architect

With the 2006 Charter Renewal coming up, one of the fundamental concerns licence fee payers had expressed was that the BBC had to shift away from its London bias and represent all of Britain in its broadcasting. While a move out of London had been on the cards for some time, Director-General Mark Thompson recognized that a new base in the north of England could help the overall transformation programme, one major element being the relocation of five BBC divisions from London to MediaCityUK in Salford, near Manchester.

During the following few years I became a regular visitor to the BBC Executive Board, particularly since the BBC's central London flagship project Broadcasting House, which had an overall budget of £1 billion, was in troubled waters. Additionally, the BBC had to upgrade a great deal more of its property portfolio to meet the goals of its 'Creative Futures' directive, with a plan of not only improving its buildings, but also opening up the BBC to its audiences the length and breadth of the UK.

The 'Project England' scheme provided new upgraded digital facilities to local radio stations in all regions. About 16 new spaces were launched during this period, each comprising roughly 10,000 to 20,000 square feet, with each one having the usual challenge of constructing new workplaces and installing complex digital broadcasting kit.

In contrast to the old-style BBC, which had typically operated behind closed doors or high, forbidding security fences, these new amenities were located in city/town centres and welcomed audiences into specially designed ground-floor public areas. The list of new facilities opened tells its own story: Birmingham, Cambridge, Coventry, Hull, Leeds, Liverpool, Leicester, Norwich, Southampton and Stoke among others.

Aside from the decision to move some operations up north to Manchester, Scotland and Wales were also factored into the transformation. BBC Scotland had been clamouring for years for a new home to replace its Victorian base in Glasgow, which had been established in the 1930s. Cardiff, the capital of Wales, became the setting of a new totally digital 175,000 square feet complex, Roath Lock. A drama factory which produces the world's longest-running medical series, *Casualty*, and the classic sci-fi programme, *Doctor Who*.

Pacific Quay – Scotland Sets the Scene
Pacific Quay in Glasgow was the first of the mega-projects which took the BBC from analogue to digital. It was a significant milestone when it opened in 2007, since it was Europe's first end-to-end digital production facility. It also heralded the BBC's transformation away from the traditional world of content and tapes to the new one of a fully digital broadcasting platform.

The decision was made that BBC Scotland's existing Queen Margaret Drive (QMD) property in central Glasgow was too costly and complex to redevelop and would also involve considerable disruption to its ongoing production and broadcasting activities. Aligning with the BBC Charter's commitment to support urban regeneration, a derelict dockland site on the banks of the Clyde, a few miles south of Glasgow, was approved in 2004. It provided the perfect location for the 364,000 square feet Pacific Quay development, which houses 1,300 staff. It also opened a fresh chapter for the BBC in Scotland, not only in constructing a new building, but also for inspiring a new way of working.

Having learned the lessons from the development of White City in London, the project was financed via a bond issue through Barclays Capital rather than Land Securities Trillium. Under this arrangement, the bondholders own the building, with the BBC holding the 30-year lease. The total capital costs of the development were £188 million, partially offset by the sale of the old BBC Scotland site for £18 million. Land Securities Trillium was assigned to oversee the design team, with Bovis Lend Lease as the main building contractor.

Following an international competition, the BBC appointed distinguished British architect David Chipperfield, who provided the architectural 'wow' factor, as well as incorporating acres of open space into the design, which was very different to the nooks and crannies of the old Victorian QMD building. It was all open plan, including the space occupied by the Director of BBC Scotland, and this in itself sent a clear signal to everyone that things were really changing.

Pacific Quay was a great opportunity to see how the organization grappled with moving not just into an open-plan office environment, but also in coping with the digital world. There were many concerns about how to make programmes with this new capability, including some industrial relations issues and the usual fear of the unknown. Of course, it all worked out in the end, as workflows were changed and people embraced the new-fangled technology. More pertinently, the project also supported BBC Scotland's efforts to achieve a 25 per cent reduction in its cost base over five years by embracing change, which was a higher target than most other parts of the BBC.

Pacific Quay owed its success to a strategy which I supported, in that it was organized as part of a comprehensive change management programme rather than just a building project. It was under the overall management of a Programme Director who spanned technology, construction, operations and transformation. The development also thrived under the leadership and executive sponsorship of the Controller of Scotland, Ken MacQuarrie, who held a strong vision of the transformational powers of technology and his management support was key in successfully aligning co-operation across multiple BBC departments. The building was also designed to provide significant public access, delivering on the BBC Charter commitment to engage communities by encouraging open admission to its facilities and live broadcasts.

New Broadcasting House – The Journey to a Creative Powerhouse

In 2000, the BBC published its London Three Hub property strategy, which was a portfolio optimization programme recognizing the upcoming issues of expiring leases and other property concerns in the capital. This meant closing Bush House, the HQ of the BBC World Service, a distinguished 1930s building in the Strand, now part of King's College, London. Additionally, several smaller buildings were closed to enable operations to be consolidated within fewer sites. As a consequence, the organization's iconic Central London W1 Broadcasting House, its flagship since 1932, would now house national and international

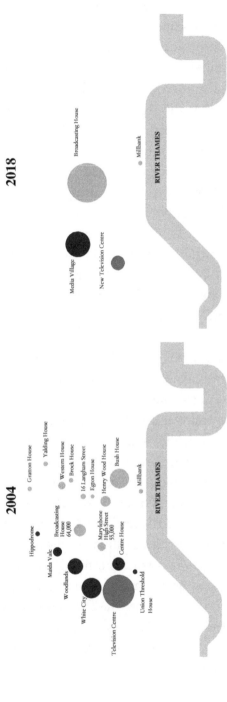

FIGURE 9.1: BBC Three Hub London Strategy

radio, television and online journalism, including the World Service, all under the same roof.

This ambitious project, with a capital value of £1 billion, presented a number of enormous and very complex challenges, as well as numerous logistical and aesthetic problems. The brief being that the legacy of the original heritage-protected Art Deco Broadcasting House had to be retained, while adding a twenty-first-century state-of-the-art production base for the BBC, with capacity for 6,000 employees, across the whole campus. Moreover, Broadcasting House is located in an architecturally sensitive area, surrounded by 13 other heritage-listed buildings, as well as being situated in a congested city centre, off central London's main shopping thoroughfares. Maintaining good relations with all our neighbours throughout the regeneration became a full-time job for Robert Seatter, the BBC's Communication Manager at the time, given its highly complex nature.

The other disadvantage was that the site is built above the London Underground network and the studio floors in the basement had to be spring-loaded to dampen the constant vibrations of Underground trains passing underneath. Especially important since broadcast quality and continuity had to be ensured, as the BBC's main radio networks based at Broadcasting House had to be kept on-air throughout the redevelopment programme.

Construction on this 'Grand Project' began in 2003. A big-name architect – Sir Richard MacCormac – was retained, along with London Securities Trillium for the capital programme management (design/construction/build), while Bovis Lend Lease was appointed as the main contractor. The project was financed via a bond issue to raise the £813 million, with the BBC contributing the additional £232 million and everything seemed set for what was to be an eight-year project carried out in two phases, to be delivered in 2011. However, things did not go quite to plan as Broadcasting House welcomed HM the Queen to open the second phase of the redevelopment in 2012!

Undoubtedly a project of this magnitude is fraught with difficulties; but back in 2003, a year prior to my arrival, the problems hit epidemic scale. Two major sub-contractors providing glazing and stone cladding went bankrupt, the 2001 terrorist attack prompted a re-think of security and safety specifications and to cap it all, the refurbishment works uncovered defects in the structure of the original Broadcasting House building. Added to this and on a sad note, the project director was struck down by a fatal illness, which left the redevelopment in caretaker hands at precisely the wrong time. Plus, the relationship with the developers and contractors had hit an all-time low, with the inevitable contractual disputes fuelling the fire.

The urgency and scale of the issues at Broadcasting House were the critical items in Mark Thompson's in-tray when he took over the helm of the BBC in 2004. Solving them almost certainly contributed to many sleepless nights for him and for me too. Nevertheless, I suggested applying a fresh approach based on a three-step strategy:

+ Restructuring the BBC client project team and introducing additional resources;
+ Re-negotiating the development agreement to re-base the budget;
+ Reviewing the design to simplify the specification and reduce costs.

At the time, what I also found overwhelming was having to deal with not one, but two potentially major contractual disputes, although it did provide me with a crucial learning point – not just opting for what appeared to be the only course of action. Even though lawyers galore were queuing up to offer the BBC their services, no doubt attracted by the rich pickings of a lengthy legal dispute.

Thankfully, through the wise counsel of external advisor Jonathan Harper, we managed not to go down the conventional route to resolve these issues. Since one of my aims was for BBC Workplace to act as an intelligent client, I suggested to BBC Legal Counsel that a full-time in-house legal advisor was needed. This request brought Peter Farrell, now Head of BBC Legal, into my life, who proved to be an invaluable asset.

I also took another unusual step with another instrumental appointment, a former Disney colleague of mine Keith Beal, who was an experienced production expert and understood broadcasting. He helped re-shape and re-energize the project team and played a pivotal role in stabilizing what had turned into a hugely problematic venture. Having steadied the construction side of the Broadcasting House project, Keith shifted his focus to help with the BBC's move up north to MediaCityUK.

The other turning point in terms of the Broadcasting House Project team was to beef it up, but not in a conventional manner. Broadcasting House Phase 1 was run as a pure construction project, yet in my mind, I always saw the regeneration of Broadcasting House as a major link in the BBC's content creation capability and one that relied heavily on technology. Therefore, as the second phase was being reshaped it provided the perfect opportunity to set it up as a fully-fledged change management programme. Until that point the BBC never had to face the challenge of moving so many live programmes into a new building, with the added complication of adapting to new technology.

The Corporation realized that the organization needed to 'up its game' and embrace programme management wholeheartedly. To this end it created a specific Corporate Programme Management office to underline the importance of this function.

Again, it was another positive way in which BBC Workplace reinforced its strategy as an intelligent client; by playing a part in nudging the Corporation in this direction and helping with the selection of the first BBC Corporate Programme Manager.

With Phase 1 completed and with construction of Phase 2 in a better place, it was time to focus on change management. In 2009, it was Head of Journalism Mark Byford who persuaded Andy Griffee to take on the onerous task of becoming full-time Programme Director for Broadcasting House and to effect its smooth transition. A broadcaster and dyed-in-the-wool BBC journalist with 25 years' experience, Andy had been Controller of BBC English Regions for nine years. This meant he had to switch from dealing with the sharp end of editorial output and immerse himself in the unfamiliar world of project management and finding the best way to maximize the efficiencies of co-location. Yet this appointment was significant since it sent a clear message to a sceptical broadcasting community that BBC Workplace took their issues on board and understood the way they worked.

Andy is a good example of an agile person transferring his skills to another sector, but also realizing that the brief required a holistic approach by bringing together editorial, property and technology in terms of how they all functioned cohesively for the benefit of the organization.

It would have been very difficult to deliver the Broadcasting House projects without Andy Griffee as overall Programme Director, together with effective collaboration from BBC Workplace's London Property Director Andrew Thornton (sadly no longer with us) and Director of Technology Andy Baker. They achieved the impossible by facilitating the move of 5,539 people from ten buildings across London, integrating them into the four that comprised New Broadcasting House. The migration schedule began in January 2012 and spanned 75 weekends of staff moves. This also involved providing 41,886 training days and 126 different courses, so that BBC personnel could familiarize themselves with the workings of the new technology and renovated building.

In hindsight, Andy commented that managing the transition at Broadcasting House was 'the most stressful and high-stakes job I ever undertook'. He also pointed out that his respect for Broadcasting House and the role it played in BBC history motivated him in undertaking this 'once-in-many-generations' opportunity to make my imprint on its next chapter and the future of a major chunk of BBC output'.

With a stable team in place and a plan to resolve the project delivery issues, the other aspect was to engage with the various professionals who would inhabit the new facility. They were identified as three distinct tribes: News, World Service, Audio and Music, all requiring bespoke technologies and distinct working practices. The key was to identify 'cultural' or 'team' differences and align these idiosyncrasies within a change management programme. They also needed encouragement to embrace new ways of working in a shared space, using common technologies. Aligning different working cultures is never an easy journey, but it is always worth investing time and effort in delivering shared solutions.

When the original plans were drawn up, the architects, designers and BBC Executives responsible for the Broadcasting House redevelopment had little idea how rapidly the pace of technological change would transform broadcasting and most people are unaware of how unique this gloriously distinctive building is in fusing the BBC's past with the present and the future. At the time of its completion, I remarked, 'Broadcasting House is not only a building for the BBC, but for London and for Britain.'

It still astounds me that it is responsible for half of all the BBC's output. It houses Europe's biggest newsroom and broadcasts globally 24 hours a day, every day of the year. The new building's central area fits 70 double-decker buses and all of the floorspace equates to 10 football pitches. In the end, despite the multitude of problems, construction cost £31 million less than the £1.05 billion stated in the 2006 budget. New Broadcasting House has trebled the financial benefits first identified in 2002 by up to £736 million over the remaining 21-year life of the bond.

The rationale for redeveloping New Broadcasting House and the validation for its transformation came from the actual people working there, by giving them a workplace which enabled them to operate together as a coherent unit. Journalists and broadcasters could now easily obtain the most comprehensive view of a news story or an unfolding situation by being able to access or meet up with colleagues from all corners of BBC journalism.

Award-winning *BBC News* broadcaster and Radio 4 *Today* programme presenter Mishal Husain remarked at the time, 'Being under one roof is an amazing moment for all of us in *BBC News*. It'll showcase our strength to the outside world and it'll create an amazing internal talent pool, so if I'm working on a story, someone who will know that story inside out will be right there, within arms' reach.' Nonetheless, I will leave the last word to veteran former *BBC News* journalist John Humphrys, who has quite a cynical reputation. His comment on the regeneration of Broadcasting House was that, 'It wasn't going to work. I thought things would go wrong endlessly and it didn't happen. It was pretty damn near seamless, I must say!'

MediaCityUK, Salford – Placemaking at Scale

The 'Out of London' policy was confirmed in an announcement at the end of 2004 and it signified that five London-based departments: BBC Children's, BBC Learning, parts of BBC Future Media & Technology, BBC Radio 5 live and BBC Sport, would transfer to the north of England, with Manchester being the preferred location. However, it would require a novel approach to secure the viability of such a large relocation out of London and inspire employees with the attraction of the 'Magnetic North'. This initiative envisaged the creation of a media zone, with the BBC as the anchor tenant, which would also appeal to other creatives in its aims to compete on a global scale.

This found me spending a day back in 2006 with Director-General Mark Thompson, showing him around the four proposed sites shortlisted for the project. When we drove into the 37-acre wasteland of disused and neglected docklands by the Manchester Ship Canal at Salford Quays, on a windswept, grey October morning, he looked perturbed. Who in their right mind would choose this out-of-the way derelict site in favour of the better-located options in the city centre?

Despite the obvious shortcomings, on walking around, he changed his mind when he recognized its potential symmetry coming from a cultural value perspective. What Mark had spotted, which nobody else had, was that the site formed the third apex of a triangle around Salford Quays. The other two were occupied by The Lowry arts complex, comprising two theatres, a drama studio and a museum dedicated to one of Britain's most recognizable artists, northerner L.S. Lowry, who was a renowned painter of industrial and landscape scenes. The Imperial War Museum North formed the second apex. This was housed in an evocative award-winning building designed by Daniel Libeskind – a popular destination which by 2005, three years after its opening, had already received its millionth visitor.

'What better neighbours could Britain's best cultural icon have?' Mark quipped, as he surveyed this ramshackle expanse of land by the canal and imagined the BBC completing the impressive, yet edifying triangle.

Ironically, and what has never been commented on so far, is the genesis for MediaCityUK did not come from Salford itself, but from Manchester City Hall. This was due to the visionary leadership of Sir Howard Bernstein, then CEO of Manchester City Council. He came up with the idea of creating a media zone which fitted nicely with the BBC's 'Magnetic North' vision for the move out of London. Howard then facilitated the 'impossible' by bringing together arch-rivals the BBC and ITV to come together and explore the concept of working together, through a series of brainstorming sessions. This was made easier as one of the potential site solutions was commercial broadcaster ITV's existing site.

The plot thickened with the arrival on the scene of Manchester's neighbour Salford, who had an optimum site, coupled with a hyper-dynamic regeneration body led by Felicity Goodey – who had led the team responsible for funding, building and operating The Lowry gallery and theatre centre. This proved to be a powerful combination for the other competing sites and much to Howard's disappointment, the media city concept was lost to Salford.

So, Salford City Council granted planning consent for a multi-use development on the Quays, involving residential, retail, studio and office space, under Felicity's indefatigable leadership, who engineered a remarkable cocktail of talent and like-minded partners to create a twenty-first-century city in record time. She led the consortium, which built MediaCityUK, consisting of the developer Peel Holdings, Salford City Council and the North West Development Association. They worked together with the BBC, local businesses and the neighbouring Lowry complex. This proved to be a great example of public/private partnership working in harmony towards a common goal.

Additionally, as this was solely a lease agreement, the BBC did not have to raise capital for the Salford project, which meant that it did not incur any direct building-related costs outside rent. So, the funds released from leasing were assigned to investing

221

in programmes and people, especially the costs of relocating employees from London. This was a crucial factor because previous attempts to decentralize production out of London had led to significant talent loss as people became tired of commuting from their home base in the capital. It was essential to the success of the project that BBC North could attract and retain talent by helping them find reasons to transfer to Salford, rather than inventing pretexts for them not to move up north.

That flexibility and effective use of space is evident throughout the facilities at BBC North and it has enabled different and creative ways of working. This is due in part to the COO of BBC North at the time, now Director of BBC Children's, Alice Webb and her insistence that nothing should be attached to the fabric of the building on a permanent basis. The absence of fixed walls and signs demarcating territories allows for more effective use of space since programmes can shrink and grow their footprint depending on production requirements. Also, people at BBC North are used to sharing space and resources so when BBC Children's need laptops for a weekday event, they borrow them from BBC Sport, who only need them at the weekend.

Currently, there are around 3,200 staff working in 26 departments, producing thousands of hours of content for BBC television, radio and online; broadcasting the nation's favourites, such as *Blue Peter*, the annual telethon *Children in Need* and the hugely popular football show, *Match of the Day*.

The success of MediaCityUK was further underpinned by ITV confirming plans to use the studio block, as well as lease office space and relocate production of the UK's longest-running, popular prime-time soap, *Coronation Street*, to a new studio lot on the opposite side of the Manchester Ship Canal. MediaCity is now considered ITV's flagship facility, with a staff of over 750 working for the UK's biggest commercial programme provider, hosting factual, entertainment, drama and post-production.

It has also become home to an eclectic and exciting mix of over 200 businesses, which are fuelling the 'northern powerhouse' – global brands such as Kellogg's and Ericsson, as well as dock10, the UK's premier television and post-production facility, and SIS, the world leader in broadcast gaming and retail betting. Shops and restaurants have been attracted to the waterside location and there is now a constant ebb and flow of visitors to the site.

The appeal of MediaCityUK was behind health insurance conglomerate BUPA's decision to stay in the same area but move their HQ 'up the road' from their present Salford Quays site to this dynamic multi-dimensional neighbourhood. This demonstrates that management are seeing and understanding that their organization's future success lies in an ability to attract and retain talent by providing amenities near or in a convivial and vibrant setting. However, MediaCityUK is not just about the 'big players'. At its core is the Landing, a hub for high-growth technology and digital start-ups, scale-ups and SMEs, incorporating 120 future-focused businesses. This environment is certainly a breeding ground for creativity, especially for the 1,500 students using the state-of-the-art facilities at the University of Salford. Additionally, Salford City College, University Technical College and the Oasis Academy have also made MediaCityUK home and are all fostering beneficial relationships with the companies around them as they develop the next generation of technological, digital and creative pioneers.

Mark Thompson had originally envisioned the siting of the BBC at Salford Quays as a complement to the 'cultural triangle' of The Lowry and the Imperial War Museum North. It has morphed into a 'cultural and social pentagon', which now includes the UK's two major broadcasters, the BBC Philharmonic Orchestra, as well as Salford University.

The BBC was certainly the impetus for the regeneration of this run-down area on the banks of the Manchester Ship Canal.

What Mark could not have foreseen on that blustery day in October 2006 was that the BBC move would bring 4,600 new jobs between 2011 and 2016 to Salford. Added to that, according to an independent report carried out by KPMG in 2015, the BBC's relocation contributed £277 million to the UK economy (as measured by Gross Value Added) in just one year.

Television Centre, White City – the BBC's Cinderella *did* go to the Ball

The venerable epicentre of the Corporation might be Broadcasting House, but for over 50 years, the real BBC magic was created over at Television Centre in West London. When it opened in 1960, the BBC's broadcasting and talent factory was one of the first purpose-built centres for television production, as well as being one of the largest in the world.

It was designed by architect Graham Dawbarn and the story goes that while seeking inspiration for the project, Dawbarn took the 50-page brief to a local pub, pulled out an envelope and drew the outline of a large triangle to mark the perimeter of the site then inserted a question mark in the middle of the triangle almost as though he had no idea what to do. As shown in Figure 9.2 below, this simple sketch featuring Dawbarn's sign of uncertainty provided an ingenious solution to design a space with eight studios, production galleries, dressing rooms, camera workshops, recording areas and offices. The tapering effect of the 'question mark' allowed for further expansion, if required.

Increasingly, over the years various extensions were added and the BBC effectively ended up 'colonizing' White City in the following decades, with the addition of six further buildings, all located within easy walking distance of Television Centre.

This sizeable complex, which eventually became Media Village W12, totalled 2 million square feet and occupied around

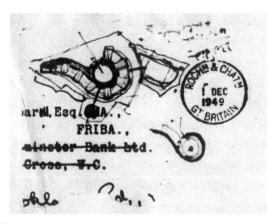

(Image: BBC)

FIGURE 9.2: Dawbarn's first design for the BBC Television Centre captured on the back of an envelope.

35 acres. It featured substantial facilities, such as White City One, a 350,000 square foot office building – its brutalist Soviet-style architecture earned it the unfortunate nickname 'Ceausescu Towers' after the despised Romanian dictator. The complex also included Woodlands, home to 1,300 staff working at BBC Worldwide. Not to be confused with BBC World, this division was responsible for selling BBC productions across the globe.

For five decades the image of Television Centre dominated the BBC's news output. It was regarded as one of the nation's favourite buildings, as well as being the familiar embodiment of 'Auntie Beeb'. This major BBC campus was home to 12,000 people involved in producing some of Britain's best-known television programmes, such as the original *Doctor Who* series broadcast for the first time in 1963, the day after President John F. Kennedy was assassinated. So many popular and interna-tionally-acclaimed TV shows were conceived and filmed there, including classics, such as *Monty Python's Flying Circus, Blue Peter, The Forsyte Saga, I, Claudius, Play for Today, Dad's Army,*

Fawlty Towers, *Top of the Pops* and *Yes Minister/Prime Minister*. More recent productions include *Top Gear*, *Only Fools and Horses*, *Blackadder*, *Keeping Up Appearances*, *Absolutely Fabulous* and *Strictly Come Dancing* (known as *Dancing with the Stars* in other countries) to name but a few. Not forgetting the numerous political, children's and sport programmes, as well as breakfast, music, variety and talk shows, fund-raising telethons, etc.

All production was in-house, which required an army of personnel, from camera operators, producers, directors, screenwriters, script producers and editors, sound recordists, lighting technicians, production, costume and set designers, art directors, make-up artists, hairdressers, props builders, post-production and sound editors, visual effects and music supervisors, etc. – all departments requiring numerous assistants, administrative and support staff to maintain the smooth running of this global TV talent factory.

Television Centre also housed the nerve centre of the BBC technical system, including the Eurovision network, which although part of the European Broadcasting Union, includes 75 broadcasting companies worldwide. I still recall Mike Eaton, Television Centre's Duty Manager, showing me around the Central Control Room on my first visit, which looked very similar and just as complex as NASA's space launch HQ. Underneath this convoluted set of buildings were thousands of miles of cables, which had expanded over the years and the ducts were overflowing with an ocean of colourful spaghetti. When Television Centre eventually closed in 2013, the salvage value of all this copper cabling generated a sum in the millions.

Depending on who one talked to at the time, Television Centre was either a sacred part of the BBC brand or an asbestos-filled labyrinth of costly real estate. Its original purpose as the world's largest production factory had already had the rug pulled out from under it as far back as the early 1980s. With the arrival of more technically sophisticated filming processes, this meant that many programmes could be made on location and much of the production space had become redundant. Another contributory factor was that Television Centre was still very much an 'old-school' multi-camera, video-production facility and most drama (except soap operas) had shifted onto film or single-camera video recording.

Another issue for me to consider, aside from English Heritage listing parts of Television Centre in 2008 and assigning it special status since it was of 'undeniable national interest and one of very few monuments to television history' was that I was dealing with something intangible beyond merely bricks, mortar and property values. This was brought home to me when it came time to move the popular Blue Peter Garden from London up to Salford. The garden was a feature of the long-running children's TV programme and was also the burial place of many of the show's beloved pets and included a statue of its first dog, Petra. The thought of relocating the remains of all these childhood favourites perplexed many viewers and caused widespread consternation.

Despite its many idiosyncrasies and the enormous cost of keeping Television Centre open, the BBC had soldiered on with this colossus for many years prior to my arrival. From 2010 onwards, figuring out the future of the BBC's much-treasured Television Centre felt like being caught in the crossfire of a brewing civil war. It was certainly a challenge to provide both public value and craft a sensible solution for this gigantic campus, riddled not just with structural problems and asbestos, but fraught with internal politics as well. There were many times when I almost threw up my hands in despair since there seemed to be no light at the end of the tunnel. However, the skills and experience gained from working on MediaCityUK gave me the tools to view the Television Centre project as potentially about innovation and placemaking, coupling the emotional connection people had to the BBC and its place in White City.

First, since the BBC had defined the eight major hubs around the UK, BBC Workplace had the overall strategy of moving 12,000 people around the estate. The question was: where would Television Centre fit into all this? Already from the 1990s, some Television Centre productions were being crewed entirely by freelance staff. By 2011 almost all the technical operators had gone, replaced by independent professionals. Freelancers were increasingly employed in the design, wardrobe, hair and make-up departments, so there was no real need to house and cater for a vast army of in-house production personnel.

As BBC Workplace had moved 'upstream' strategically, it had acquired a much better grasp on occupancy levels and had developed the ability to advise the BBC Executive board using real data, rather than merely speculation. This was a first for the organization as it removed the ability of the various production divisions to make unjustified claims for space and resources.

In 2007 the inevitable conclusion was reached by the BBC Executive board that Television Centre was to be closed and sold so a coherent strategy had to be figured out, not just for Television Centre, but also for the five other facilities which made up the BBC's White City campus. A dedicated group was formed from BBC Workplace to tease out the myriad of issues involved in the closing and sale of White City, called the Major Asset Disposals team. Known by its acronym MAD – obviously somebody somewhere had a great sense of humour! However, to be fair to the MAD team they did frame a strategy based on a phased withdrawal of the BBC from its position as the dominant occupier in White City. This involved a move down to about 4,000 people from 12,000 and this was made possible, in part, by the introduction of agile working practices across the BBC's workplace.

Additionally, from 2007 until 2009 decisions had to be made in shaping the portfolio optimization strategy for this vast 35-acre White City estate with the heritage-listed 'doughnut' Television Centre sitting as the single biggest surplus asset. Plus, dealing with the reality that the general consensus of the property market considered White City as a 'BBC desert' and not particularly appealing to other occupiers. Further adversity piled on with the onset of the 2008 global financial crisis, which severely dampened interest in commercial real estate at that time. All this conspired to add to the difficulties of disposing surplus property in a neglected, unglamorous and depressed neighbourhood – BBC White City was indeed the proverbial white elephant!

The only option for the BBC at the time was to mothball large swathes of real estate in London and just hope for an improvement in the years to come. It was a great price to pay but there seemed to be no other viable course of action. Consequently, the MAD team was disbanded and a complete rethink in approach was required.

Funnily enough, it was Walt Disney who proved to be my inspiration in engineering how the BBC's 'Cinderella' could go to the ball. During my early days at Disney, I was part of the Imagineering team, which is the research and development division of the Disney empire, responsible for the conception and construction of its attractions and theme parks worldwide, as well as the organization's real estate management. It was at the corporate HQ in Burbank, California, in a cluster of industrial buildings that a rather wet-behind-the-ears, former chartered surveyor met some of the most creative minds in the world. Undoubtedly, I was enthralled by the world of Disney and working with fellow Imagineers and their talent for ingenuity and resourcefulness encouraged me to think differently and follow Walt Disney's mantra: if you could dream it, you could do it!

I needed to stand back and take a fresh look at how the BBC's Gordian knot of a problem could be cut. So, one day I went up to the highest floor of the Television Centre complex and looked around the entire neighbourhood. Indeed, I had one of those rare eureka moments – in order to secure the disposal of BBC surplus assets, the whole of the White City area had to be reimagined or re-imagineered to make it more attractive. This led me to develop a methodology called 'Land + Brand', which was subsequently refined into the Smart Value formula, and it comprised of three core principles:

+ Optimizing the disposal of Television Centre by harnessing the power of the BBC's iconic brand;
+ Consolidating all the other BBC facilities in one campus through agile working;
+ Creating a White City marketplace which would be attractive to investors and occupiers, which subsequently turned into 'Creative London'.

Serendipity did play a major part in helping me to see things in a different light. While I was looking down across the 'BBC desert' from on high, I could not help but notice the scale of our new neighbour the Westfield shopping complex, which had recently opened in 2008. At the time it was the largest shopping mall in London. A decade later it attracts over 30 million people per year and has over 360 retailers across its 2.6 million square feet of lettable space, now making it the largest shopping centre in Europe.

Looking at the vast expanse of Westfield London took me back to the Disney Imagineers' playbook and to the creation of Disneyland Paris. While everyone knows about the famous theme park, very little is known about the wider picture and the Walt Disney Company's involvement in the creation of a new town – Marne-la-Vallée – and the Val d'Europe shopping outlet, which opened in 2000. It was designated an 'international tourist destination' by the French government in 2016 for its capacity to attract 15 million people annually. To put this in perspective, that other great Parisian landmark, the Eiffel Tower, welcomes 7 million visitors per year.

This connection between Disneyland Paris, Marne-la-Vallée and the Val d'Europe shopping mall framed my views of place-making for White City from a corporate perspective. It was my impetus for reasoning that if 23 million people visited Westfield shopping mall in its first year of opening alone, surely some of them might see the Television Centre neighbourhood as an attractive place to live or work in. Could the nostalgia factor of those well-known and much-loved BBC programmes move people to buy into the area? Or perhaps the buzz associated with Television Centre's glory days producing prime-time TV shows starring so many famous names? Could the allure of the BBC brand be harnessed to attract people to White City?

As a result of my rooftop inspiration, BBC Workplace went back to the drawing board to come up with an alternative approach and devised a product development exercise based around my ideas for a demand-led scheme, which would lever-age the value of the BBC brand. Labelled 'Smart Value', it aimed to develop a mechanism for collaborating with a developer part-ner to optimise the value of both the BBC brand and its land. In parallel, BBC Workplace also tried to improve the market's appreciation for the wider White City area.

In May 2010, we presented an ambitious new proposal called 'Creative London', where White City anchored by a re-purposed Television Centre could become the conduit for a multimillion-pound urban regeneration project to transform a deprived area of West London, which had been hit hard by the recession, and turn it into a vibrant, new 'creative London quarter'.

The concept was an evolution of what the BBC had achieved in Salford with MediaCityUK, which meant that the Corporation would work as a catalyst in collaboration with public and private partners. The aim was to build a showcase creative media hub for London around the adjoining White City estate. In this way the BBC would still retain a presence on the historic Television Centre site by leasing studio and exhibition space, while providing opportunities to promote the creative sector. The development of the area would replace dilapidated buildings with exciting new spaces for independent production, media and arts companies.

The 'creative quarter' concept, while more complex than merely selling off the BBC's White City estate to a developer, presented exciting opportunities for the Corporation to align itself with its original 'Creative Futures' agenda. It also endorsed the BBC's obligation to deliver both economic and public value, with the added bonus of creating social value in this neglected part of London.

In January 2011, the BBC approved a twin-track approach to the disposal, which called for the market testing of 'Smart Value' alongside a conventional freehold sale to identify whether this approach would drive out additional value to its White City properties. As if that was not difficult enough, the BBC made life even more challenging by inserting further business expectations into the equation:

+ Maximize value to the Corporation;
+ Minimize risk during the handover from the BBC to the new owner;
+ Protect the legacy of Television Centre.

In 2012, the BBC sold Television Centre to property developers Stanhope Plc for £200 million. The BBC retained the ownership of the building, but sold the lease with the understanding that this could be bought by Stanhope at some point in the future and in this way, the BBC would also take a share of future profits from the development. The joint venture of the BBC and Stanhope formed Television Centre Developments, which was tasked to dispose of the 1 million square foot landmark building and redevelop it into residential properties, in addition to a mix of leisure and office facilities.

BBC TV broadcasting might have moved out of White City, but the commercial side of the organization, BBC Studios (the former BBC Worldwide), responsible for selling BBC programmes operates in the newly refurbished studios, which formed part of Television Centre.

In 2018, BBC Studios returned £243 million (EBITDA) to the organization through its overseas sales, proving its creativity still informs, educates and entertains millions worldwide. The BBC's other commercial venture Studioworks brought in a revenue of £37 million in 2017/18, by providing production and post-production facilities from the now-renovated, former Studio 1, where many of its hit shows were once filmed.

Other parts of the BBC's White City complex – Broadcast Central and Lighthouse – also provide office space, broadcast and production centres not just for the BBC, but also for commercial stations Channel 4, Channel 5 and BT Sport among others. Again, giving the BBC a working link to a set of buildings which had played such an important role in its history over the years.

The whole Television Centre site has now been redeveloped, the old car park turned into a landscaped square open to the public and there is a vibrancy about the place as other media companies have moved in, attracted by its numerous restaurants, bars, cafes and cultural activities. No doubt the allure of fashionable private members' club Soho House, with its rooftop pool and panoramic views over London, is also a great draw.

The original Television Centre with its distinctive dough-nut-shaped 1960s exterior has been retained, together with the renovated gilded statue of Helios, the Greek god of the sun over-looking the central rotunda, where he had stood guard for half a century. An emblematic connection to the BBC, Helios sunrays symbolize television radiating around the world. At the base of the monument lie two figures representing sound and vision – a powerful visual reminder that BBC TV's legacy is still fostering and encouraging a creative environment in White City.

White City – A Placemaking Phoenix Rises in West London

The redevelopment of the BBC's Television Centre and Media Village W12 was one piece of the jigsaw in the overall regenera-tion of White City. The other was the enormous transformative impact of Europe's largest shopping centre, Westfield London, in conjunction with the UK's premier science and research university, Imperial College. The formidable trio of the BBC, Imperial College and Westfield were the cornerstones which really turbocharged this 60-acre West London site.

To put it all in context and from a property market perspec-tive, in the beginning of the twenty-first-century White City was considered a bit of a wasteland, dominated by the vast expanse of 'BBC desert'; it was a ramshackle oddity with no real purpose, despite its interesting history. In 1908 the site was chosen to hold the Franco–British Exhibition to commemorate improved Anglo-French relations. The exhibition featured an artificial lake surrounded by a 'city' of buildings with white stucco facades, which gave the area its name 'Great White City'. Later that year, and with the addition of a newly constructed stadium as its centrepiece, the Great White City hosted the fourth modern Olympic Games. The new stadium was designed to be located exactly 26 miles from Windsor Castle, the starting point of the Olympic marathon, and since then this distance was adopted as the standard for all modern marathons.

White City was subsequently used as an international exhibition centre up until World War I, with the stadium eventually becoming a speedway and greyhound racing track. Ultimately, the area took a downmarket turn. White City Stadium was demolished in 1985 to make way for the BBC's White City complex, now White City Place and the Media Village, W12.

In parallel with the BBC, Imperial College was also facing some significant challenges in its 102-year history, which were defined more by the university needing to maintain its growth and innovation capacity. This was severely hampered by its existing built-up central London campus, which was established in 1893 behind the Royal Albert Hall in South Kensington and was becoming increasingly unfit for purpose.

Like the BBC, Imperial College has an international reputation for excellence – in this case for science, engineering, medicine and economics. It ranks consistently among the top ten universities in the world. This prestigious institution attracts students from 140 countries, undoubtedly drawn in by the fact that its alumni include 13 Nobel Prize winners – notably Sir Alexander Fleming, who discovered penicillin.

Imperial College realized that in order to maintain its pre-eminent position in the scientific field, collaborating effectively with other experts worldwide was vital. So, attracting and retaining the brightest and best faculty talent, students and researchers was a paramount concern, together with providing them with affordable accommodation in London. One solution to Imperial's problem of space was buying a vacant lot in White City from the BBC in 2009. At the time BBC Workplace was developing its Smart Value initiative, which would eventually culminate in its plans for 'Creative London' and central to its thinking was taking a more holistic approach to master-planning in White City. This meant devising ways to engage with neighbouring landowners to present a unified front to the local Planning Authorities. I was helped to persuade them to buy into this unusual approach by the BBC's long-standing planning manager Andrew Fullerton, who was also an experienced architect. This formed the basis for Imperial College becoming lead partner in the W12 Alliance to redevelop and regenerate White City alongside the BBC.

Together with its £3 billion investment, the university has added considerably to its landholding in White City from its original 2009 purchase from the BBC. It now extends over 23 acres. Furthermore, Imperial's intention for its new West London campus was to provide an innovation ecosystem complete with 3,000 researchers working on pressing scientific challenges.

At the heart of Imperial's newly-developed campus is a £200 million Research and Translation Centre containing 484,000 square feet of laboratory and office space for academics to work, collaborate and innovate with established technology companies, as well as start-ups. It also contains 198 apartments designed to provide affordable housing for young academics to help drive innovation across the site. In addition, Imperial College's Advanced Hackspace and Thinkspace brings together over 2,000 like-minded entrepreneurs with the aim of turning their most forward-thinking and inventive ideas into reality.

The other side of the White City triangle and the incentive behind my 'Smart Value' concept for the BBC and White City was the retail colossus Westfield, owned by French–Australian consortium Unibail-Rodamco-Westfield. Marking its tenth anniversary at White City in 2018 also coincided with its second phase £600 million extension comprising of an additional 750,000 square feet of new retail space and 1,522 new homes. This also required a £170 million investment in local infrastructure, which benefits the wider neighbourhood. More crucially, Westfield has provided 8,000 new jobs to add to the 12,000 they originally created when the mall opened, with neighbouring residents getting first choice on employment. Westfield estimates that a further £300 million a year will be generated to the local economy through the 2018 expansion.

White City's regeneration sits at the intersection of commerce and industry in the scientific and medical fields, as well as incorporating a variety of new high-end residential and office developments. This has now attracted other global corporations to this once unmarketable and neglected area of London. In turn, they also offer scale, market power and even financial support to projects in White City. Companies such as Colt, Verizon, Virgin Media, Vodafone, Swiss pharmaceutical leader Novartis and recent addition L'Oréal now have their London corporate bases there. They join aerospace giant Airbus and the UK government's Defence and Security Accelerator department, responsible for finding inventive solutions to key defence-related challenges in collaboration with Imperial College. Yet the creative arts are also well represented in the regenerated White City, carrying on the BBC's legacy by adding another vibrant dynamic to the placemaking mix. Among them is the world's largest online luxury fashion retailer Yoox Net-A-Porter, which opened a 70,000 square foot state-of-the-art tech innovation space in White City Place. Tech Hub is already partnering with Imperial College to offer free coding classes to local children, with an emphasis on boosting digital skills among girls.

The Royal College of Art located its communication, animation, digital art and technology design departments to BBC Media Village, taking advantage of London's newest research and creative quarter. Another cultural dimension was added when the 1,200-seater Troubadour Theatre opened. This unique 'pop-up' theatre is capable of staging full-blown West End/ Broadway-scale shows on the site of the BBC's former car park.

The key lesson behind the successful regeneration of White City is that first, it was beneficial that both BBC and Imperial concurred that their shared aims and visions laid the foundations for subsequent bonds to be forged between academics, scientists, entrepreneurs and corporations, as well as – and just as importantly – its neighbours and the local community.

Second, the productive synthesis of the BBC, Imperial College and Westfield London fortified these bonds in the various amenities available in White City: the restaurants, shops, bars, cafes, gyms, cultural centres and green spaces, while also fostering and supporting a culture of research and innovation on an unprecedented scale in central London.

Sources

1. 'Being under one roof is an amazing moment for all of us in BBC News, it'll showcase our strength to the outside world and it'll create an amazing internal talent pool, so if I'm working on a story, someone who will know that story inside out will be right there, within arms' reach and I'll be wanting to make the most of that.' Mishal Husain, Appendix 3.

2. 'it wasn't going to work, I thought things would go wrong endlessly … and it didn't happen. It was pretty damn near seamless, I must say!' John Humphrys, Appendix 1.
   APM Awards Report (2013) 'The BBC's W1 Programme', p. 4

3. 'undeniable national interest and one of very few monuments to television history'.
   English Heritage Report. '"Auntie" honoured in recommendation to list parts of BBC Television Centre', 2008.

Epigraph

Brady, T. 'Kevin Roche: "I'm basically a problem-solving construction guy"', *The Irish Times*, 2017.

GLOSSARY AND DEFINITIONS

ABW Activity-Based Working

ADWAC The BBC Architectural Design Workplace Advisory Council. Chair: Frank Duffy. Members: Ricky Burdett, Paul Finch, Carla Picardi, Philip Ross

AWA Advance Workplace Associates

B2C Business to Client

BIM Building Information Modelling

BOMA Building Owners and Managers Association International (US)

CAPEX Capital Expenditure

CIPD Chartered Institute of Personnel & Development

CRE Corporate Real Estate

CSR Corporate Social Responsibility

EBITDA Earnings Before Interest, Taxes, Depreciation and Amortization

ESG Environmental, Social and Governance

FASB Finance Accounting Standards Board (US)

FM Facilities Management

FRI/IRI Full Repairing and Insuring/Internal Repairing (Lease Definitions)

GVA Gross Value Added

HR Human Resources

IASB International Accounting Standards Board

IDRC International Development Research Council (Replaced by CoreNet Global)

IFMA International Facility Management Association

IFRS International Financial Reporting Standard

IWFM Institute of Workplace & Facilities Management (US)

KPIs Key Performance Indicators

MBWA Management By Walking About

NIA/GIA Net Internal Area/Gross Internal Area

NLA Net Lettable Areas

REIT Real Estate Investment Trust
RIBA Royal Institute of British Architects
RICS Royal Institution of Chartered Surveyors
SME Small and Medium-Sized Enterprises
TI Tenant Improvement (US)
ULI Urban Land Institute (US)
VUCA Volatile Uncertain Complex Ambiguous

Agile Working Maximum flexibility and minimum constraint in the way employees work.

Chartered Surveyor A professional who advises on property and construction, also undertakes property valuations and structural surveys of buildings.

C-Suite Board level management, e.g. CEO, CFO, COO.

Dilapidations Repairs required at the end of a tenancy or lease, predominantly in the UK.

Distributed Work Employees work in separate locations and communicate virtually, with no physical office.

Fit-out The process of making interior spaces suitable for occupation.

Flexible working/Flexi-working A full range of working practices agreed between the employee and their employer.

Flexible workspace/Flexi-space Refers to any type of space outside of the conventional lease market.

Gearing Ratio A type of financial ratio which compares a company's debt in relation to different financial metrics.

Headcount Forecasting The process in which a business predicts the number and type of employees it requires in the future.

Net Usable/Occupiable The method of measurement of the area for which an occupier will pay a square-foot rate.

Privity of contract A contract which confers rights and imposes liabilities only on its contracting parties.

Remote Working/Telecommuting Employees work in separate locations but also touch base in a physical office.

Reversion Property automatically reverts back to the original grantor after a period of temporary ownership by another person/party.

Co-working Spaces A shared working environment in which a number of organizations work side by side in one building, usually charged on a monthly membership basis.

Hybrid Space Refers to an amalgamation of serviced offices and co-working spaces within the same building.

Serviced Offices Managed by a specialist operator, who rents fully-equipped individual offices or floors to organizations on a cost-per-desk basis.

REFERENCES

CHAPTER 1

Daykin, J. 'Intrapreneurship'. *Forbes*, 2019. https://www.forbes.com/sites/jordandaykin/2019/01/08/intrapreneurship/#745432f34ea3

Gellman, L. & Brown, E. 'WeWork: Now a $5 Billion Co-Working Start-up', *Wall Street Journal*, 2014 https://www.wsj.com/articles/wework-now-a-5-billion-real-estate-sartup-1418690163?autologin=y

Harter, J. & Mann, A-M. 'The Worldwide Employee Engagement Crisis'. Gallup, 1, 2016.

Joroff, M. 'How is the New City-making Industry Evolving to Help Cities Create Extraordinary Economic Value?'. Atheneum Partners Forum GmbH, 2015. http://www.forum.atheneum-partners.com/author/michael-joroff/

Kane, C. & Anastassiou, E. 'Perceptions and Perspectives: Fresh Thinking Required?'. 2019.

Corporate Real Estate Journal, Vol. 9, No. 1, Henry Stewart Publications, pp. 87–9.

Kane, C. 'Mistrust and misunderstanding: Lessons for the Property Industry on How to Align Itself with Corporate Occupiers'. *React News*, 2019.

reactnews.com/article/mistrust-and-misunderstanding-lessons-for-the-property-industry-on-how-to-align-itself-with-corporate-occupiers-from-the-bbcs-former-head-of-real-estate/

Kenny, P., Purton, T. & Wynne, G. 'The Growth of the Serviced Office'. *Financier Worldwide*, 2018. https://www.financierworldwide.com/the-growth-of-the-serviced-office#.Xhj3GkeeTIU

'Dreamers Who Do'.

Pinchot, G. 'Four Definitions for the Intrapreneur'. *The Pinchot Perspective*, 2017. https://www.pinchot.com/2017/10/four-definitions-for-the-intrapreneur.html

Spatial Agency Database, 'DEGW 1971–2009'. https://www.
spatialagency.net/database/degw

We Company/HR&A Advisors, Global Impact Report 2019, p. 17.

CHAPTER 2

Bateman, C. 'A brief history of Queen's Park in Toronto'. *BlogTo*, 2013.
https://www.blogto.com/city/2013/04/a_brief_history_of_queens_
park_in_toronto/

British Property Federation. PIA Property Data Report 2017, pp. 5, 9, 17, 21.

Crosbie, T. 'Dilapidations: a necessary cost or a money-making
exercise?' *Making Moves*, 2017. https://makingmoveslondon.co.uk/
dilapidations-a-necessary-cost-or-a-money-making-exercise/

Department of Justice: Canada. 'Where our legal system comes from'. 2017.
https://www.justice.gc.ca/eng/csj-sjc/just/03.html

DLA Piper. Real World Law: Commercial leases 2019. https://www.
dlapiperrealworld.com/law/index.html?t=commercial-leases

Dover, M. 'Capital & Counties JV wins Covent Garden'. *Property Week*,
2006. https://www.propertyweek.com/news/capital-and-counties-jv-
wins-covent-garden/3071263.article

Hower, M. 'Redirecting Building Waste from Landfill to LEED Projects'.
Planet ReUse/Sustainable Brands, 2014. https://sustainablebrands.
com/read/waste-not/planetreuse-redirecting-building-waste-from-
landfill-to-leed-projects

MSCI. UK Lease Events Review 2018. Prepared in association with BNP
Paribas Real Estate, 2018, pp. 9–10.

Nareit Research. 'Estimating the size of the Commercial Real Estate
Market in the US'. Based on CoStar Analytics 2018 Q4 and S&P
Global Market Intelligence, 2019.

Ruhmann, M. & Wijnmaalen, J. 'Country by country guide of
commercial leases'. TELFA, 2018. https://www.dirkzwager.nl/
Media/publicaties/ebook/37711/telfa-country-by-country-guide/
pdf/937078.pdf

Wolfe, L. 'Calculate commercial leases with square feet formulas'.
2018. https://www.thebalancecareers.com/calculating-commercial-
rents-3515436

CHAPTER 3

ACAS. 'Guidance: Flexible working and work–life balance', 2015,
pp. 7–15.

Advanced Workplace Associates. 'The difference between agile working and flexible working'. https://www.advanced-workplace.com/difference-agile-working-flexible-working/, 2017.

Alos, J. 'Effective ways to keep your Millennial and Gen Z employees productive'. Undercover Recruiter. https://theundercoverrecruiter.com/millennial-gen-z-productive/, 2019

Apgar IV, M. 'What every leader should know about real estate', *Harvard Business Review*, 2009. https://hbr.org/2009/11/what-every-leader-should-know-about-real-estate.

Applied Workplace. 'The Evolution of Office Design', 2015. https://www.appliedworkplace.co.uk/blog/the-evolution-of-office-design/

Beaudoin, L. 'What millennials really want in the workplace'. CBRE website https://www.cbre.com/configuration/global%20shared/content/articles/agile-real-estate/what-millennials-really-want-in-the-workplace

Bhanot, V. Hubble Raises £4m Investment to Build World's Largest Online Office Broker. Hubble HQ, https://hubblehq.com/blog/hubble-raises-4m-investment, 2019.

Bloodworth-Rivers, T. 'Outsourcing Facilities Management: 3 pros and cons to consider'. iofficecorp. https://www.iofficecorp.com/blog/3-reasons-to-outsource-your-facilities-management-and-3-reasons-not-to, 2019.

British Land, News and Views (press release) 'British Land flexes its space with Storey Club'. 2019. https://www.britishland.com/news-and-views/press-releases/2019/29-04-2019.

Cave, A. 'Mark Dixon: the Briton who wants to build a new Google'. *Telegraph*, 2009. https://www.telegraph.co.uk/finance/financetopics/profiles/5219967/Mark-Dixon-the-Briton-who-wants-to-build-a-new-Google.html

CBRE Report. 'Wellness in the workplace – Unlocking future performance'. 2016. pp 13

CBRE Report. 'Top trends in facilities management: How society, demographics and technology are changing the world of FM'. 2017, pp. 2–4, 9.

Cision PR Newswire. 'Tishman Speyer introduces studio co-working spaces in select global markets', 2018. https://www.prnewswire.com/news-releases/tishman-speyer-introduces-studio-co-working-spaces-in-select-global-markets-300720841.html.

Conlan, T. 'BBC cancels Land Securities contract'. *Guardian*, 2005. https://www.theguardian.com/media/2005/may/12/broadcasting.bbc3,

CoreNet Global Report. 'The bigger picture: The future of Corporate Real Estate'. 2016, pp. 28, 36–7.

Deloitte. 'The new organization: Different by design'. Global Human Capital Trends Report, Deloitte University Press, 2016, pp. 1, 9, 32.

Deloitte. 'Millennials disappointed in business, unprepared for Industry 4.0'. Deloitte Millennial Survey, 2018, p. 17. https://www2.deloitte.com/content/dam/Deloitte/global/Documents/About-Deloitte/gx-2018-millennial-survey-report.pdf

Dexus Website. 'Commercial space, your way. Explore your future space with Dexus'. 2019. www.dexus.com/leasing

Dixon, S. 'Learning from remote work's biggest fail'. *Distant Job*, 2018. https://distantjob.com/blog/yeah-but-yahoo-learning-from-remote-works-biggest-fail/

Dukes, E. 'Activity-Based Working is making a positive impact on the workplace'.2019. iofficecorp.com. https://www.iofficecorp.com/blog/does-activity-based-working-actually-work-the-surprising-data

Garner C. 'Working anywhere: A winning formula for good work?'. The Work Foundation Report 2016, University of Lancaster, 2016, p 5

Gaskell, A. 'Is your organisation a bus or a taxi?'. DZone, 2014. https://dzone.com/articles/your-organisation-bus-or-taxi

Green, R. 'How to manage a multigenerational workforce'. *Business News Daily*, 2019 https://www.businessnewsdaily.com/4636-generational-differences-management-challenges.html

Grewal, H.K. 'Social value should be primary consideration in contracts. Front Desk Analysis'. *Facilitate Magazine*, 2019, p. 11.

Hall, B. (2017) 'How Millennials are redefining employee satisfaction'. Human Resources Online, https://www.humanresourcesonline.net/how-millennials-are-changing-businesses/

Hannon, K. 'Work/Life balance, job satisfaction and retirement'. *NextAvenue*, 2017 https://www.nextavenue.org/older-workersworklife-balance-job-satisfaction-retirement/

Harter. J. 'Employee engagement on the rise in the U.S'. Gallup, 2018 https://news.gallup.com/poll/241649/employee-engagement-rise.aspx

International Workplace Group. 'A proven business model: Fine-tuned for success'. IWG Website. https://franchise.iwgplc.com/en-gb/iwg-franchise-business-model

Landsec Media Press Release. 'Landsec launches new flexible office brand'. 2019. https://landsec.com/media/press-releases/2019/landsec-launches-new-flexible-office-brand

Leesman Data Report. 'The Rise and Rise of Activity Based Working: Reshaping the physical, virtual and behavioural workspace'. 2017, p. 6.

Ma, M. 'The workplace of 2050: According to experts'. *Wall Street Journal*, 2020. https://www.wsj.com/articles/the-workplace-of-2050-according-to-experts-11578499235?mod=foesummaries

McFeely, S. and Wigert, B. 'This fixable problem costs U.S. businesses $1 trillion'. *Gallup Workplace*, 2019. https://www.gallup.com/workplace/247391/fixable-problem-costs-businesses-trillion.aspx

McGrath, J. 'Blackstone launches impact platform'. ESG Clarity, 2019. https://esgclarity.com/blackstone-launches-impact-platform/

Meister, J.C. 'Survey: What employees want most from their workspaces'. *Harvard Business Review*, 2019. https://hbr.org/2019/08/survey-what-employees-want-most-from-their-workspaces?utm_medium=social&utm_source=twitter&utm_campaign=hbr

Price, Waterhouse, Cooper. 'IFRS 16: The leases standard is changing. Are you ready?'. 2016, pp.1–3, 9. World Economic Forum. https://www.weforum.org/agenda/2016/01/the-fourth-industrial-revolution-what-it-means-and-how-to-respond/

Starkman, J. & Nadal, A. (2018). 'How to manage a multigenerational workforce'. *The Business Journals*. https://www.bizjournals.com/bizjournals/how-to/human-resources/2018/04/how-to-manage-a-multigenerational-workforce.html

The PeopleFluent Edge. 'Headcount planning strategies to drive success'. 2018. https://www.peoplefluent.com/blog/performance/headcount-planning-strategies-tactics

VanderWeele T.J. 'On the promotion of human flourishing. Proceedings of the National Academy of Sciences'. 2017 https://hfh.fas.harvard.edu/measuring-flourishing

Varcoe, B. and Hinks, J. 'CRE & FM's Choice: Cost-centric collusion, or a customer-centric convergence on integration'. CRE & FM Disruptive Thinking Series, Zurich Group Plc, 2014, pp. 5, 9.

WeWork website. Locations and Statistics, 2019. https://www.wework.com/locations; https://www.wework.com/mission

Weller, C. 'IBM was a pioneer in the work-from-home revolution — now it's cracking down'. *Business Insider*, 2017. https://www.businessinsider.com/ibm-slashes-work-from-home-policy-2017

World Green Building Council Report. 'Health, wellbeing & productivity in offices: The next chapter for green building'. 2014, pp. 2, 6, 7–11, 13, 16–17, 78–9.

CHAPTER 4

Aviva Newsroom. 'One in four UK workers have quit roles for greater flexibility'. 2019. https://www.aviva.com/newsroom/news-releases/2019/03/one-in-four-uk-workers-have-quit-roles-for-greater-flexibility/

Bloom, N.A. Liang, J., Roberts, J. 'Does Working from Home Work?'. Working Paper No. 3109. Stanford Business School, 2013. https://www.gsb.stanford.edu/faculty-research/working-papers/does-working-home-work-evidence-chinese-experiment

BT Group Plc Annual Report 2019, p. 2.

CIPD Report. 'Megatrends: Flexible working'. 2019, p 46 https://www.cipd.co.uk/Images/megatrends-report-flexible-working-1_tcm18-52769.pdf

Deloitte/Timewise Solutions. 'A manifesto for change: A modern workplace for a flexible workforce'. 2018, p. 3 https://timewise.co.uk/wp-content/uploads/2018/05/Manifesto-for-change.pdf

Forbes Top 100 Digital Companies. 2019. https://www.forbes.com/top-digital-companies/list/#tab:rank

IWG Global Workspace Survey. 'Welcome to generation flex – the employee power shift'. 2019, p. 4 http://assets.regus.com/pdfs/iwg-workplace-survey/iwg-workplace-survey-2019.pdf

Kane, C. & Waters, C. 'Workplace dodos can survive and prosper'. *Work&Place* Vol 3. Issue 1. *Occupiers Journal*, 2014, pp. 19–23.

Nicks, L., Burd, H. & Barnes, J. 'Flexible working qualitative analysis: Organisations' experiences of flexible working arrangements'. Government Equalities Office, 2019, p 25.

Owl Labs/Global Workplace Analytics. 'State of remote work'. 2019. https://www.owllabs.com/state-of-remote-work/2019

Pochepan, J. 'Here's what happens when you take away dedicated desks for employees'. Inc.com, 2018. https://www.inc.com/author/jeff-pochepan

US Bureau of Labor Statistics. 'Job flexibilities and work schedules summary'. Data from the American time use survey, 2019. https://www.bls.gov/news.release/flex2.nr0.htm

Vodafone Business Report. 'Global survey reveals rapid adoption of flexible working', 2016. https://www.vodafone.com/business/news-

and-insights/press-release/vodafone-survey-reveals-rapid-adoption-of-flexible-working

Waters, C. 'BT senior manager's view: Flexibility pays'. EFC website, 2013. https://www.employersforcarers.org/membership/what-employers-say/item/92-bt-senior-managers-view

Weiler Reynolds, B. 'FlexJobs 2018 Annual Survey: Workers believe a flexible or remote job can help save money, reduce stress, and more', 2018. https://www.flexjobs.com/blog/post/flexjobs-2018-annual-survey-workers-believe-flexible-remote-job-can-help-save-money-reduce-stress-more/

CHAPTER 5

Begum, P. 'The Changing Workplace: A Digital World'. *The Psychologist*. Vol.30. 2017, pp 20–29

Graham, J. Dr & Mawson, A. 'The Workplace Management Framework', Version 1.0. Advanced Workplace Associates, 2014, pp. 12, 17, 25, 28, 31, 35, 37, 39, 41, 45, 48.

Hirschhorn, L. & Gilmore, T. 'The new boundaries of the "boundaryless" company'. *Harvard Business Review*, 1992. https://hbr.org/1992/05/the-new-boundaries-of-the-boundaryless-company

Kaiser Family Foundation/US Census Bureau. '61.5 million office workers'. 2017. https://senion.com/whitepaper/office-workplace-survey/

McKinsey Survey. 'What successful transformations share'. McKinsey & Co., 2010. https://www.mckinsey.com/business-functions/organization/our-insights/what-successful-transformations-share-mckinsey-global-survey-results

Miller, L. 'The secret meaning behind Leonardo da Vinci's Vitruvian Man'. *Truth Theory*, 2017. https://truththeory.com/2017/11/03/secret-meaning-behind-leonardo-da-vincis-vitruvian-man/

Swanson, L. 8 Changes Chatbots Will Bring to the Workplace. CMS Wire. 2018 https://www.cmswire.com/digital-workplace/8-changes-chatbots-will-bring-to-the-workplace/

CHAPTER 6

Bank of America Securities. 'Can ESG investment strategies outperform?'. Bank of America Global Research U.S. Equity & Quant Strategy, 2019. https://www.bofaml.com/en-us/content/esg-investing-research-report.html

Newman, K. 'Cities with the world's worst traffic congestion'. *US News*, 2019. https://www.usnews.com/news/cities/articles/2019-02-12/these-cities-have-the-worlds-worst-traffic-congestion

Talty, A. 'Work from home 2019: The top 100 companies for remote jobs'. *Forbes*, 2019. https://www.forbes.com/sites/alexandratalty/2019/01/15/work-from-home-2019-the-top-100-companies-for-remote-jobs/#3ae487491544

Phipps, A. 'Technology 2020: What is the real estate sector scared of?' Cushman & Wakefield, 2019, pp. 4, 6.

Property Week. 'Making social value stack up', 2019. https://www.property-week.com/features/making-social-value-stack-up/5101297.article

CHAPTER 8

Baker, S. 'How a 60-year-old BBC radio show may be one of the only things keeping the world from nuclear war'. *Business Insider*, 2019. https://www.businessinsider.com/bbc-radio-show-may-be-preventing-nuclear-apocalypse-2018-8?r=US&IR=T

BBC Media Centre. 'BBC international audience soars to record high of 426m', 2019. https://www.bbc.co.uk/mediacentre/latestnews/2019/bbc-international-audience-record-high

BBC Press Office. 'Radical reform to deliver a more focused BBC', 2007. http://www.bbc.co.uk/pressoffice/pressreleases/stories/2007/10_october/18/reform.shtml

BBC Royal Charter Archive. History of the BBC Research https://www.bbc.com/historyofthebbc/research/royal-charter

Castella de, T. 'How the Coronation kick-started the love of television'. *BBC News Magazine*, 2013. https://www.bbc.co.uk/news/magazine-22688498

The Center for Organizational Design, 'Developing High Performing Teams: What they are and how to make them work', 2009 http://www.centerod.com/developing-high-performance-teams/

CNN News, 'UK press mauls Hutton "whitewash"'. CNN.com. 2004 http://edition.cnn.com/2004/WORLD/europe/01/29/hutton.press/

Irvine, J. 'Hodge concerned by BBC sale'. Economia/ICAEW, 2015. https://economia.icaew.com/news/january-2015/hodge-concerned-by-bbc-sale

Kane, C. 'Putting public value at the heart of cultural excellence: Exploring a transformational journey of workplace strategy at the BBC'. *Corporate Real Estate Journal*, 2013, Vol. 2, No. 4, pp. 279–99.

Stillito, D. 'Where were you when man first landed on the moon?'. *BBC News Magazine*, 2019. https://www.bbc.co.uk/news/entertainment-arts-49003296

Tryhorn, C. 'BBC "chaos" as TV Centre hit by power cut'. *Guardian*, 2003. https://www.theguardian.com/media/2003/nov/28/broadcasting.bbc1

CHAPTER 9

BBC Group. 'Annual Report and Accounts 2018/19'. Strategic report: commercial operators, pp. 68, 74.

BBC News. 'BBC Television Centre Up for Sale', 2011. https://www.bbc.co.uk/news/uk-13746250

Bishop, T. 'A Year in the Shadow of Westfield'. BBC News, 2009. http://news.bbc.co.uk/1/hi/england/london/8327455.stm

Butler. S. 'Net-a-Porter Owner Opens Tech Hub in London'. *Guardian*, 2017. https://www.theguardian.com/business/2017/jun/27/lap-of-luxury-net-a-porter-opens-new-tech-hub-in-london

Conlan, T. 'BBC Cancels Land Securities Contract'. *Guardian*, 2005. https://www.theguardian.com/media/2005/may/12/broadcasting.bbc3

Eiffel Tower At A Glance. 'The number 7m visitors a year'. Eiffel Tower website. https://www.toureiffel.paris/en/the-monument/key-figures https://web.archive.org/web/20080701122654/ http://www.english-heritage.org.uk/server/show/ConWebDoc.14079

Griffee, A. 'W1 Project Comes to a Close'. BBC Blog, 2013. https://www.bbc.co.uk/blogs/aboutthebbc/entries/9b8bb03e-159b-3cd5-97b5-a931da3b43c4

Imperial College London Website. 'White City Campus: Campus Development'. https://www.imperial.ac.uk/white-city-campus/about/campus-development/

Irvine, J. 'Hodge Concerned by BBC Sale'. Economia/ICAEW, 2015. https://economia.icaew.com/news/january-2015/hodge-concerned-by-bbc-sale

Kane, C. 'Television Centre – Shaping the Next Chapter'. BBC Spaces & Places blog, 2012. https://www.bbc.co.uk/blogs/spacesandplaces/2012/09/television_centre_-_shaping_th.shtml

Kane, C. 'Putting Public Value at the Heart of Cultural Excellence: Exploring a Transformational Journey of Workplace Strategy at the BBC'. *Corporate Real Estate Journal*, Vol. 2 No. 4, Henry Stewart Publications, 2013, pp. 279–99.

Kane, C. & Gaskell, A. 'Corporate Occupiers Strengthen Place Making Initiative in London's White City: The BBC's and Imperial College's Role in Adding Value'. *Corporate Real Estate Journal*, Vol. 8, No. 3, Henry Stewart Publications, 2018, pp. 235–52.

Kane, C. with Anastassiou, E. 'Place-making: A New Strategic Role for Corporate Real Estate'. *The Leader*, CoreNet Global Publishing, 2019, pp. 38–9.

Kempton, M. 'An Unofficial History of BBC Television Centre', 2007. https://web.archive.org/web/20070907085244/http://www.tvstudiohistory.co.uk/tv%20centre%20history.htm

KPMG Report. 'The Role of the BBC in Supporting Economic Growth', 2015, pp. 1–2, 17.

Légifrance website. Arrêté du 5 février 2016 délimitant une zone touristique internationale à Serris dénommée « Val-d 'Europe » en application de l'article L. 3132-24 du code du travail, 2016. https://www.legifrance.gouv.fr/eli/arrete/2016/2/5/EINI1602342A/jo/texte

London Borough of Hammersmith & Fulham Report. 'BBC TV Centre Plans Approved', 2013. https://web.archive.org/web/20150222010606/http://www.lbhf.gov.uk/Directory/News/BBC_TV_Centre_plans_approved.asp

London Borough of Hammersmith & Fulham Report. 'The Transformation of White City has Really Taken Off', 2018. https://www.lbhf.gov.uk/articles/news/2018/06/transformation-white-city-has-really-taken

Love, B. '"Casualty" enters Guinness World Records'. Digital Spy, 2010. https://www.digitalspy.com/soaps/casualty/a277037/casualty-enters-guinness-world-records/#~p1b3d0b7rvI2Rk

Palmer-Brown, A. 'MediaCity UK: The BBC's Move to Manchester'. *Meanwhile Creative*, 2019. https://meanwhilecreative.co.uk/coworking-office-space/manchester/mediacity-manchester/

Prynn, J. 'Former BBC Car Park in White City Makes Way for a Meccano-style Pop-up Theatre'. *Evening Standard*, 2019. https://www.standard.co.uk/go/london/theatre/pop-up-theatre-troubadour-white-city-car-park-a4052626.html

Royal College of Art website. 'RCA White City'. https://www.rca.ac.uk/more/about-rca/our-campus/rca-white-city/

Westfield website. 'Regeneration & Economic Benefits'. http://westfieldlondon-plans.co.uk/regeneration-and-economic-benefits/

BIBLIOGRAPHY AND FURTHER READING

INTRODUCTION
Drucker, P. *The Landmarks of Tomorrow*. New York: Harper, 1959.

CHAPTER 1
Sundararajan, A. *The Sharing Economy: The End of Employment and the Rise of Crowd-Based Capitalism*. Cambridge, MA: The MIT Press, 2016.

CHAPTER 2
Cryer, M. *Curious English Words and Phrases: The Truth Behind the Expressions We Use*. Auckland: Exisle Publishing Ltd, 2012, pp. 270.
Federal Trade Commission Decisions. Vol. 105, Washington: US Government Printing Office, 1986, p. 111.

CHAPTER 3
Handy, C. *The Second Curve: Thoughts on Reinventing Society*. London: Random House Publishing, 2015, p. 4.
Shea, G.P & Solomon, C.A. *Leading Successful Change: 8 Keys to Making Change Work*. Philadelphia: Wharton Digital Press, 2015, pp. 2–3, 21.

CHAPTER 5
Usher, N. *The Elemental Workplace: The 12 Elements for Creating a Fantastic Workplace for Everyone*. London: Lid Publishing, 2018, pp. 21, 39.

CHAPTER 8
Jackson, N. *Building the BBC, A Return to Form*. BBC London, 2003, pp 16, 155.
Webb, A. *London Calling: Britain, the BBC World Service and the Cold War*. London: Bloomsbury, 2014, pp. 1–12.

Further Reading

Anderson, M. & Jefferson, M. *Transforming Organisations: Engaging the 4Cs for Powerful Organisational Learning and Change*, Bloomsbury, 2018.

Axelrod, R. *The Evolution of Co-operation*, Penguin, 2013.

Baer, J. & Naslund, A. *The NOW Revolution: 7 Shifts to Make Your Business Faster, Smarter and More Social.* Wiley & Sons, 2011.

Berkun, S. *The Year Without Pants*, Jossey-Bass, 2013.

Brower, T. *Bring Work to Life by Bringing Life to Work: A Guide for Leaders and Organizations.* Bibliomotion, 2014.

Clapperton, G. & Vanhoutte, P. *The Smarter Working Manifesto*, Sunmakers, 2014.

Coplin, D. *The Rise of the Humans: How to Outsmart the Digital Deluge*, Harriman House, 2014.

Crawford, M. *The Case for Working with Your Hands: Or Why Office Work is Bad for Us and Fixing Things Feels Good*, Penguin, 2010.

Daisley, B. *The Joy of Work: 30 Ways to Fix Your Work Culture and Fall in Love with Your Job Again*, Random House Business, 2019.

Denning, S. *The Age of Agile: How Smart Companies are Transforming the Way Work Gets Done*, Amacom, 2019.

Donkin, R. *The Future of Work: Robots, AI, and Automation*, Palgrave Macmillan, 2010.

Edwards, V. & Ellison, L. *Corporate Property Management: Aligning Real Estate with Business Strategy*, Blackwell Publishing, 2004.

Ee, S. *Value-Based Facilities Management*, Candid Creation Publishing, 2015.

Gillen, N. *Future Office: Next-Generation Workplace Design*, RIBA Publishing, 2019.

Godin, S. *Tribes: We Need You to Lead Us*, Penguin, 2015.

Gratton, L, *The Shift: The Future of Work is Already Here*, HarperCollins, 2014.

Gratton, L. & Scott, A. *The 100-Year Life*, Bloomsbury Business, 2016.

Groves, K. & Marlow, O. *Spaces for Innovation*, Frame, 2016.

Grulke, W. *(10) Lessons From The Future*, Financial Times/Prentice Hall, 2001.

Handy, C. *Understanding Organisations*, Penguin, 1993.

Handy, C. *The Empty Raincoat: Making Sense of the Future*, Random House, 1995.

Handy, C. *Beyond Certainty: The Changing Worlds of Organisations*, Random House Business, 1996.

Handy, C. *The New Alchemists*, Hutchinson, 2004.

Handy, C. *The New Philanthropists: The New Generosity*, W Heinemann, 2007.

Handy C. *Myself and Other More Important Matters*, Arrow, 2007.

Heath, P. & Sept, C. *The Emergent Workplace: Understanding and Creating Adaptive Workplaces*, Business Place Strategies Inc, 2013.

Heath, C. & Heath, D. *The Power of Moments: Why Certain Experiences Have Extraordinary Impact*, Corgi, 2019.

Hines, A. *ConsumerShift: How Changing Values Are Reshaping the Consumer Landscape*, No Limit Publishing, 2011.

Hinssen, P. *The Network Always Wins: How to Influence Customers, Stay Relevant, and Transform Your Organization to Move Faster than the Market*, McGraw-Hill Education, 2014.

Karlsson, C & Picard, R.G. *Media Clusters: Spatial Agglomeration and Content Capabilities*, Edward Elgar Publishing, 2011.

Khanna, P. *Connectography – Mapping the Global Network Revolution*, Weidenfeld & Nicolson, 2017.

Laloux, F. *Reinventing Organizations: A Guide to Creating Organizations Inspired by the Next Stage in Human Consciousness*, Nelson Parker, 2014.

Maitland, A. & Thomson, P. *Future Work (Expanded and Updated): Changing Organisational Culture for the New World of Work*, Palgrave Macmillan 2004.

Maitland, A. & Thomson, P. *Future Work: How Businesses Can Adapt and Thrive in the New World of Work*, Palgrave Macmillan, 2011.

McAfee, A. & Brynjolfsson, E. *Machine, Platform, Crowd: Harnessing the Digital Revolution*, WW Norton, 2017.

Meister, J. & Willyerd, K. *The 2020 Workplace: How Innovative Companies Attract, Develop, and Keep Tomorrow's Employees Today*, Harper Collins, 2010.

Meister, J. & Mulcahy, K. *The Future Workplace Experience: 10 Rules For Mastering Disruption in Recruiting & Engaging Employees*, McGraw-Hill Education, 2016.

Miller, Paul & Marsh, Elizabeth. *The Digital Renaissance of Work: Delivering Digital Workplaces Fit for the Future*, Routledge, 2014.

Morieux, Y. & Tollman, P. *Six Simple Rules: How to Manage Complexity without Getting Complicated*, Harvard Business Review Press, 2014.

Myerson, J. *Design for Change: The Architecture of DEGW*, Birkhauser Verlag AG 1998.

Myerson, J. & Ross, P. *The Creative Office*, Laurence King Publishing, 1999.

Myerson, J. & Ross, P. *Space to Work: New Office Design*, Laurence King Publishing, 2006.

O'Mara, M. *Strategy & Place: Corporate Real Estate and Facilities Management*, The Free Press, 1999.

Pein, C. *Live, Work, Work, Work, Die: A Journey into the Savage Heart of Silicon Valley*, Scribe, 2018.

Pfeffer, J. & Sutton, I. *The Knowing-Doing Gap: How Smart Companies Turn Knowledge into Action*, Harvard Business Review Press, 1999.

Propst, R. *The Office, A Facility Based on Change*, Birch, 1986.

Rifkin, J. *Third Industrial Revolution: How Lateral Power is Transforming Energy, the Economy, and the World*, Griffin, 2013.

Rowland, D. & Higgs, M. *Sustaining Change: Leadership that Works*, John Wiley & Sons, 2008.

Saval, N. *Cubed: The Secret History of the Workplace*, Anchor Books, 2015.

Schwab, K. *The Fourth Industrial Revolution*, Portfolio Penguin, 2017.

Semple, E. *Organizations Don't Tweet, People Do: A Manager's Guide to the Social Web*, John Wiley & Sons, 2012.

Sinek, S. *Start With Why: How Great Leaders Inspire Everyone to Take Action*, Penguin, 2011.

Sterling, A. *The Humane Workplace: People, Community, Technology*, Kindle Editions, 2015.

Suarez, R. *The Coworking Handbook: Learn How To Create and Manage a Successful Coworking Space*, CreateSpace Independent Publishing Platform, 2014.

Talwar, R. Wells, S. Whittington, A. Koury, A. & Romero, M. *The Future Reinvented: Reimagining Life, Society, and Business* (Volume 2), Fast Future, 2017.

Tapscott, D. *Growing Up Digital: Rise of the Net Generation*, McGraw-Hill, 2000.

Tett, G. *The Silo Effect: Why Every Organisation Needs to Disrupt Itself to Survive*, Little, Brown Book Group, 2016.

Veldhoen, E. *The Art of Working*, Academic Service NL, 2005.

Veldhoen, E. *You-Topia: The Impact of the Digital Revolution on Our Work, Our Life and Our Environment*, XLIBRIS, 2013.

Waldcock, B. *Being Agile in Business: Discover faster, smarter, leaner ways to work*, Pearson, 2015.

Ward, C. *Out of Office: work where you like & achieve more*, Blue Dot World, 2013.

Williams, A. & Donald, A. *The Lure of the City – From Slums to Suburbs*, Pluto Press, 2011.

ACKNOWLEDGEMENTS

Writing this book would not have been possible without many factors falling into place. Most importantly, the loving support and infinite patience of my wife, Loreto. When starting out on this venture I didn't realize for one moment just how challenging it would be. All I knew was that I wanted to tell a story and suggest a few ideas which might help others deal with this crazy world of ours. Thanks go to my friend David Pearl, who provided lots of little story-telling gems and support along the way, plus engineering an introduction to Charles Handy. For this, I am eternally grateful as the advice and inspiration Charles provided at breakfast in Putney set me on the right path.

Of course the whole endeavour would not have started without the advice of my former colleague at the BBC, Pat Loughrey, who advised me to keep a journal of my adventures. These 26 notebooks brought to life not only a complicated and convoluted storyline but reminded me of a whole host of great people who came on the BBC journey with me. It is impossible to mention everybody in this book, but you all know who you are so please accept my appreciative thanks. Looking back, we truly lived the BBC values, especially the one about 'great things happen when we work together'!

This book is six years in the making and there were times when I felt like giving up. Early on, I stumbled upon Nigel Roberts, a former BBC journalist who helped me frame the narrative and coached me in the art of writing a book. In 2015, Nigel was taken from us and this was a big loss. It took me a couple of years to fill this gap and during this period I realized that the task of explaining my complex world to readers was bigger than I had anticipated. I needed a sounding board and editor for my thoughts and a collaborator to explain this veritable bowl of spaghetti in a simple and engaging way. Thankfully, I found the very capable Eugenia Anastassiou, whose journalistic skills kept me on track and who has been instrumental in helping me get *Where Is My Office?* across the finish line. Amassing all the research, writing papers and carrying out interviews was a task I had completely underestimated. I am very grateful for the contributions of Ciara O'Connor, Colm Devereux, Adi Gaskell, Nick Perry and Marina Kostadinovic, who helped eat the elephant in manageable pieces.

Also, thanks go to the Bloomsbury team, Ian Hallsworth and Matt James, who had faith in Eugenia and me to produce this book. As a complete novice it was fantastic to get their backing and to receive the support from Allie Collins and the wider team during the publishing process.

I also owe a debt of gratitude to former BBC Director-General Mark Thompson for taking time out of his hectic life leading the *New York Times* to write the foreword for this book and for all the encouragement he provided when we were at the BBC. While on that note, I wish to acknowledge the help of Keith Beal, Tim Cavanagh, Dilys Foster, Andrew Fullerton, Andy Griffee, and John Smith for helping to fill in the gaps for the BBC story and to BBC Head of History Robert Seatter for his support and permission to use BBC material in the book.

During the last six months of writing there were several people who made the journey more bearable by acting as sounding boards, reviewing draft ideas and generously providing their input and time to the project. These include Max Luff, Caroline Waters, Peter Miscovich, Neil Usher, Ronen Journo, Tomas Blatte, Martin Laws, Mark Eltringham and Simon Heath. When it came to review rough drafts, I sought out friends who had no idea of my world to see what they made of it. Thanks to the following for taking the time to review and comment: Julie Gilligan, Maureen Martin, Ciara McLoughlin, Peter Edgar and David Connole.

I badgered and interviewed a wide range of people across the globe, all of whom had something useful to say. The following is a list of contributors/interviewees in alphabetical order that I have maintained over the years, which I hope covers everybody who has contributed, and I am extremely grateful for their input:

Chris Alcock, Ben Almond, Doctor Monique Arkesteijn, Paul Bagust, Ann Bamesberger, Guy Battle, Professor Franklin Becker, Giovanni Bevilacqua, Steven Boyd, Tracey Brower, Angela Cain, Fiona Calnan, David Camp, Antonia Cardone, Mark Catchlove, Kevin Chapman, Peter Cheese, Martin Clarke, Rupert Clarke, Brian Collins, Michael Creamer, Don Crichton, Dave Crocker, Mark Dixon, Angus Dodd, John Duckworth, William Dunne, Juliet Filose, Ian Foulds, Francesca Fryer, Mark Galbreath, Thais Galli, Kevin George, Nicola Gillen, Lis Gleed, James Goldsmith, Professor David Good, Richard Graham, Sir Malcolm Grant, Charlie Green, Michael Grove, Kursty Groves, Michael Graham, Franco Guidi, Andrew Hallissey, Steve Hargis, Doctor Rob Harris, Roy Hirshland, Guy Holden, Chris Hood,

Bill Hughes, Professor Michael Joroff, Luc Kamperman, Despina Katsikakis, Jamie Kinch, Judy Klein, Bryan Koop, Andy Lake, Su Lim, Sir Stuart Lipton, Kate Lister, Doctor Paul Luciani, Roger Madelin, Reza Marchant, Patrick Marsh, Melissa Marsh, Andrew Mawson, Danny Meaney, Denis McGowan, Francisco Vázquez Medem, Juliette Morgan, Chris Moriarty, Debra Moritz, George Muir, Jane Muir-Sands, Doctor Clare Murray, Kate North, Tim Oldman, Nick O'Donnell, Marta O'Mara, Roelof Opperman, Caleb Parker, Russell Phimister, Lisa Picard, Polly Plunket-Checkemian, Dror Poleg, Jack Pringle, Doctor Marie Puybaraud, Steve Quick, Danial Quinn, Doctor Amanda Rischbieth, Philip Ross, Doctor Peggie Rothe, Kay Sargent, Kevin Sauer, Helmut Schuster, Euan Semple, Natalie Slessor, Anthony Slumbers, Ryan Simonetti, Kate Smith, Robert Teed, Perry Timms, Fons Trompenaars, Frank Van Massenhove, Doctor Barry Varcoe, Tim Venable, Damian Wild, Stephen Wild, Clive Wilkinson, Glen Wong, Bridget Workman, Workplace Evolutionaries and Tim Yendall.

Last, but not least, I want to acknowledge the input of the CRE leaders group USA, who generously allowed me time to sound them out on my thinking at their annual board meeting.

INDEX